ONLY

IN

MAINE

SELECTIONS FROM

DOWN EAST MAGAZINE

Edited by DUANE DOOLITTLE

*Down East Enterprise,
Incorporated
Camden, Maine*

Cover design by Bonnie Bishop. Cover photo of Burnt Island
Lighthouse, Boothbay Harbor, by David Hastings.

4   5

Down East Enterprise, Inc. / *Camden, Maine*

CONTENTS

FOREWORD

KENNETH ROBERTS inclined to the iodine theory. He felt that the sea, in pounding rockweed against the jagged Maine shore, bruised it until iodine was released, and this came to the lungs of Maine people and made them write. All over Maine, he noticed, he was forever bumping into these school teachers, crossing tenders, housewives, physicians, bankers, and retired sawmill operators who kept asking him where they ought to send their manuscripts. No other state, of course, has such an incidence of literary production, and it must be the air. Methodically pursuing this thought, author Roberts began with James Rosier, which is as far back as you can go in Pine Tree *belles lettres*, and he established that Rosier seemed to have a flair, but that he never really got a grip on his pen until he stood on the *Archangel* and looked upon the beauties of Georges River — breathing as he gazed.

From this, Kenneth Roberts proceeded to list Maine authors,

and they ran on and on like the Catalog of Ships in the Homeric epic until the topic was belabored into cumulative boredom. He mentioned in particular a book of Maine poetry published in 1888 which ran to eight hundred and fifty pages, with over four hundred Maine poets contributing. Iodine, he said — Iodine.

Poet Robert Peter Tristram Coffin did something of the same in one of his books, and he found a few writers Roberts had missed. And, again, the list extended from Cranberry Horn School to The Gurnet, and got tiresome. Yet in this state where 215 per cent of the people have written something, and the others are getting ready, there is a dearth of publications in which the collective output, or some part of it, might reasonably appear. Clarity, grace, vigor, readability, and what Aristotle called pleasing language are hardly the touchstones of Maine journals and periodicals. Nothing fanciful seems to appear except the weather forecasts. From Seba Smith to Fred Owen, Portland used to print something once in a while. The old Bangor *Commercial* loved to turn an unexpected phrase. Bill Nye (born in Shirley) stated this well when he wrote one time that he now had a new and very smart editor who permitted him to put things in the paper "if they were news or not." But even this is a misleader — the old Lewiston *Journal* had Sam Connor, Holman Day, Roy Atkinson, Vincent Canham, and the great Bateman, who could write plain news in enthusiastic essays that made a Grange supper sound like a banquet of the immortal gods, or a Republican caucus assume the dignity of a septuagint translating the Bible. But when Arthur Staples went his way the era ceased here, too. Let us remember that it was a small, obscure, highly mortgaged, far-down Maine weekly that found room, once upon a time, for the scurrilous libels of Stephen A. Douglas Smith, who sold plows. Mr. Smith became Justice William R. Pattangall, and it may be stated as a reasoned fact that if Bill sent his manuscripts to any Maine publication today they would remain unpublished.

The exception, of course, is *Down East* — the magazine of Maine. Here, in the heavy iodine reek of the Camden waterfront, its editors sit in tranquil meditation and cultivate the school teachers, housewives, and sawyers of the State of Maine, and gladly publish things if they are news or not — consequently offering something to read as opposed to the other and more modern forms of writing. This is their second compendium of selections from their unique magazine, and each page gives off its iodine to edify one and all. The authors herein are truly down east authors. They are the present and current representatives of that surging herd, led by James Rosier and supported by Kenneth Roberts and Rob Coffin, that marches on and on like the Chinese, who, it is said, will never pass a given point, because they keep on coming.

— John Gould

MAINE SPRING

People who do not live in Maine seem to be under the
impression that a State-O-Mainer stands looking
out of his storm-window all through the
long-delayed Spring, waiting for the
Fourth of July sun to melt the snow.
Not so!
All kinds of interesting things
take place in
Springtime.

SPRING BURNING

BY DARRELL A. ROLERSON

SPRING CREPT IN, but we didn't need a town crier to tell us of its arrival. The birds sang about it during the day, and the frogs during the night. The crocuses knew it, and it was certainly no surprise to the budding maples. Spring was in the air, but more importantly, it was in the soul. It brought with it baseball games in the afternoon and smelt dipping at night in the tidal brooks. Spring pushed before it that indescribable feeling that makes a boy glad just because he's a boy — a surge of joy that starts as an itch in a boy's toes and leaps up through his body to explode from his throat in a whooping big "Yahooooo!" There's no scientific name for it, but it's unavoidably contagious — spring fever!

To all the people of an island town like Islesboro, spring brought another kind of adventure. The snow, which had hovered in great hilly drifts during the past months, had dribbled away into the ocean. Earnest sea breezes had probed the closely tangled fields until they were dry enough for burning. I don't know now how the word got around, but suddenly the right day of the season was at hand and the townspeople congregated after supper for that important community purpose — to burn the fields.

For us boys spring burning week was a glorious one. Nights were ablaze with dancing flames that hypnotized and mystified as they capered across sprawling straw carpets, devouring all traces of last year's grass and fallen foliage in their paths. We watched intently for frightened ground moles as they scurried away from the advancing fire. When we were boys old enough to be on our own, we would sneak into the darkness, just beyond the flames' revealing light, and steal manly pleasures by smoking the straight hollow stems of dried milkweed.

Before the main section of field was touched off, a safety line was burned snug against the edge of the woods. With this precaution danger was at a minimum, so that when the entire field was ablaze, the burning crew withdrew to a comfortable knoll to watch the gyrating spectacle as it slashed into the wavering darkness.

If the fire should wander, we'd pound it out. Standard equipment was a thick fir bough, and everybody toted one. The men often carried entire trees, eight and nine feet tall, to thrash down the fire, should it spread out of bounds.

Field burning was a sport which attracted everybody in town. Those who were too old to participate sat rocking in the windows of their darkened homes, or in one of the many vehicles that lined both sides of the road. The youngest citizens squirmed under the watchful eyes of moms, who had come to join in the excitement of the evening.

Every last brown blade of grass was burned right down to the water's edge. As was the custom at old-fashioned corn husking bees or barn raisings, after each successful burning the fire crew was invited to the field owner's home to feast. We boys were gluttonous with hot coffee and chocolate cake, stuffing without reproof while the men boasted of hunting escapades, and the women exchanged housewifely talk, spiced with a tidbit or two of gossip.

"The morning after the night before," smelling remotely like somebody's old compost heap, and with eyes still red from smoke, we marched off to school. Teachers greeted us with up-turned noses, for the raw odor of burnt grass was still in our clothes. We were unconcerned, restlessly anticipating the fact that we'd be at another burning that very evening, as well as the next, and the one after that, if we were lucky, until eventually every last field in Islesboro was transformed to a blackened expanse of powdery ash.

It was not always the fields alone that were burned, as I well remember the night we cooked old Ada's rhubarb. To this day it remains a mystery how every last adult seemed to melt into the darkness, as the spry old lady strode across the smouldering field to see if we weren't just a mite too close to her rhubarb patch. The confirmed rumor about town was that Ada used the sour stalks as a base for home brew, letting the tart wine age until winter and then having a "spring fever" all her own. She was beside us before we could run, shaking her white head and clucking her tongue. "I don't know what I'll ever use it for now," she told us boys. "You've frightened the pucker right out of it!"

But spring has marvelous powers of regeneration, especially after the burning. As I remember it, that very next week when the black fields greened overnight and began to flourish, so did Ada's rhubarb. And the next December, according to rumor, Ada had a private case of spring fever.

SMELTING

BY W. ALAN HENDERSON

I HAD SCARCELY HUNG UP my city clothes and donned my Maine overalls when my neighbor Percy said to me one night, "Let's go smeltin'."

"O.K., Perc, I'll be glad to go with you some day."

"I mean right now — tonight," said Percy.

"Tonight? It's ten p.m. — time I was in bed."

"Maine folks don't go to bed when the smelt are running," Percy said.

"But, Perc," I argued, "I've got a pair of boots, but no net, or whatever you catch them with."

"You've got two hands, haven't you? That's all the law allows you to use when smelt are spawning. You don't use nets."

I didn't like the picture at all: me standing in the water dipping out smelt with my hands, as I'd seen movies of bears doing to catch salmon. But I couldn't get out of it.

We got into my car and drove seven miles up a lonely country road.

"Shut 'er off," said Percy, "and let's go."

We stumbled down a wooded hillside, following a path that
even an Abnaki Indian would have cursed. All of a sudden,
Percy aimed his flashlight up into the trees and picked out a
sign: "Private Property — No Trespassing."

"This is it," he said. "Here's where we turn off."

He ignored the sign completely, and we plunged through
more brush. Finally we heard the brook, and we heard voices.
Obviously, we weren't the only borderline cases out at that
time of night.

There was a fire blazing, and we could make out dim forms
bent over in the brook and strung out a distance from each
other. Flashlights were playing their beams on the purling
water. It was an eerie sight, and it set me tingling.

In we splashed into a foot of fast-moving water, and I received my initiation into the most primitive way of catching
fish that I ever experienced.

I dipped. I dripped. I slipped. I dropped the flashlight into
the brook. Miraculously it kept right on shining. I stabbed and
I grabbed, but I never felt a smelt.

Every now and then some bossy-sounding guy would yell,
"Everybody out of the brook." And we'd obey him like little
children and scramble up the bank. Yet I liked this recess part.
It gave me a chance to get warm around the fire. Bear in mind
that this was in April, and the damp night air could sift through
long johns in fifteen minutes.

But just as I was getting comfortable, the self-appointed
leader would yell, "O.K., everybody back in the brook." Secret-
ly, I wished he would make up his mind.

I was told that the reason for this "in-again-out-again-Fin-
negan" routine was to fool the smelt into thinking we had
gone home. As if the smelt cared one way or another. They had
one idea in mind: to spawn before dawn, the females swim-

ming up the brook first, with the males rushing after them. I don't think we fooled them one bit.

I was amazed to find several women bent over in the brook snagging smelt. The weaker sex? Haw! They were nowhere near as cold as I was.

The evening wore on in this hit-and-miss fashion, and I finally plucked up courage to ask Percy, "What time is it?"

"Two a.m.," he said.

"Great balls of fire!" I said. "Let's go home." I had caught exactly three smelt in three hours.

"Wait a little longer," said Percy. He had twenty smelt, but was in the grip of smelt fever, and didn't know when to quit.

It was pretty near three a.m. when we left. Everybody else had gone home long ago. My score still stood at three smelt. I was doing some mental arithmetic.

"Let's see. Six dollars for the doctor's visit and three dollars for penicillin, that's nine dollars: three dollars per smelt! I could have bought lobster for a lot less than that."

Sportsman that he was, Percy wanted to divide his catch with me, but I waved the offer aside.

"To the victor belongs the smelt. You earned 'em, you keep 'em."

"Oh," said Percy, "you'll do better tomorrow night, now that you've got the hang of it."

I hadn't reckoned on tomorrow night. I hemmed and hawed and said that I didn't think I could make it; I had to catch up on some correspondence.

Guess where I was the next night?

Right! Standing in a different brook this time. We were the first ones there, which I discovered gave us the authority to holler, "Everybody out of the brook." It goes by seniority. I let Percy do it, for it didn't seem proper for a city guy to order the Maine people around. We had more status with Percy in command. But I sure would have liked to yell it just once.

This night we had a ball. I had brought hot coffee and sandwiches, and they tasted mighty good around the fire. The night was a lot warmer, too. I even caught one more smelt than the previous night, and it built up my ego when a guy said, "Boy, those are big ones you got!" I felt that at last I was making the Maine grade.

Percy got thirty smelt this time. He made me take some by threatening to give them to the cat if I didn't want them. I'm glad I took them, for four fried smelt are just a tease.

MAINE TOWN MEETING

BY J. MALCOLM BARTER

SOME OF THE FLAVOR of an honest-to-goodness, knock-down town meeting still exists Down East in Maine, as real as clam chowder and boiled, live lobster and just as savory. Such a town meeting is conducted about the beginning of mud time in Bremen, Maine, a small coastal community on Muscongus Bay about 25 miles southwest of Rockland. It numbers about 400 souls in the winter and perhaps twice as many more in the summer time, with lobstering and clamming its principal occupations.

Town meetings in the surrounding towns may be cut and dried affairs, but one can always count on an old hurrah-boys when the voters of Bremen assemble in the basement auditorium at the consolidated school for their annual election of officers and action on articles in the warrant. Visitors make a special point of getting down to Bremen the Saturday night of the meeting just to stand in the back of the hall and watch the show. The selectmen usually hire an extra constable or two in case the party gets rough.

Bremen town meeting last March was no exception. Rival candidates ran for every important town office except that of school committee member, and rarely is that disputed. All day, hard liquor flowed and cigars were passed about freely as the various contestants for selectmen, town clerk, tax collector, and treasurer hauled their supporters to the polls. And the candidates circulated outside the hall between the time the polls closed at 7 o'clock and the night's business really got started with action on the warrant of fifty-eight articles at 8 p.m.

When the moderator banged his gavel down sharply at 8:00 to call the meeting to order, the ballot clerks were busy inside the guarded door of the selectmen's office tallying the vote. Anyone who wanted to sit down had a chair, and all waited for the fireworks to begin. They didn't have to wait long. Before the moderator could finish reading the first article of business, an ex-Army sergeant was on his feet demanding that four articles, Numbers 43, 44, 45, and 46, be chucked right out of the warrant and not even be considered because they had been submitted by the local postmaster. The sergeant cited the Hatch Act about federal employees staying out of politics and a few private reasons of his own, which had more to do with the personality of the postmaster than his duties with the mail. The sergeant said his piece, but he didn't get very far. The moderator ruled him out of order and told him he would have his chance to move for dismissal of the articles if he so chose when the meeting got to them, but until it did, the articles stayed put.

So it began. The sergeant may not have won his point, but he set a tone to the meeting which never changed all evening — one of belligerent determination to have one's say, of passionate demand for a detailed explanation of anything which looked the slightest bit fishy, and of personal confrontation of anybody in town who might be suspected in any way of trying to get away with something.

The selectmen were raked fore and aft for overdrafts. The bill for legal services in a successful tax dispute had to be paid, "no question 'bout that, but why couldn't the selectmen have waited to pay it 'til the town gave its approval?" As for the budget committee, it might as well have stayed home and never made any recommendations at all, for its batting average on what it advocated in an effort to keep taxes down ranked pretty low. The school superintendent fought all alone for pay raises for his teachers. He didn't doubt the sincerity of the six men on the budget committee in not approving the raises, but as he pointedly reminded them and the town, they had no authority to set teachers' salaries. He got the money for the pay hikes, but he lost funds for hot top for the school driveway.

"Good idea to let the driveway go through a mud season to see if the gravel will hold up for tarring," the postmaster said.

The four articles which the ex-sergeant wanted to have heaved out of the warrant had to do with property revaluation. When they came up, the postmaster and his wife, with the assistance of a former selectman, battled it out on the floor with the sergeant. After about an hour's discussion and six amendments, the postmaster came off with a $1500 appropriation for professional outside assistance and a special town meeting in August to start the process of reassessing buildings in the town. So important was the matter to the non-resident population that one summer visitor and his wife came all the way up from New York to attend the meeting. He asked for permission to speak, and, hearing no objection, the moderator gave him the floor. He spoke briefly, said how much he liked the town but didn't like his taxes, applauded the move toward revaluation, and sat down. No one rose to argue with him.

From property taxes the voters turned next to town officers' salaries and gave them a thorough revision. The selectmen were voted $25-a-year pay boosts across the board, the first select-man's salary going to $325 and that of the second and third selectmen to $200 each. The moderator even received a $1.50 increase from $8.50 to $10, but the constable took a pay cut from $15 down to $5. After all, it was argued, he never had to make an arrest; and never did much more than tack up a town meeting warrant once or twice a year.

The article on "miscellaneous bills," catch-all for various town expenses not specifically authorized in separate articles, occupied the voters of Bremen for a full half-hour. An item of $28.95 for insurance was seized upon and chewed over for fifteen of the thirty minutes. A few years ago the town built a three-room consolidated grade school to replace its one-room schoolhouses. Included in the new building was a basement auditorium for town meetings and school functions. No longer needing the old town house, the town leased the building for $1 a year to the local woman's club, known as the Bremen Patriotic Club. As the town still holds title to the building, it pays the fire and liability insurance and the Patriotic Club reimburses the town. One fisherman couldn't understand how this transaction was handled under miscellaneous bills in the town report and teed off in great shape against "the town's paying $28.96 to insure a luxury group in case they get hurt, while the fishermen have to scramble up and down the town wharf, and if they break a leg, won't get a dime." The select-men, a member of the Patriotic Club, and even the moderator, had to do some tall talking to explain how credits and debits must be treated in town accounts.

Only once was the extra constable, hired from out of town because he would be less likely to take sides, called into action by the moderator. A defeated candidate got into a hassle in a corner of the hall with the husband of the woman who licked him for office. There was bristling and hot words. The husband shook his finger under the nose of the losing candidate, who in turn grabbed the husband by the front of the shirt. But the con-

stable and friends stepped in before either party started swinging. Before the evening was over the two would-be combat-
ants were chatting like old friends.

It took six hours and five minutes to get through the warrant,
article by article, amendment on amendment. The only breath-
er came when the treasurer was called upon to read a list of
tax liens placed on the property of taxpayers who had failed
to pay their taxes. A few people listened, others stretched their
legs, some napped, and the moderator took advantage of the
lull and sat down to rest his feet.

Legally, a town meeting on a Saturday night must end at
midnight. At 12 o'clock, however, the voters of Bremen had
progressed only two-thirds of the way through the warrant and
were still going strong. The moderator noted the time, informed the clerk he was "covering the clock," turned his watch
upside down on the table, and kept the meeting going. So hot
did the discussion get throughout the night that nobody bothered to keep track of mounting appropriations. When the gavel
went down to adjourn the session at 2:05 a.m., the voters of
Bremen had appropriated $6700 more than they did the previ-
ous year at the rate of better than $1000 an hour. They had,
in effect, jacked up their own taxes another 15 mills. But that
is the privilege one has at a real town meeting — taxation with
personal representation. "It was quite a night down in Bremen."

DOWN TO THE SEA

To many, Maine means the down east coast and the sea —
lobstering and fishing, old schooners,
and Maine-built ships
that sailed round
the Horn.

CAPTAIN "SHOTGUN" MURPHY AND THE "SHENANDOAH"

BY RICHARD B. NOBLE

WHEN THE BEAUTIFUL *Shenandoah* slid into the waters of the Kennebec in November of 1890, some 8000 people were on hand to watch the event because, among other things, this was the largest sailing vessel that had ever been built in the United States up to that time. There was then only one other ship in the entire world that exceeded her in size, the five-masted French vessel *Ville De Paris*. The *Shenandoah* was to create a sensation in every port she visited, and the American people liked her looks so much that the federal government put her portrait on all master mariners' licenses for sailing vessels from then on.

At the time the Sewalls planned the great *Shenandoah*, there was endless argument as to whether a wooden ship of such great length could possibly be successful. She was just three inches shy of being 300 feet long, with a beam of 49 feet, 1 inch and a depth of 28 feet, 6 inches. Her gross tonnage was

3406; net 3258; and two acres of canvas could be spread from her yards and spars, which towered as high as 217 feet above the deck. She cost $175,000 to build.

Old-timers said that a ship of that size would be unwieldy and behave badly in a heavy sea. How wrong they were; Captain James F. Murphy later reported that she sailed like a knockabout sloop in any kind of weather! He claimed that the reason she handled so well was because he himself directed just where the masts should go. The Sewalls had called Captain Murphy to Bath in 1889 to superintend the rigging of the new vessel, and he saw to it that she was. "sparred right." She was rigged as a four-masted bark, or a "shipentine," as American seamen sometimes called her.

Captain Murphy — or "Shotgun" Murphy as he was known — took the *Shenandoah* out on her maiden voyage and commanded her for nearly nine years. She completed her first voyage from New York to San Francisco in 125 days, of which fifteen were in calms and light breezes. She had clawed out to windward ahead of the British vessel *Kensington* off Cape Horn, and Captain Murphy was ready to race her against all comers.

He sailed from San Francisco at 10 a.m. on August 1, 1891 in company with four other grain ships, the Down Easters *M. P. Grace* and the brand new *S. D. Carleton*, both of Bath, and two Britishers. The whistles of the Farallones could be heard in spite of the strong head wind as the tugs cast off their various charges. Captain Edwin T. Amesbury tacked the *Carleton* to the north and Murphy headed south. On November 18, 109 days later, Murphy sailed the *Shenandoah* into Havre, France, having averaged 278 knots for twenty straight days during the passage. The *Carleton* made it on November 21, 112 days out.

Captain Murphy, who was strictly an extrovert and could boast with great gusto, claimed that he had discharged his cargo and sailed away for New York before anyone else had showed up. Captain Amesbury of the *Carleton* had a different version.

"If Jim sailed from Havre before I came in," he said, "how come he came aboard my ship at her wharf and took hot biscuits out of my cook's oven?"

On March 24, 1892 the *Shenandoah* sailed from New York in another race with the *Carleton* (Captain Amesbury) and also the *Tam O'Shanter* (Captain Peabody). This time the destination was San Francisco, and the three captains had heavy bets on who would reach there first. Captains Murphy and Amesbury bet $1000 on their ships, and Murphy also placed a side bet of $2000 with Captain Peabody that he would beat him.

Captain Murphy got a big surprise and disappointment to find that the *Tam* was already docked when he came in to Frisco, having beaten him by only three hours. It was rather rough on Murphy's pocketbook. Both the *Shenandoah* and *Tam O'Shanter* made it in 11 days, and Murphy always claimed he reached the Golden Gate first but was hung up there by fog. Captain Amesbury said he didn't see much fog, but he and his *Carleton* were well behind. She got caught in heavy weather and took 142 days to make the trip.

Another time off the Golden Gate, heavy fog lifted just enough for Murphy to set a course for San Francisco Bay before it closed in again. He bent on all sail and raced for the harbor. The pilot boat hailed him, but he was busy looking the other way. Later, after the vessel had slackened speed, a tug spoke him and asked if a man and his wife could come aboard to see how a square-rigger was worked.

"I let them come aboard," Captain Murphy related, "but I didn't have much time for entertaining visitors, for the harbor was full of moving craft, and I only had three miles to get the sail off my ship and bring her to anchorage."

All hands were swarming over the deck and rigging, and the sharp orders from the *Shenandoah*'s master were obeyed with such alacrity that Murphy heard the visitor say to his wife, "Isn't he the old pirate! See how scared these poor sailors are of him."

On still another occasion off the Golden Gate, the *Shenan-*

doah was standing by near the channel waiting for the fog to lift when a U.S. transport from the Philippines came steaming by, all glittering with gold braid and brass. The captain, with his new-fangled navigating equipment, decided to help the "poor unprotected sailing ship" and hollered out, "My position is 37 degrees 40'!"

"Huh," roared Murphy, "my position is 37 degrees 30'!" The transport captain looked disdainfully at the *Shenandoah*'s master and passed by — straight onto the rocks at Point Montera. Later, when the fog lifted, the *Shenandoah* sailed past the point and safely to her anchorage.

Many of the master mariners in those days received their licenses at an early age, because a lot of them went to sea as young boys; some were even born at sea. James F. Murphy got his master's ticket when he was twenty-two, and his first command was the clipper ship *David Brown*. The young captain was a hearty Irishman, quick-witted, with a natural talent for the sea. It wasn't long before he developed into one of the most efficient captains in the Cape Horn trade. He was popular with ship owners, because he was a good money-maker, and his passages were as short as possible. He was a hard driver who got the most out of his ship and his crew. Some of his officers were real "buckos." They could fight their way with fists from one end of the forecastle to the other — and most of them enjoyed it.

Captain Murphy found his *Shenandoah* listed in the "Red Record," a few times, but nothing ever came of it. Once he was cited for not trying to rescue a man who had fallen overboard from the royal yardarm. Murphy countered that there was a gale blowing and he could not lower a boat.

The "Red Record" was a unique section of the *Coast Seamen's Journal*, the official newspaper of the National Seamen's Union of America, published at San Francisco. It was printed from September, 1888 until November, 1895 to try to stem brutality at sea. It listed sixty-four cases of murder and cruelty, principally covering vessels in the Cape Horn fleet, many of which were Maine ships. Rarely was anyone who had been accused ever bound over for trial. If a case did reach court, the defendant was usually freed for lack of evidence or on the grounds of justifiable discipline.

One of the unusual customs of the enthusiastic Captain Murphy was to fly an Irish burgee — green with a yellow harp on it — beneath the Stars and Stripes when entering port. This practice became the subject of a poem, composed by a sailor named Johnny Clark and sung to the tune of "The Banks of Newfoundland":

We'll wash her and we'll scrub her down, and work without a frown, for on board the saucy Shenandoah, *flies the harp without a crown.*

The entire epic can be found in Joanna C. Colcord's book, *Roll and Go.*

In July, 1898 while the *Shenandoah* was in England, Captain Murphy received a cablegram from the owners, A Sewall & Co., directing him to insure the ship against war risks. The Spanish-American War had begun, and Spanish gunboats were lurking off the British Isles. Murphy, always thirsty for action, decided that the best kind of insurance was two 4-inch guns, which he mounted on his ship, one at the bow and the other on the stern.

Sure enough, when only a few days out of Liverpool off the coast of Ireland, Murphy fell in with a Spanish gunboat. It fired a shot across his bow, which meant for him to heave to. Instead, Captain Murphy, who was doing fifteen knots at the time, fired two rounds at the Spaniard, but missed, much to the crew's disappointment. A chase ensued, but it was useless for the gunboat to try to catch the speedy *Shenandoah*. In four hours the big bark was hull down on the horizon.

Once off Cape Horn, the *Shenandoah*'s captain had an opportunity to compare the sailing qualities of his ship with those of one of the much-publicized British tea clippers. This partic-ular ship, the *Jerusalem*, decided to show off one morning when she found herself to leeward and a little ahead of the *Shenan-*

doah, which was close hauled with a strong northwest wind.

The British captain, thinking to display the superior point-ing ability of the *Jerusalem,* discourteously put his helm down and crossed the Bath ship's bow, taking a berth well to wind-ward. Captain Murphy stood on his quarter-deck and watched the maneuver, his temper boiling. He let the Englishman attain a position well on his weather bow, and then roared a string of commands. The *Shenandoah's* helm went down and her lee braces were hauled well aft. The bark leaped forward with ease to windward of the impertinent Britisher, blanketing her almost to a standstill. Not many hours later the *Shenandoah* had left the Britisher astern and was out of sight.

An officer of the U.S.S. *Wabash* once wrote a thrilling ac-count of a chance meeting of his vessel and the *Shenandoah* in mid-Pacific one Fourth of July morning in the early 1900's when square-rigged sailing vessels were not too common. The *Wabash* was returning to the States from the Far East, and, according to naval custom, had "dressed ship" in honor of the holiday. Here is part of the officer's story:

"The crew was lolling around on the decks when the lookout yelled, 'A sail!' The sail was a skys'l, still and tiny as the link of a lady's lorgnette chain, on the outermost verge of the south-eastern horizon. A sailing ship approaching you at sea seems to make at you in bounds when you yourself are driving for her, and by the time we took a second long look at the approaching ship, her huge royal bellied out by the fresh breeze shone clear and brilliant in our eyes, reflected by the bright morning sun. Our gaze was then focused on the bit of bunting — the Stars and Stripes of our Republic! I think a bit of a chill ran over the spines of all of us when we saw that, in the middle of the Pacific Ocean on this 4th of July.

" 'The *Shenandoah,* out of Bath,' shouted the signal quarter-master on the bridge.

"It would be hard to describe the feelings we all experienced when the *Shenandoah* swept by within 100 yards of us, her crew just as excited as we were, and she did not wait for us to dip, but just as she swung by us like a princess in the pride of her finery, again and again was the banner dipped in reply to our dipping at the mizzen, and the ship's crew, ranged along the weather rail, mingled their hoarse shouts with the tremendous cheering of our man-of-war's men."

Captain Murphy left the *Shenandoah* in 1898 to supervise the repairs to the *Kenilworth*, another Sewall ship. Captain William Starkey took command of the *Shenandoah* for one voyage to San Francisco and nearly sailed her to glory. While the ship was caught amid icebergs, with the blocks, sails and rigging frozen into a solid mass of ice, a meteor came out of the heavens like a great green ball of fire with a long fiery trail behind. Captain Starkey thought it was going to strike the ship, but it passed overhead and blew to pieces before striking the water.

In 1902 Captain Murphy was back on the quarter-deck of the *Shenandoah* once again and sailed her from San Francisco to Liverpool and then to New York. Later that year Captain Omar E. Chapman took command of the ship and stayed with her until 1910. In that year Captain Murphy came aboard for the last time and sailed the *Shenandoah* on her final voyage before she was cut down for a coal barge.

The last years were lean ones for the *Shenandoah*. Most of the transoceanic carrying trade had been taken over by foreign shipping, and much of the domestic traffic was diverted to railroads and steamships. High insurance rates shut the wooden *Shenandoah* out of the long-distance cargoes she had once carried, and she was too big and too expensive for short hauls. For three years she lay at anchor waiting for a cargo which never came, and at the end her discouraged owners sold her to a barge company for $36,000. With her top hamper removed, she made her first trip as a coal barge at the end of a tow line in October, 1910. For a few years she suffered the degradation of this service up and down the coast. On October 29, 1915 she ended her days when she was rammed and sunk by a steamer off Fire Island, New York.

BRUIN—MAINE LOBSTER DOG

BY WILLAN C. ROUX

IF ELROY JOHNSON'S DOG, Bruin, wasn't the smartest dog in the State of Maine, as Elroy claimed, he was mighty close to it.

Elroy is a Maine lobsterman. In fact, he is *the* Maine lobsterman. For, when a statue of a typical Maine lobsterman was sculptured in 1939, Elroy was the model. Displayed at the New York World's Fair, the statue was seen and admired by thousands. Presently, it is at the Boothbay Harbor Sea and Shore Fisheries installation. And, in the near future, a bronze replica will be cast and erected in a permanent location on Maine Avenue in Washington, D.C.

While Elroy is undeniably proud of the statue and happy that it will soon go to the Nation's Capital, he has always had, as he put it, a "foolish notion" about it and his dog, Bruin.

Bruin was a duly licensed "lobsterman." Soon after the statue of his owner was completed, Bruin was issued a license by the Commissioner of the Sea and Shores Fisheries Department. It was hung on his collar in a special ceremony and, just as Elroy became the representative of all Maine lobstermen, Bruin qualified similarly for all dogs that go lobstering with their masters.

From the time he was a puppy until the day he died, Bruin never missed hauling traps no matter the season or the weather, except for one week when he was recovering from an accident. Bruin's station on Elroy's boat was the after deck. He would lie there quietly until a trap was hauled aboard, then he'd get up and look into it as eagerly as Elroy and show pleasure or disappointment at what it contained. His judgment was unerring: he knew when a lobster was legal and when it wasn't. If a trap held nothing but shorts and crabs, he'd turn away, lie back down on the deck and wait for another to be pulled up. Legal lobsters he greeted with happy yips and hearty tail waggings. Elroy, of course, measured the catch to be sure they were "counters" but he said there was no need to. "Bruin was never wrong. All I ever did — and I did it only once — was show him a counter alongside a short. I pointed to the short, shook my head and threw it back. Then I nodded at the counter and put him into the basket. Bruin caught on all right and never forgot."

On many occasions, Bruin caught lobsters on his own in the shallow water near Elroy's lobster shack. He'd wade in, grab the lobster by the back and carry him ashore in his mouth. He had great respect for flailing claws and never once got nipped, which is more than some lobstermen can say.

When he was very young, Bruin looked like a teddy bear. He grew to be about the size of a springer spaniel, though there was little, if any, of that strain in him. Elroy never could decide what he was mostly, and it didn't matter: he was all dog and all understanding.

Elroy never talked down to Bruin, never scolded him, never shouted at him. His talk was man-to-man. When the dog did something out of order, which was very infrequent, Elroy just said quietly, "Bruin, you shouldn't have done that. Twasn't

nice." And the dog would wince and go lie down, his eyes on
Elroy, waiting for a gesture or a word that told him he was
forgiven. It was never long coming. For Elroy was as unhappy
as Bruin when they failed to see eye to eye.

Uncle Ev Sinnett, who owned the general store at the head
of Steamboat Wharf on Bailey Island, was inclined to discre-
dit Bruin's smartness. And there were others among the lobstermen gathered at the store of an afternoon who agreed.

Elroy, who was more than a little annoyed at their skepti-
cism, was telling about the time he and Bruin went duck hunting at Land's End. When they arrived at their vantage point,
Elroy discovered that all but one of his shotgun shells had
fallen out of his pocket somewhere along the line of approach,
and were probably scattered over a considerable stretch. "All
I said to him was, 'Bruin, we've lost all but one of our shells.
Seems as though the rest of them are back where we came
from. Go find them and bring them to me.'

"I showed him the shell," he continued. "He didn't even
sniff at it. He simply looked at it and started back-tracking.
He returned in a minute with a shell in his mouth and dropped it into my hand. Off he went and retrieved another, then
another and another until he got them all. I thanked him and
we settled down to the business at hand and soon had all the
ducks the law allowed."

Uncle Ev sniffed. "You can't tell me that dog knew what
you were talking about. Or, just by looking at something
knew what you wanted him to find." Several of the other
men nodded.

"Well," said Elroy, " he *did* find the shells just as I told you.
I know, sure as I'm sitting here, that Bruin understands what
I say and knows things by name as well as by sight. How many
times have you been here when I'd say to him, 'I forgot my
dinner pail. Do you mind getting it for me?' And he'd go right
down to my shack, pick it up and bring it to me."

"That may be so," answered Uncle Ev, "but I think he just
knows your scent and once you got him in the habit of fetch-

ing your dinner pail, he kind of automatically goes for it when you tell him."

"May be," said Elroy, "but I know it's more than that. And I'm going to show you right now." He called the dog to him. "Bruin," he said, "I left my mittens down there at the shack next to my dinner pail. These fellows don't think you know a mitten from a dinner pail. What I want you to do is fetch me the mittens. You can get the dinner pail later."

Bruin barked twice and ran the fifty feet from the store to the shack on the beach. Without any hesitation he picked up the mittens and trotted back with them.

"There," said Elroy, triumphantly, "I told you he'd know the difference and that ought to prove to you once and for all that he knows what I'm saying. He understands English same as you and me. And a darned sight better than some of you. Now, Bruin, go get my dinner pail."

Uncle Ev and the other doubters were finally convinced and never again seriously questioned the dog's prowess. In fact, they came to think he was something special and were as proud of him as Elroy was.

Bruin had at least two brushes with death. Both had happy endings. The first occurred one midwinter day when he, Elroy and his helper were hauling traps just this side of Halfway Rock lighthouse. It was rough, bitter cold, and there were frequent snow flurries. Elroy said afterward that it was just about as wicked a chunk of weather as he'd ever been out in. The boat pitched and rolled and suddenly the bait tubs upset in the cockpit. Between cleaning up the mess of ripe fish and keeping the boat from broaching as they set out for home, they forgot all about Bruin.

It wasn't until they were in the lee of Jaquish Island, three miles in, that they missed the dog. He was nowhere on board. Evidently he'd slipped off the stern and was somewhere out there in the water.

Elroy figured the chances of finding him were slim, but he could no more go home without trying than he could if it had been any other member of his family. So they started back, hoping that Bruin hadn't gone overboard too far out.

If anything, the water was rougher, the wind icier and the snow flurries thicker. Elroy, up forward, looked in every direction as they drove the boat back toward the lighthouse. They'd gone more than a mile when he sighted Bruin off the port bow. The dog must have seen them at the same time because he changed his course and swam toward the boat. Soon he was alongside and Elroy hauled him aboard. He shook himself thoroughly, nuzzled Elroy, barked his thanks and stretched out by the stove in the deck house.

"That dog," said Elroy, "must have swum a good mile and a half in that freezing water. And he wasn't any the worse for it once he dried out. Darned if I don't think he'd have made land under his own power if he'd had to. He knew which way home was. Always did when we were out. I swear his sense of direction was every bit as reliable as a compass reading."

Bruin's second narrow escape was a result of pure carelessness. "He wasn't what you'd call a careless dog," said Elroy. "But this once his mind must have been somewhere else. Usually he stayed close to the house. 'T wasn't often I had to call him or go look for him. On toward dark one day, I realized all of a sudden that Bruin wasn't anywhere around. I called, walked up the road and followed it to Uncle Ev's store. No one there had seen him. Finally I went over to my shack and, as I stood there at the head of my dock, I heard a whimper. It was coming from my punt which was tied up to the float. There was Bruin lying in the bottom of it and I could see he was in considerable pain. There was blood on him from a gash in his hind leg and another along his side. When I spoke to him he just wagged his tail weakly and begged me with his eyes to help him. Knew I'd take care of him as I always had.

"I carried him all the way back home, cleaned him up and dressed his wounds as best I could and made a bed for him next to the kitchen stove. He sure looked like death and I think that's what was on his mind. Later I found out he'd been hit by a truck. It was his own fault. Just got careless crossing the road and the truck couldn't stop. Instead of trying to get home, he went off by himself, figuring his time was up. Somehow he eased himself into the punt he knew so well and lay there waiting to die.

"Of course," Elroy went on, "he didn't. He was tougher than he thought and with a week or so of resting and healing he was back on the job as good as new."

Bruin died of old age many years ago and Elroy, now in his seventies, has never wanted another dog. "None could replace him," he says. "You know, I kind of wish they could have included him in that statue. Maybe it's a foolish notion to anyone but me."

His eyes glistened as he looked out the window. "But I've always thought it would have been fitting, — mighty fitting."

UNTIL THE SEA RUNS DRY

BY ROBERT NEALEY

As with the fore-and-aft schooners, Maine's seagoing farm-ers were not the originators, but the ingenious designers and perfecters in the long evolution that culminated in the artistic and practical success known as the dory.

A waterfront reporter once called down to us from Portland's Commercial Wharf:

"How long will those flimsy things stand by you?"

Dropping an affectionate fist on the nearest dory, our skip-per answered with a misquote from Bobby Burns:

"Until the sea runs dry, chum! Until the rocks melt in the sun!"

No truer eulogy was ever uttered.

I learned about dories as a crew member of one of the last topsail schooners ever to clear a Maine port and drive north-east under sail-power alone.

Her dories were cupped, one in another on both sides of the

foremast. In the shelter of these nested dories, we dorymen were already settled into our first work of sharpening hooks in hook sets, fastening them to our main trawl by short lines called gangins, and knocking the ice and snow from our wooden trawl tubs; while some of "the old ones" grumbled about "the good old days" when such "tubs" were actually canvas sacks that were much lighter to handle and took up less space.

We all wore the uniform of the trade: yellow oilskins, storm hats and cowhide sea-boots, just as the Newfies, Bluenoses, Gloucestermen and all the Grand Banks peoples did. None of us were Portuguese, Scandinavian, Boston Irish or Italian. We were all down east Yankees of British descent, whose ancestors were either Puritans, pirates — or both.

Our skipper was one of us — older and wiser. He would never have become our master if he had not once been a good doryman. Everything about us centered on that one object, the dory. Without dories, even our schooner would have been useless, for we would never have accumulated a fishy cargo or a penny.

By the ancient 50-50 "lay," half our gross profit, when any, went to crew and master, while the balance went to the owners, who were private investors and/or fish company executives. If unlucky, we were paid nothing. If lucky, we received from two to five dollars for each hour we worked.

We dorymen belonged to no trade union and obeyed nobody except the lord-god who was our master and skipper. We paid for all of our shipboard food and for most of our gear. It was the best money could buy, as long as our credit was good. In hard times and penury, we ate less well and worked much harder to improve our luck. The skipper purchased all stores, accepting a commission therefrom.

We ate and drank well in season: spring lamb, summer vegetables and fruits, prime fall beef, winter preserves and fresh shortening bread, Canadian rum, coffee and tea — while the shack locker contained cheese and pilot biscuit, plus "hermit" and "brownie" cookies, for off-watch snacks.

A rose-colored down east sunrise or sunset meant nothing to us except that we had to drop one sail after another and steer up a cove channel to Herrin Wharf, where the herring-chokers brought samples down from their icehouse, as we made fast to a gull-soiled and tide-warped pile.

Our skipper, a master at buying bait, ran a dirty thumbnail down a herring belly and sniffed it alertly to test its alleged tenderness and freshness. We always got good bait, which was stuffed with chipped ice below decks. By the grace of God we expected, eventually, to exchange the herring for cod. This did not mean we were a pious lot, although before ever a dory was launched, the skipper had us, one by one, place a meaty fist on his Bible and solemnly swear that if it ever came to a choice between saving ourselves or our catch, we would give the fish priority.

Loaded with bait, we were off with the first flood tide. In the cabin our skipper began consulting his charts, although he had long since committed them to memory. The charts were unlike those used today. They were yellow and thin and cracked with age. They were seagoing-farmer improvements and variations of accumulated knowledge passed from father to son for endless generations. No doubt, some still exist in some farmstead attic or woodshed loft.

"Western Bank," such charts would read. "71,000 mixed fish, February 14, 1893. Le Havre, 92,000, August 13, 1901."

When our skipper got us to such a spot, he poked his old gray head from the scuttle and proclaimed: "We're on fish! Haul the duck down!"

The skipper had his own fish-scope in his homemade charts and his total-recall memory. We knew he had seen on one of his charts, the symbolic "VFS." Next, he ordered out the eight-pound deep-sea lead, which we flung overboard and then retrieved hand-over-dripping-hand and passed to him, realizing as we did so that the sea was not full of fish by any means, and that it was easy to err if you did not know your business.

We watched intently as the skipper turned the lead upside-down to examine the tallow stuffed into a slot there. With thick thumb and forefinger he pinched a bit of the tallow. Then, making doubly sure that what he felt with his trained fingers was the "Very Fine Sand" his charts had indicated, he tasted the tallow with the furry tip of his tongue. Without looking up he ordered:

"Bait, boys!"

So we started chopping herring into bait sizes, slipped them on the hooks, and again coiled them into the tubs, until the skipper called:

"Dories down!"

When the dory Dave Conrad and I shared — number three — came up, Dave got in first. He was a broad-backed, thick armed, pale eyed, ruddy-faced, short, heavy man who hated to shave. He had the heavy muscles developed by toil that was just a step above galley-boat slavery. As had been the case with the first two dories, four dorymen, two at each painter, heaved number three dory and then Dave Conrad over the side. Dave then took the oars and the buoy-kegs, the trawl tubs, the bull-stick for leveraging the trawls into the sea, the rum jug and the cracker box which he stored in the sideboards.

The remaining dorymen heaved me into the dory next, and when I managed to land on my feet, they jeered:

"Siddown, chum, you're rockin' the boat!"

Among seagoing farmers of the day that was considered a very funny joke.

The skipper pointed in the direction of the "set," and I placed the oars and began to row with quick, deep strokes as the schooner sailed away to drop other dories. The schooner never stopped in those days. If a doryman made a misstep for one reason or another, and fell into the Atlantic, he was, when possible, fish-hooked out on the run as if he were a frozen pollock.

In our dory Dave flipped up the red flag as though he were posting mail in a rural letterbox, and heaved the first buoy-keg and anchor into the sea, then rhythmically lifted the top

coil with the bull-stick and flipped his wrists over as if he were
turning over hay to dry in the sun. Thus the bait sank to the
"Very Fine Sand" twenty-five fathoms below.

I kept rowing easily, occasionally raising my head to "find
the sea and the wind." It wasn't yet officially winter, but the
air was cold and the weak sun couldn't break through the
heavy clouds. Since Banks gales arrived with little warning,
we had to keep alert. The schooner became invisible and left
Dave, the dory and me alone. We were riding a roller-coaster
that dropped us breathlessly into the depths and shot us up-
ward into the clouds. Only one dory plank separated life and
death.

Dave and I had been dorymates long enough to know that
neither one could get along without the other. We said little.
Our actions spoke louder than words. Our thoughts were identical, as we concentrated on the job that gave us our daily
bread. Dave dropped the last hook glistening down, then sent
another buoy afloat.

I inquired, "Lay here?"

"Ayeh," Dave said.

So we anchored to a buoy and waited for the schooner to
sound the fishing signal, in two hours or so. Dave decided to
catnap on the bottom boards out of the wind. While the cod
swallowed hooks I kept warm by exercising at the oars, to keep
us into the tide. Eventually, out of sight, but not sound, the
schooner's foghorn started a melancholy moaning. That was
the signal to twenty dorymen that our skipper figured the cod
had finished their breakfast.

I fished in the buoy to which we had been anchored, spiral-
ing it to Dave as he arose stiffly and stretching, still half asleep.
Automatically, he slipped the trawl line into the pulley set into
the gunwale aft, and hand-over-bare-hand, started hauling up.
He was one of the few I knew who could do such work bare-
handed. His hands were enormous, leathery, black, the palms
crisscrossed with permanent scars that sometimes cracked open
under the trawl line and bled until the wound coagulated in

the cold, salt water. Twenty pound "steakers" came flapping up via the same type of fish harvest that had started in the Sea of Galilee.

As the hooks appeared, Dave flipped the fish free and into the stern-sheets with a deft backward motion of his wrist. Hour after hour, as fish filled the dory, I coiled empty hooks into empty tubs, sometimes scratching my hands through the water-logged canvas "palms" I wore, so that the salt water in the little cuts felt like wood splinters and were very uncomfortable. The live fish died. The wind strengthened. Dave and I jackknifed and straightened, hauled and coiled, never spoke, and occasionally changed places.

When the last hook was up, I hoisted the sail. Sticking one oar in the sculling notch aft, I steered for the schooner. Eventually we sighted other sails, red like our own, heading in the same direction. We were the seventeenth dory to be picked up on the run. As we came alongside, the cook javelined pitchforks down and I threw a line up. Dave and I pitched cod after cod up over the rail into deck bins. Then, as our dory was decked with the pulley-whip, I pulled the plug and let brine, fish scales, and blood drain out.

On deck, we went to the troughs to rip and gut cod. I ripped down with my sheath-knife. Dave caught the cod and, gutting it, tossed it into a cleansing tub, while carrion streamed into the sea for the waiting sharks and screeching terns. Any doryman with a spare moment stirred the cleansing tub with a broken oar, and then dumped the fish into the hold where they were stuffed and packed in ice chips.

Where herring had been, cod now were. It had taken fish to catch fish. Although it was not yet noon, we had all put in nine hours work, with more to come. Eventually the cook poked his head from the galley and bawled:

"First table!"

After dinner we went above to make another set. It was dark before we got finished with the aid of lantern-light. Finally Dave and I had our turn at catnapping in our forecastle bunks.

Before dawn we were back on the ferris-wheel again for another twelve or eighteen hours or so.

Once more the skipper called, "Number Three!" and we
were alone at sea again — Dave, the dory and I. We hauled a
second set until late afternoon, our muscles and nerves strained
to the utmost. Vapor seeped from our mouths and nostrils.
Frost formed on our oilksins. Snow-heavy clouds bounced
on the restive sea. Black rollers smashed hard against our
dory. The salt brine froze on us. But finally the schooner's
horn signalled us to fish. For the second successive day we
filled our dory full of fish, until the weak sun was swallowed
by the high sea.

"Weather don't look promisin'," I said. "You think it'll
improve, Dave?"

"Daow!"

We heard no storm-warning horn from the schooner. We saw
no other dories. We waited, but the schooner did not come.
It grew very black. I thought: *Having been among the first
dropped, we'll be among the last retrieved.* We waited. The
sea didn't. It suddenly hurled a tidal wave at the dory, and as
we yawed, despite my efforts at the oars, a flurry of snow slapped our faces. I mumbled to myself:

"The skipper will circle in until he finds us. The dory will
stick by us until the sea runs dry and the rocks melt in the sun."

We stared. We listened. The dory sank into troughs so deep
that the oars and my arms, up to the elbows, were submerged
in icy water.

"Shall we dump a buoy and anchor?"

"Daow!" Dave said.

"Then the trawl tubs, chum?"

"Daow!"

"Then these cod?"

"Shuddup," Dave said.

"I ain't got room to really row, Dave. And how you goin'
bail us out with all this gear and fish aboard?"

"We ain't goin' ditch no fish," Dave said. "You know that!"

Before I could answer a sea dropped down on us, heavy and hard, half filling the overloaded dory. While I labored at the oars to keep us into it, Dave bailed out water and some fish. The dory worked just as hard, if not harder, than we did, to stay afloat.

Time passed. If we could hold our position the skipper would find us. But the gale grew stronger and we didn't. I wondered if the schooner could sail in this blow, or would she have to heave to?

"Dave," I said. "We're in for it!"

"Yeh." Dave held a pocket compass cupped in his hands, close to his eyes, trying to read it in the dark.

It snowed, rained, hailed — in flurries, gusts, torrents, freezing on us and the dory. My mittens were frozen to the oars. This helped me to hang on to them, and hold our position via the compass readings. When Dave wasn't reading, he was bailing. But the dory remained up to her gunwales in the sea. So steep were the rollers that we sometimes seemed to be upside-down. But it was better to ride them than fall off and have them drop on us.

Finally, Dave, who was thirty years my senior, sat down on the piled fish, his eyes as glassy as theirs. My tongue was too dry to wet my mouth. Our rum and biscuits were gone. Dave was going. He smelled a deadly fish smell. The wind cut through my oilskins and woolen underclothing as though I were naked. Dave sprawled supinely out and moved only when the fish under him moved. The dory seemed unconscious, or dead, too, ready to give up the ghost. Suddenly I could not collect my wits. My mind wandered crazily. My arms and back ached, but the hard rowing had kept my blood circulating.

There was more water than fish in the dory now, and Dave's body sloshed about as if it might be washed overboard any minute. From a doryman's habit, I still glanced dog-like over one shoulder at every fifth stroke. So I saw our schooner come over a crest and down at us. Dave and I and the dory lived to fish many times again.

"PUT THE DIMITIES TO HER"

AS TOLD TO STUART FORD BY ELROY JOHNSON

In the early summer of 1917 the Maine fishing schooner *Albert W. Black* lay quietly against the wharf at Bailey Island, her change of gear from winter trawling to sword fishing nearly completed. A pulpit was in place at the end of the bowsprit, where Jack Drakes, the striker, would spend day after day with his dart-tipped pole ready and his eyes straining from under his long-visored cap for a glimpse of the two stiff fins that would mark the presence of a swordfish near the surface. Aloft, narrow seats had been lashed from stay to stay on the fore topmast as lookout stations. They would be manned, when the schooner reached the fishing grounds, by all of her crew except the striker at his position in the pulpit, Skipper Granville Johnson at the helm, and Henry Doughty, the cook. It would be Henry's job, once a fish had been ironed, to throw overboard one of the keg floats that stood, wrapped with fathoms of line, on the starboard side forward. Spare poles and lances were fastened to the main shrouds; rigging and sails had been overhauled, and waterways, cabin hatches and rails glistened with fresh paint. As a precaution against what might lie ahead when a swordfish ironed by the striker was pursued and played from a dory, the top dory nested in the schooner's waist had a light platform built into the stern. It would serve as an island of refuge for the dorymen if a swordfish, only lightly ironed, should turn and punch its 500 pounds of muscle, sword first, through the half-inch planking. After a quarter of a century of fishing since her launching at Hodgdon Brothers shipyard at East Boothbay in 1892, the 72-foot *Albert W. Black* was ready to leave on another trip to Georges Bank.

As soon as the crew was on board, the schooner cast off lines for a quick sail to Portland to take on stores and additional gear, then back to Dingley Island, Harpswell, where twenty tons of ice were stowed in her hold. Leaving the New Meadows River, the vessel took her departure from Seguin — course southeast by south, a half south for the southeastern edge of Georges Bank. The discomforts of winter fishing over, her only apparent danger was being caught in a rare summer hurricane or being run down by a trans-atlantic liner, which was to be her fate fourteen years later.

The schooner reached the bank safely, found fish and returned with a catch that netted each man $85, which at that time would buy a lot of groceries for families ashore. Fishing continued good, but on a later trip, after icing down twenty-seven swordfish, the schooner had the misfortune to break her propeller shaft. Although power was not needed when the vessel was under sail, its loss did hamper her during early morning calm on good fishing days, and the old-fashioned way of taking to the dories to chase and harpoon fish was inefficient. So rather than lengthen out the trip without an engine, Skipper Johnson decided to return to Portland for repairs. Mending the broken shaft did not take long, and the *Albert Black* was soon back on Georges and striking fish. Toward dusk, as the lookouts were climbing down from their stations aloft, Elroy

Johnson called over to Jimmie Garaway, "Well, we have another twenty-seven fish. I wonder what bad luck will happen
this time."

"Oh, probably the Kaiser in the morning," Jimmie jokingly
replied.

Next morning Elroy was aroused by the 5 o'clock call for
breakfast. The boom of seas on the weather bow and the drawn
slide of the companionway told that a nasty, wet easterly was
blowing. The schooner was hove to under foresail and jumbo
with the wheel lashed hard down. As this would be no day for
fishing, Elroy went down in the hold to "trig" the last fish
caught and then relaxed in the cabin on the long seat outside
his bunk. Suddenly there was a dull boom, followed in a
moment by another.

"Must be I left a cake of ice loose in the hold," Elroy said
to Jimmie.

Without answering, Jimmie darted on deck and called back,
"Ice cake be damned! Come up here and I'll show you what
it is!"

There to the south'ard, about two miles away, lay a German submarine, firing warning shots to round up the fleet of
ten fishing vessels. The long black hull came nearer and took
up a position to windward of the schooners. Already her commander had begun ordering the fishermen into their dories
while German sailors clambered aboard to place explosives
that would later sink the vessels.

At the time, the *Albert Black* was about a mile to leeward
of the rest of the fleet. Never having been burdened with insurance on his vessel, Skipper Johnson decided it would be
a lot safer somewhere else. He saw a chance to escape and
took it.

"Put the dimities to her, fellows," he cried. There was a rush
of feet for the mainmast pin rail, and as the big mainsail was
hoisted, he unlashed the wheel while one of the crew started
the 35 horsepower engine. Almost before the peak of the sail

could be jigged up, Skipper Johnson spun the wheel over and the schooner took off before the wind.

When she had been hove to, the schooner had headed more or less toward the submarine; hence the hoisting of the mainsail was not immediately noticed by the Germans. But as the boom swung over, the broad expanse of the sail showed the U-boat commander that one of his sitting ducks was on the wing.

As the schooner's crew rushed the balloon jib forward from the lazaret, the submarine opened fire with her deck gun. The first shot sent up a fountain of water about 300 yards astern. The second landed close abeam. Out on the bowsprit, his feet on the foot ropes, Austin Snow tugged away at the big sail, while Elroy stood in the pulpit facing aft and snapped the hanks of the ballooner onto the stay. Ephram Eastman and Ezra Nickerson stood by the halyard and sheets. A third shot shrieked by them and splashed 200 feet ahead. By now, however, the distance to the sub was over a mile and rapidly widening. The schooner fled northwesterly in the general direction of Cultivator Shoal.

It did not require more shots to keep the *Albert Black* moving, nor were any forthcoming. Yet the possibility remained that the submarine would try to overtake the schooner once she had destroyed the other nine vessels. The only sure way to escape was to go where the submarine would not dare to follow. That was into shallow water, and that's where Granville Johnson sailed her.

At the start of her flight, the *Albert Black* was somewhere near the 90-fathom curve, about Latitude 41, with well over 500 feet of water beneath her keel. Now the water was shallower, and the schooner was deliberately exchanging the strange new hazard of the U-boat for one that was more familiar — Cultivator Shoal. If seas were breaking on the shoal, they might be seen in time; if not, the lead line could be relied on.

Skipper Johnson heaved the lead himself, standing on the

cabin house and throwing the line as far forward as he could. But the vessel was traveling so fast that the lead could not reach bottom by the time the line came opposite where he stood. Ordinarily, the vessel would be turned into the wind to lose way so soundings could be made, but in this emergency it seemed better to keep her going until very shoal water allowed the lead to reach bottom in spite of the speed. After four or five hours of running, the lead finally sounded in five fathoms.

"If he follows us here, he's got to come on top," the skipper said. He let the vessel come up a few points, then, after awhile, brought her still closer to the wind, steering more to the east. In a few hours, as soon as the water deepened, he swung the vessel off northwest for Portland Lightship.

The next day, around midnight, the *Albert W. Black* sailed into Portland Harbor. Bert Lubee and Elroy were out on the bowsprit taking in the ballooner as the schooner swept by the Coast Guard picket boat.

"That does it," Bert shouted as he fisted the sail. "That licks the Kaiser!"

THAT MAINE SPIRIT

There is something about living in Maine
that tests the character
and improves the spirit:
"Unshakable, self-sufficient,
and with an eye out to help
one's neighbor."

CONQUEROR OF LOUISBURG

BY RICHARD HALLET

WILLIAM PEPPERRELL, commanding general of the colonial English at the siege of Louisburg, was not a military man by profession. Like his father before him, he was a Kittery merchant and trader; a builder of ships, and a dealer in lumber, salt fish and naval stores.

But for those times, his business was on a vast scale; he was a Croesus of the New World. It was said of him that he could walk from the Piscataqua River to the Saco, a distance of thirty miles, without stepping off his own soil.

Born in 1696 at the height of a relentless Indian warfare which would go on until 1713 and all but exterminate the white settlements in Maine, young Pepperrell grew up in a mischancy time. From Kittery to Falmouth, Indians were on the war-path. Even in church men prayed with their firelocks between their knees and with sentinels posted at the door. At

sixteen, William Pepperrell bore arms in patrol duty and in
keeping watch and ward.

He had little formal education, but he was far from being
the rough frontiersman. The Pepperrell firm had a Boston
branch; young William spent much time there, and was early
appointed to the Governor's Board of Councilors. In Boston
he married the granddaughter of the learned Judge Samuel
Sewall, and acquired in Boston society the courtly manners
which later so well suited his status as an English baronet.

His reputation for skill in handling men and reconciling
their conflicts with his peculiar blend of firmness and affability
made him the logical choice for commander of the expedition
against Louisburg. When earlier he had been made Chief Justice of the Court of Common Pleas in Piscataqua, he "immediately after his appointment endeavored to qualify for his duties
by the study of law." Now again he must put the cart before the
horse by studying the art of war after being made a lieutenant
general in charge of siege operations. This might well give him
pause, even in that makeshift age. He was, it is true, already
colonel of all the Maine militia; but up to now he had commanded these rough-and-ready soldiers only on the parade
ground.

At this time the celebrated English preacher George Whitefield — the Great Awakener — was his guest in Kittery, and
Pepperrell asked for his advice. Should he risk all on this cast
of the dice, or no? The preacher thought the omens far from
good. "If you fail, the widows and orphans of the slain will
reproach you. If you succeed, envy will poison your days and
eclipse your glory."

Flat against this sage advice, Pepperrell accepted command,
and contributed 5000 pounds out of his personal fortune to
equip the expedition. The dubious Whitefield then gave him
this motto for his flag: *Nil Desperandum, Christo Duce* (With
Christ as your leader, you need not despair).

Certainly if Louisburg were taken, it would have to be by
a kind of special miracle of God's own Providence. The war

of the Austrian Succession between France and England had now been raging in Europe for a year; but long before this France had been preparing to defend her possessions in the New World.

The fortress of Louisburg, on the southeast tip of Cape Breton island, stood guard over the mouth of the St. Lawrence and at the same time threatened Boston. The French had made it one of the strongest places in the world, probably second only to Gibraltar.

William Vaughan of Damariscotta, originator of the "mad scheme" to take it, well knew that it was strong. He had been there. He had seen its ramparts of stone 30 feet high, and its ditch 80 feet wide; he had counted its cannon, and marked how shallow the sea was in the neighborhood of the fort.

But Vaughan was headstrong, and his courage was fabulous. Like Lord Cochrane of later times, he believed that "the impossible has the best chance of success, because nobody guards against it."

Vaughan argued with Governor Shirley of Massachusetts that some of these colonists had the blood of Cromwell's Ironsides in them, and every manjack of them had been a marksman from youth up. "And then in winter the snowdrifts sometimes bank up against the ramparts so high that men on snowshoes can scale them easily, walk into town, and take the frightened French like so many hens in a coop."

Governor Shirley was an audacious man himself, but this notion of attacking Louisburg in the dead of winter made him quake a little. Better to wait until April, and even then it would be best "to rely on surprise and swarm into Louisburg at night, while the French were asleep."

Vaughan had made his main point good, and the plan to conquer Louisburg was carried in the Boston Assembly by a single vote.

A fleet of 100 small armed vessels carrying 4000 troops rendezvoused at Canseau in Nova Scotia on April 1, 1745, and was reinforced by three British warships under Commodore Peter

Warren. The people who stayed at home in Boston bade adieu
to the Louisburg soldiers in a kind of "it's-been-nice-knowing-
you" mood. A letter from Boston to one Colonel Hale reads:
"I hope this will find you at Louisburg with a Bowl of Punch,
a Pipe, and a P-k of C-ds in your hand and whatever else you
desire (I had forgot to mention, a pretty French Mademoiselle).
Your friend Luke has turned poor B. out of the house for saying he believed you would not take the place . . . 'Damn his
blood,' says Luke, 'Let him be an Englishman or a Frenchman, and not pretend to be an Englishman when he is a
Frenchman at heart.' If drinking to your success would take
the place, you must be in possession of it now, for it's a Standing Toast."

It would take more than drinking to success to compass the
fall of Louisburg, for the French were not to be taken in their
sleep. Yet the hearts of the besiegers were bold. Parson Samuel
Moody of York, an uncle of Pepperrell's wife, had been appointed chaplain to the army. He was seventy years old, but
still hale. His book *The Doleful State of the Damned* preached
hell-fire at its hottest, and to this fire the doughty chaplain now
consigned the French.

His friends tried to dissuade him from the dangerous mission, but he said scornfully: "No, there was never a bullet made
to hit me." When he stepped on board the transport at Boston,
he seized an ax and cried, "Here is the sword of the Lord and
Gideon."

In his prayer at the start of the siege, he said, "Thy people
shall be willing in the day of Thy power," and so indeed it
proved.

General Pepperrell landed his troops skillfully on the first
of May, and laid siege to the town. The breaks favored him,
as they so often do the bold. He must first take the grand battery to the east of the fort. This battery had thirty heavy guns,
and might well be thought impregnable. But the redoubt-
able William Vaughan, who was sent to take it, had passed his
life in making hard things easy. His ruse was to set some naval

stores on fire behind the battery. Black smoke from burning pitch rolled across it; the French defenders took fright, spiked their guns and ran away. The smoke cleared, and Vaughan surveyed the battery cautiously. It looked deserted. With a flask of brandy he bribed a Cape Cod Indian to take a closer peek. The Indian came back and reported that the battery in fact was empty.

Vaughan sent a note to Pepperrell: "May it please your Honour to be informed that by the grace of God and the courage of 13 men, I entered the Grand Battery about 9 o'clock, and am waiting for a reinforcement and a flag."

Reinforced, Vaughan drilled out the big forty two pounders and turned their fire against the fort.

Benjamin Franklin in Philadelphia had written his brother in Boston: "Fortified towns are hard nuts to crack and your teeth are not accustomed to it; but some seem to think forts are taken as easy as snuff."

The grand battery had been taken as easy as snuff; but the fort was almost as hard a nut as wise Ben had prophesied.

Pepperrell then began his siege. Wading through icy surf, his soldiers brought their munitions and food ashore on their heads. They dragged cannon across the spongy marsh on sledges, each pulled by 200 men. The morass quaked under them; more than once they were at the point of foundering, guns and all; but they pulled through to solid ground. Although many of them had lost their shoes and socks in the muck, they plied the guns fiercely, and the fort replied with equal fierceness.

The siege dragged on. Pepperrell's men had their daily dram of strong New England rum, and needed it. They fell sick of marsh fever, until only half of them were fit for duty.

General Pepperrell was everywhere among them with encouraging words, but now he was having trouble with Commodore Warren. The Commodore had captured a French 64, the *Vigilant*, trying to slip into the harbor with 600 men and military stores.

"For God's sake," the arrogant seaman wrote to Pepperrell, "let us do something and not waste our time in indolence. . . Pray how came the island battery not to be attacked? Pray let me know."

Pepperrell then attacked the island battery, and was beaten off disastrously; but he was firm in his refusal to turn the land expedition into a sea expedition by putting his soldiers aboard Warren's ships.

Instead he pressed the assault by land. By mid-June the French had shot away most of their cannonballs and were nearly out of food. The circular battery was a ruin, the west gate punched in; and hardly a house in town was still fit to live in. The forty-eight-day siege had taken its toll of the morale of the French troops; 9000 cannonballs and 600 bombs had fallen in their midst, and the women and children, trembling inside half ruined casements, were at the point of exhaustion.

The Governor therefore capitulated; and on the forty-ninth day of the siege, Pepperrell's army marched in and took possession. Commodore Warren had written a separate letter to the Governor demanding surrender of the town to himself; but it was Pepperrell who received the keys, and in fact the victory was his.

At a banquet given by Pepperrell to his officers, many feared that grim Parson Moody would be too long-winded in his prayer. But for once he was short. "Good Lord, we have so many things to thank thee for that time will be infinitely too short to do it; we must therefore leave it for the work of eternity. Bless our food and fellowship on this joyful occasion, for the sake of Christ our Lord. Amen."

The victory at Louisburg, won by raw militiamen, was reckoned one of the wonders of the world, and General Pepperrell's reputation now eclipsed even that of the great Sir William Phips. Boston got the news in the middle of the night; and long before sunrise, bells were ringing, cannon roaring, and people swarming on the streets as thick as on election day. In Philadelphia old Ben Franklin had to eat his words about "taking forts as easy as snuff"; and even in faraway London, the Tower guns were fired by order of the Lords of the Regency.

On behalf of His Majesty, the Duke of Newcastle wrote a gracious letter to Pepperrell, touching "the event which does so much honour to His Majesty's arms" and expressing the Duke's great satisfaction in being able to "acquaint the General that His Majesty has thought fit to distinguish him by conferring on him the dignity of a Baronet of Great Britain."

Sir William Pepperrell it was from that day forth; and Sir William to the end of his days wore nothing but scarlet clothes trimmed with the most brilliant of gold lace. The Kittery merchant had well earned the honors that were thrust upon him. The British ministry, recognizing the high strategic value of his victory, instantly ordered two Gibraltar regiments to be shifted to Louisburg as a permanent garrison.

There is an interesting way to measure how great a victory Louisburg really was. For it was possible in those days too to win a war and lose a peace. Three years after the siege, France got the place back without bloodshed by the Treaty of Aix-la-Chapelle. A decade later, the British appeared before Louisburg in full force and laid siege again.

In place of Warren's three ships, they had twenty-three ships of the line and eighteen frigates. In place of Pepperrell's 4000 New Englanders, their transports carried 11,000 British regulars. In place of the Kittery merchant as commander-in-chief, this expedition had one of the best of Britain's professional soldiers, Sir Jeffrey Amherst. And the man chiefly in charge of siege operations was the man who would be known as one of the most notable of all British soldiers — James Wolfe, who later took Quebec.

And the result? With approximately the same number of Frenchmen behind the ramparts, this second siege, like the first, lasted exactly forty-nine days. From which the British might have drawn an omen as to what lay in wait for them.

Louisburg was a rehearsal for the Revolution, and the same

drums that marched into that French stronghold would later
rally the attack on Bunker Hill. A member of the House of
Commons in 1775 warned that the Colonists were no mean
antagonists, and that "they took Louisburg from the French
,single-handed — as mettled an enterprise as any in our history."

The great Sir William was probably lucky in dying in 1759
before disaster overtook him. For he was a Crown man to his
marrow; and in his Kittery mansion, on a console under the
paintings of angels' heads in the hall windows, lay a gold snuff-
box given him by the Prince of Wales, who would become
George III. Pepperrell's loyalty to the throne was inherited
by his family; and by the Confiscation Act of 1778 his princely
fortune was stripped from his heirs, and his two daughters were
saved from the poorhouse only by the charity of friends. "Surely
every man walketh in a vain show," lamented a local preacher.
"He heapeth up riches, and knoweth not who shall gather
them."

But the riches of his fame as conqueror of Louisburg were
subject to no Confiscation Act; and today as a fitting symbol
of Maine enterprise, both in peace and war, Sir William Pepperrell's portrait hangs over the governor's desk in Augusta,
Maine.

AROOSTOOK PIONEERS

BY MARY ELIZABETH BARKER ROGERS

RECOLLECTIONS HAVE REMAINED with me from my earliest child-hood in the form of a series of pictures. One of the first is of a bright morning in early spring, 1856. A group of people were moving in a forest that was just beginning to show a mist of green. By a rude trail, the first promise of a highway through swamp and over hill, they followed a horse, hitched to a sled commonly called a jumper. My grandfather drove this horse. The jumper was loaded with trunks, bags and various house-hold utensils. Following the load, walked my father with some small bundles. There was also a lad of sixteen ·who was my uncle and an older boy — son of new neighbors, the Sewalls — who bore me, a child of three, perched on his shoulder.

We were a small band of pioneers, common enough at that time, going into a temporary home at Island Falls while a permanent one was being built. Grandfather and two sons, Rodney and Stephen, had come first and selected five lots of

160 acres. This was uncleared land situated on a beautiful ridge
which to this day bears the family name of Barker Ridge. He
then transported his family and all his belongings by team from
Barker's Mills, near Lewiston, a distance of more than 200
miles, and now my father had arrived and was getting his family settled before he began the slow task of making a farm and
permanent home.

The little log camp to which we were bound was built by
some men who for a time lived in it while they cut cedar and
shaved shingles. The log house stood in a small opening from
which the trees had been cut to build it. The surroundings
were rough with stumps still standing, and rocks and roots and
brush covered the ground. The house was very comfortable
with a stone fireplace in the middle of one side wall. The furniture was all made on the spot, for the nearest place to purchase
anything was Patten, twelve miles away, and the only vehicle
fit to go over the trail was a hand-made jumper. A bed stood
in one corner with a trundle bed for the children which
shoved under the larger one in the daytime. All the cooking
was done at the fireplace and served on a rough table at the
end of the room near the door. A small shed attached covered the woodpile, and a log hovel housed the horse and the
cow.

At this time there were only two families — the Sewalls and
the Craigs — living at the Falls, afterwards incorporated as
Island Falls. Grandfather occupied an abandoned house (built
by a man who went with the Forty-Niners for gold), making a
third family.

Settlers paid the state for their farms by doing a certain
amount of road work each year. Our men had already made
considerable improvement in the trail from the Falls by working odd days. All of the men began felling trees and clearing
a portion of land for next year's crop. Logs were transported
to the nearest mill and men were found to begin preparing the
frame for Grandfather's barn. Each morning Father went away
with his dinner pail on the jumper drawn by the horse, and

did not come back until sunset. Mother and we children stayed in the cabin, tended the cow and hens and watched over the garden. There were wild animals, especially bears, in the woods, but we considered them harmless if left to themselves.

One evening in midsummer Father and Mother were looking over the garden, when they suddenly became rigid, listening intently. A faint halloo came from somewhere on the hill. "Someone calling for help?" asked Mother under her breath. Father looked thoughtful for a moment, then replied. "No, it's probably Rod exercising his lungs. Doctor's orders, you know." The following night, as he was preparing for supper, he said, "It was not Rod who was calling last night. It was Steve. He was treed by a bear." Mother looked startled. Two nights before she had been searching in the woods for the cow. She sprang up on a big fallen log and stepped down on a sleeping bear who slipped from under her foot and bounded off with a loud woof. Then I listened to my father relate how Steve had fired a shotgun at the bear, escaped from its charge up a tree and was forced to remain there until his dog drove the bear off.

There was no law on game, and deer, moose, caribou and partridges could be obtained with but little effort, so that there was an abundance of meat, including much stored for winter use. There was a good crop of vegetables from the garden. Through the summer wild berries were to be had, but no other fresh fruit at any price. Grandfather was skilled in fruit raising and he began at once to plan an orchard with apples, plums, pears, cherries, grapes and smaller fruits. Meanwhile he spent the winter cutting and hauling lumber to a mill in an adjoining town for the house he hoped to erect the next summer. When the snow covered the ground, Father hired with a lumber operation not far away. He came home on Saturday night and sometimes for a night during the week.

My memories of that first winter are mostly a series of pictures of Mother reading or knitting, during the evenings, by the light of the log fire. New energy came with the budding

trees and flowers of spring. The cleared fields were sowed to
wheat and oats, and while these grew, more trees were felled.
One morning I was told I could go to the Falls with Father
and spend the day with Grandma. I did not return until the
following morning, when I found Mother in bed and a neighbor from two miles away was holding a new baby in her lap,
my baby brother.

Again the crops were harvested, the shed filled with wood and
everything again made ready for winter. Once more Father
went to work for the lumber company. The snow covered the
ground and the cold, lonely winter days were here.

A month passed by, then one day Grandfather drove into the
yard with the horses and sled. When he opened the door,
Mother said sharply, "What is it? Is Addison hurt?"

"Yes," said Grandfather, "a log fell on him."

"Oh, Father!" and she fell on his shoulder and shook with
sobs.

They were bringing Father to my grandfather's house and,
as Mother listened to an account of what had happened, she
got herself and the children ready to go there, too. Certain
pictures are retained in my memory of what happened in the
following days.

The first picture is of several men in a room where Father
lay in bed helpless. "There is no feeling in the legs, hips or
arms." There was a short stout man with gray hair and a young
face who said but little, but that little was apparently of im-
portance. In later years I knew him well. He was Dr. Luther
Rogers of Patten and the family physician of most of the families in several townships.

When I went in to say goodnight to Father, they had tied
scarfs to his hands to lift them towards the ceiling. "To rest
my arms," he told me with his quiet smile.

The third day I was conscious that something strange had
happened. I did not know what it was, but everyone was much
distressed, and early in the day I was sent across the river to stay
with the Sewalls.

There was one more picture — a room full of men and women, my own people whom I knew and others who were strangers. In the midst my father so white and silent in his strange new bed.

There was a break now in my life. Mother's people wanted her to go back to her own family and this she did. For three years we lived near Franconia Notch under the shadow of the White Mountains.

I was eight years old when, with my little brother Addison — named for our father — and my mother, I journeyed back "Down East," as everybody called the new country. In that time much had been done to develop it. My aunt, whom I had never seen, met us at Patten village, which was the terminus of a hundred-mile stage route. Mother, weary with the long journey and the care of two children, was glad to see her. It was too late in the day to go the ten miles to Grandfather's, but friends living about half the distance made us welcome for the night.

No longer need people travel with a jumper. The road was good, at least in winter, and the comfortable sleigh drawn by a spirited horse — which Grandfather had brought with him from his former home — had replaced the old makeshift. Improvements were no less marked in the Barker homestead. The buildings were finished except the upstairs rooms which were partitioned with carpets, curtains and blankets, instead of with walls.

To the south and west stretched wide fields, but to the north and east the forest of lofty beeches and sugar maples was left untouched. Back of the buildings a thrifty young orchard was growing. Small fruits were already bearing, and in summer the vegetable garden was a delight to behold. Grandma loved flowers and raised all the old-fashioned varieties. It was a pleasant, comfortable home and Grandma was its presiding genius.

A few nights later Mother kissed us two children goodnight, and when we awoke in the morning she was gone — back to a

life of toil for her daily bread. It was three years before we saw
each other again.

I had no difficulty fitting into the family and the busy, loving atmosphere at Grandpa's.

Steve and Rod were still members of the household, though
both worked in the woods in the winter. Father's farm had
been sold to his brother-in-law, whose family was living there
in a roomy log house. There were three boys and one girl,
Jane, who was one year my senior. The next lot on the road,
which had belonged to Steve, had been sold and that family
contained several boys and girls. Two more families belonged
in the Barker Ridge colony, but in these there were no children.

When again the deep snow covered the ground, Addison and
I had to keep to the yard or the road when we went out to
play, since children did not travel on snowshoes as men did.
But there were rides on the sled behind the gray horses, and a
particularly interesting tramp behind the herd of cattle when
they were driven each morning down the long path to the
spring in the woods for their drink of water.

We were never tired of tending sheep, and when the young
lambs began to appear, my enthusiasm soared. Often Grandfather brought one wrapped in a blanket into the kitchen to be
warmed and fed, and they became my especial care and pets.

The pleasantest part of the day was in the evening when,
the work all done, Grandpa sat by the fire with his pipe and
Grandmother with her knitting, and I read aloud to them
from some book brought from the Sunday School library at the
Falls, or borrowed from the neighbors. Sometimes it would
be something from the weekly newspapers. Not much money
was spent for books by ordinary people. There were in the
house a few on agriculture and orcharding, a church history,
several books of travel and biography, and one prize, *Robinson
Crusoe.* Occasionally Grandpa and Grandma told stories of
things which took place in the first years of living in the wilder-

ness — stories of battles with moose in the hunt, or of wolves and bears.

The evenings were not always quiet and uneventful. Neighbors frequently dropped in for an hour's chat. They even came occasionally from the Falls, to bring some piece of news or on some other errand. It was the winter of 1860-61. The papers were full of discussion for and against the policy of the administration. Both Grandpa and Grandma had long been enthusiastic abolitionists, and Abe Lincoln was their chosen leader.

The news of the attack on Sumter ran like fire throughout all our frontier towns. Uncle Rodney came home from his work. "Mother, I'm going to enlist." Nine men enlisted from Island Falls, only recently organized into a town. Before mobilization was complete, two, George Sewall and William Craig, were brought back dead of measles. Steve came home from bidding Rodney goodbye, and said, "I've had a letter from Brother Silas. He has enlisted and is at the Capital. I've got to go, Mother, but I'll stay until the crop is harvested." So he went, and with him or soon after went ten others.

A disease had broken out about which little seemed to be known. The doctors called it diphtheria. It became an epidemic in all the towns about us. Hardly a family escaped and many households lost all the children. There were funerals every day. The neighbors helped each other and the funerals were all public. Fred Sewall and two Craig girls, besides several children, died in our town. When spring came and restored health to the land, there were many sore hearts and empty homes.

I did much light work out of doors to keep the routine going: planting potatoes in the burnt land, corn, beans and pumpkins in the orchard, and helping with the cattle and sheep. The task I enjoyed most was hunting the cows. They had very little pasturage, picking their living wherever they could find it, in the woods, on little meadows and swales, often getting two miles from home.

In that year the down east boom reached its height. People

from all over New England traveled down to Aroostook, where
rich lands were to be had for a song. They appeared at all
times of day and night. There were no hotels or boarding
houses in our town. The three or four families with the best
accommodations had to feed and house these pioneers. Our
house was often full, as were also those belonging to the Sewalls and Craigs. The newcomers were mostly a good class and
many of them became permanent residents. They came to
Grandpa for all sorts of supplies. Crops were good in that new
country and brought excellent prices during the war. A sawmill had been built at the Falls which supplied the settlers with
lumber for building purposes. A log schoolhouse had been
built at the Falls three years previously and a school established,
two terms each year of twelve weeks each. On every Sunday
there was a Sunday School, and twice a month a minister came
from Patten to preach in this primitive house. We children
on the Ridge used to walk to the Sunday School, the distance
being two miles and a half, and the road rough and muddy in
places.

The town had a grand celebration on the Fourth of July of
the following summer. There was a beautiful poplar grove in
the edge of the settlement, and here were built tables and a
stand for speakers, and flags were hung to decorate the place. The
day was ideal and I remember with what anticipation Addison
and I set out from home quite early in the morning. There was
plenty of noise, helped out with a fife and a drum or two. The
"horribles" were sufficiently horrible, and the guns were a delight. But the best of all were the pails of lemonade and the
board shanties where we could buy for a cent a thick stick
of striped candy.

A large crowd had gathered from our own and other towns.
The tables were loaded with bread, butter, cakes, pies and
doughnuts. Everyone worked like mad dishing up the hot
baked beans and vegetables, but — alas — the rain came down
in torrents. Instead of sitting down to the tables the people
crawled under them, into the booths, the barns, houses, any-

where for shelter. The rain ceased shortly but everything was wet and the food was a mess. Nevertheless they straightened out the best possible and sat down and ate what was not utterly spoiled. Afterwards there were speeches and patriotic songs which everyone sang. The sun came out from behind the clouds, and the fun went merrily on, until the west began to glow with the setting sun.

Late in autumn Grandma remarked one day, "It's time we dipped the candles." The butchering was all done and there was a large supply of beef and mutton tallow. This had all been tried out in the farmer's big boiler.

Next day began the task of making the year's supply of candles. Balls of wicking were cut and twisted into the proper lengths. These were strung on small wooden rods long enough to reach across a wash tub. Enough of these rods were used to cover a tub, carefully keeping the wicks apart lest they interfere with each other. Another tub was then filled with hot tallow and each rodful of wicks was dipped in it and returned to the empty tub to cool. This job lasted two or three days for it took a lot of candles to light our house through the long winter.

"The corn meal is getting low," said Grandma one morning as Grandpa brought in the foamy pails of milk. In the granary, a long room over the wood shed and a wagon house, were bins of oats, wheat, rye, barley, buckwheat and barrels of beans. But I admired most the bins of shining ears of yellow corn. It was husked on the barn floor and the ears were put in this airy room to dry.

That night Grandpa brought into the kitchen a basket of corn, an empty tub and a board with an iron strap nailed along the edge and a hole six inches long just back of the strap. Grandpa placed the board across the tub, sat on it and, thrusting the fingers of his left hand into the hole, took an ear of corn in the right hand, moved it against the iron, and quickly scraped the kernels off the cob. Other baskets followed on successive evenings and soon a load of corn and rye was ready to be carried to Houlton to be ground into meal for the johnnycake and "Injun" loaves.

Grandfather had other work with which he busied himself in the long winter evenings. He repaired all rips and breaks in the harnesses. He made moccasins for himself and mended his shoes, which were made by a shoemaker in the town. His shoe mending bench was a fascinating object. The top was divided into little compartments — one for the ball of shoe thread used to sew leather, another for wax, made by himself, to wax the thread after doubling and twisting it, another for hogs' bristles which he fastened by some mysterious process to the waxed thread and used like needles. There were awls to make the holes in the leather to be sewed, and little pieces of leather to make patches or taps. One corner was full of tiny wooden pegs to fasten the tap to the sole of the shoe, and a cute little hammer to drive them in. Our hands were small so it was our task to find if any points were sticking up inside the shoe. These points he would wear down to smoothness with an iron rasp. All our shoes for common wear were made in like manner. In summer I wore, as did most women, cloth shoes with leather soles and elastic at the sides.

When the housework was done in the morning, Grandma would spin. I sat on my favorite seat, a low stool, busy with my "stint," knitting a certain number of rounds on a stocking or doing "over and over" on a sheet. I often paused to watch Grandma's swift, graceful movements at her spinning wheel. She spun coarse yarn for mittens, medium for stockings and a fine quality for cloth and blankets. Grandpa's ordinary working clothes were always of homespun cloth which Grandma cut and made.

Grandma also made her dyes: indigo for blue, copperas and alum for yellow, cedar boughs for brown, sumac for red, and green was made by combining other colors. She combined black wool with white for gray.

The supplies for the household were bought at Patten. A ride to the town meant a day off from work and a list of things needed to last for perhaps three weeks. Addison and I always remained at home to keep the fires. A man attended to the stock. It was on one of these journeys that they brought home the first kerosene oil and a glass lamp. There were in the house whale oil lamps with tubes for wicks, but for some reason — prabably scarcity of oil — they were never used. This new kerosene lamp was very superior to candles.

Our household was awakened one cold morning about four by a loud knock on the door. It aroused me, and directly I heard the excited tones of Grandpa and Grandmother, mingled with a deeper, yet familiar voice. I awoke Addison and we hurried into our clothes and ran downstairs. Stephen was there, and even old Tom, the cat, sprang straight into his arms at sight of him. He had walked all night, thirty-five miles, because he was too impatient to wait for the next day's stage. He had been promoted to a captain, with a few days' furlough. It was the last time Addison and I ever saw him.

In the casualty lists from the battlefield there were frequently names known to us, either from our own or neighboring towns. Our own loved ones were still untouched, though Uncle Steve wrote of very narrow escapes.

This was the year Grandfather built the new barn. He hired two men to prepare the frame. They hewed the big timbers until they were squared to the proper dimensions for the foundations, uprights and great beams to hold the roof. Then they were morticed at the ends and the proper places to insert the cross pieces and braces. Lastly the rafters and ridgepole were cut and piled ready to be quickly used without confusion. Finally wooden pins were made to fasten the frame together. The day was set for the raising and the men of the town were invited to come in the morning and help. Meantime Grandma, with my help, was preparing the dinner.

The men baked the beans, which was the important dish of the meal. They borrowed two iron pots — holding enough to feed fifty men — from a lumber camp cook. The night before the raising they dug holes in the ground, somewhat larger than the kettles. In the holes they built fires of hard wood, dropping in half a dozen small rocks to heat. When the wood was burned, they shoveled out the coals and rocks; then set in the pots previously filled with parboiled beans, a sufficient quantity of fat salt pork, seasoning, a cup of molasses and water to fill each kettle. The covers were carefully put on, the bails lifted upright, and the hot coals and rocks put back around and over the pots. The whole was then covered with earth, and left to be shoveled out at noon next day, when the beans were served piping hot and done to perfection. This was and still is the lumberman's method of cooking beans for crews of men.

We had no granulated sugar at that time, but a rather expensive loaf of crust sugar in irregular lumps, used only when we had company. Most people made maple sugar or syrup and we bought molasses and brown sugar of a coarse quality. So there were no elaborate frosted cakes, such as would be found on most tables now at country gatherings. There were cookies, gingerbread and doughnuts; pies of custard, mince, pumpkin and squash. There were loaves of home-grown wheat and steaming plates of Indian cornbread, pickles and cucumbers from the garden, and there was tea. Some of the neighborhood women came to help and on the whole it was quite a gala day. To all the children it was as exciting as a circus.

There was little social life in the town during this time. Anxiety for those at the front and for the outcome of the war, also sorrow for those taken by sickness at home, were like a weight inescapable. The three years for which the first men enlisted had expired. Most of them reenlisted, but a few for various reasons came home. Among those who returned because of the entreaties of their parents were my Uncle Rodney and his friend Luther Rogers of Patten, whose brother had been killed.

A circle was formed at the Falls for the purpose of swelling the fund for church expenses. The people took turns opening their houses to these semi-monthly gatherings, where each person attending paid a small sum. Uncle Rodney announced to the young people of the Ridge that he would give them a straw ride to their socials, and we were a merry party packed into the two-horse farm wagon or, later, the sled, spinning over the road to the accompaniment of songs or bells. The houses were always filled with people happy to have an evening together with games and singing, mostly the war songs of the period. At that time, in all the town there were only two musical instruments, a violin which George Darling played principally for kitchen dances, and a piano which the Pratts, quite newcomers, brought with them.

People did much visiting in those days and we came to know many who lived in other towns and who sometimes rode long distances to spend the day. I remember we had several parties of young folks from Patten who came for overnight.

Uncle Rodney often saddled the horse and rode to the village on mail night. There came a night when he did not return, but sent a neighbor who happened to be in town to tell us that he had a letter from Steve, who was wounded, and he was going to him. The letter was only a pencil scrawl, written on the battlefield where Steve fell, and where he lay for three days before he could be moved to a hospital. The case was pronounced hopeless, and both nurses and surgeons were so driven there was little prospect of any attention being paid to hopeless cases. It was not until Uncle Rodney got there that anything was done.

Under Rod's watchful care Steve slowly recovered until two months later he could sit in a wheel chair; then Rod left him to the care of the doctors and nurses and came home. Not for very long, however. A crutch slipped and a bad fall sent Steve back to bed again, and a large part of the work of recovery had to be done over. Rod went back to him, returning in midwinter. Uncle Steve gained slowly and in August, after eighteen months in the hospital, he began the journey home. He traveled as far as his uncle's near his former home, when his wounds broke out afresh. Grandfather and Grandmother went to him, but he died in a short time.

In March we had a visit from my beloved teacher and her newly acquired husband. He was Luther Rogers, the son of Dr. Rogers and an officer in the same company as Uncle Rodney. He was tall, with a very military bearing and rather a stern face. I was afraid of him and kept out of his way. However, the men went off for deer and we three womenfolk had a pleasant time visiting together. When they left us, I decided that when I married, I would have a husband very like the man Matilda had married.

The following two years were filled with school work for me; at home when our own school was in session, and in other towns where I worked my board.

We had another Fourth of July celebration which I remember very well because I had a part in what was supposed to be an important feature of the program. Some new neighbors who were college graduates and professional teachers were the Committee of Arrangements, and asked me to sing the first song in a pantomime, illustrating two popular songs.

I was much excited, since it was my first attempt at theatricals. The entertainment was staged in a new building destined for a barn. A rough stage was built and seats arranged. A small gallery was also made to accommodate a portion of the audience. I peeped through the stage curtains at the people coming to their seats. In the gallery was quite a party from Patten, including several ex-soldier comrades of Uncle Rodney, with their newly-wedded wives. Lieutenant Rogers was there, but Matilda had died several months before, leaving a babe who was being cared for by her mother. I thought the lieutenant looked very personable in his black civilian suit.

For two years Grandpa had been slowly failing in health, and one morning he quietly and silently passed into the unknown. After that, Grandma spent much of her time with her daughter, who had moved to a farm near Patten village.

I began to think of earning some money for myself. Therefore one summer day found me in a small room in a log house, the mistress of a dozen scholars. Though barely large enough to seat the children, it was light and sunny and overlooked the beautiful Mattawamkeag Lake. We all did our best together and wound up the term with a little entertainment to which all the people came.

That autumn my grandmother made a long visit among old friends and relatives, and took me with her for a year as a student at the Lewiston High School. I made warm friends in my own class, and wanted to remain in the school and graduate, but because of finances I came back to Patten and finished the year at the Academy, then taught a school in the town during the summer.

When the first snows of winter began to fall, on December 7, 1869, I married Lieutenant Luther Rogers, and settled down to homemaking in Patten.

CHRISTINA

BY MARGE COOK

CHRISTINA WAS SITTING, very erect, on the back doorstep. She was looking out across the field to the sparkling Georges River — exactly as Andrew Wyeth later painted her in his 1947 tempera. We had come to Cushing to fetch our winter's supply of Green Mountain potatoes from her brother Al, and while the men folks loaded them into the car Christina and I sat and talked about flowers and kittens and kids. The brilliant Maine September sunshine ricocheted off the water, warming our faces and the unpainted silver shingles.

Perhaps no other Maine person ever has traveled so widely or been viewed by so many people as Miss Olson has without actually moving far from her back doorstep. Christina and the Olson farm have been the source of many of Andrew Wyeth's most successful paintings. Who is not familiar with perhaps the most famous of all — "Christina's World," painted in 1948, depicting the slim figure crawling across the wide expanse of field toward the huge farmhouse? Or the compassionate portrait of Christina cuddling a sick kitten? The latter, entitled "Miss Olson," is owned by a world-famous family, who wish to remain anonymous, but who so value the portrait that it has replaced their family patriarch in the place of honor in their home!

In the dry brush "Wood Stove," millions of people see Christina in a rocking chair, at her accustomed place beside the stove in her own kitchen. And Wyeth's "Wind from the Sea," reproduced on the cover of *Maine and Its Role in American Art* (Viking Press) so movingly pictures curtains billowing in the breeze from an opened window of a long-unused room at the Olson farm that it was the favorite of all paintings he had ever seen to the late poet Robert Frost.

The Olson farm originally was the Hathorne place. Christina's grandfather was the Captain Samuel Hathorne, veteran of shipwrecks and cannibal encounters, who ran the summer boarding house described by the late Caroline Burr in "Summer at Captain Hathorne's" (DOWN EAST, June 1961). This same boarding house, built in 1800 by Captain Hathorne's father, is the Olson house immortalized in fully a dozen famous Wyeth paintings. Square and imposing, originally painted a sparkling white, it has time-tempered to a weather-washed grey and is a landmark overlooking the river and surrounding neighborhood on Hathorne Point.

Katie Hathorne, the captain's daughter, was still unmarried at thirty-five when, late one fall, Captain John Maloney, their neighbor across the field, brought a young Swedish sailor home with him. Captain Maloney was skipper of a vessel hauling lime from Thomaston. The river froze over and the vessel could not navigate, so John Olson stayed on at the Maloney home and went to school with the local children to learn to speak English. And he courted Katie. Captain Hathorne died in the spring and soon afterward John married Katie and took charge of the boarding house. He never went to sea again. He said he had been "anchored" for life.

On May 3, 1893 Christina was born, the next year Alvaro,

followed a year and a half later by Samuel. Baby Fred arrived seven years after Sam. Christina barely remembers the boarding house days as her father decided he had boarders enough of his own and quit catering to city folks.

When she was three and a half years old, Christina became ill with an undiagnosed childhood ailment. When she recovered it was noticed she did not walk right; one foot refused to behave itself. In those days little was known about polio. She continued to do all the things other children did. She walked the mile and a half to the village school where her teacher, Mrs. Minnie Newbert, remembers her fondly as an exceptionally bright pupil.

"Christina could remember anything and used to get impatient because there wasn't time for her to recite all that she had learned, so I used to keep her in at recess and after school and hear her out. She was definitely college material."

There was plenty of work to be done at home. Christina helped her mother can and cook, paint and paper. They even made their own soap. There was a special bond between mother and daughter and each tried to spare the other. When Katie was ill for a spell Christina took over the family wash and never again allowed her mother to scrub clothes. She became a fabulous cook and a skilled seamstress. Her airy cakes and fine stitches are legend.

"We always took Christina's lameness for granted, never thought anything of it," says Nellie Maloney, who grew up with her. "She was just like anybody else." Nellie was a frequent supper guest at the Olson farm, where the menu usually included yeast bread, fresh from the oven, and stewed prunes. She also recalls the old-fashioned parlor, kept shut up except for special occasions, and the display of lovely curios brought back by Captain Hathorne from his cruises all over the world.

When Christina was twenty-five, at the urging of friends, she agreed to be examined by a specialist and entered a Boston hospital. The doctor told her that if she lived in the city he would prescribe the country for her. So she came home.

John Olson developed arthritis, used a cane, then crutches. He spent the last fifteen years of his life in a wheel chair. After his father became incapacitated Alvaro, an excellent fisherman, took up his lobster traps and fish weir, stored his dory in the barn, and became a truck gardener and teamster. He hauled wood, cut ice and hay, took care of the livestock — horses, cows, pigs, poultry — and raised Green Mountain potatoes. Katie died in 1929, followed by husband John in 1935. Sam and Fred married and moved to their own farms nearby. Alvaro and Christina never married. They stayed on at the farm, caring for each other.

In her younger days Christina went everywhere the other young folks went — to Grange affairs and to dances; she traveled on boats and went all around the city of Malden, Massachusetts by herself while visiting relatives there. Her mother made knee pads to protect her when she fell, trying to keep up with the other children. But she has never "given in" to crutches or a wheel chair. Although very thin in her youth, she developed great strength in her arms, training them to compensate for the legs that were gradually losing their power. As she put on weight and could no longer walk she crawled, with the strong arms doing double duty, as in "Christina's World."

Christina and Alvaro still live at the farm, looking out for each other as best they can.* The sister cooks the meals on the wood stove, sitting in a chair. The brother dishes up the food, pours the coffee, and sees that the woodbox doesn't go dry. Their chores are few these days. Al's farming and fishing days are over, the hayrack and mowing machine left standing in the field where they were last used. Somebody else mows the grass and tends to the blueberries. The brooder houses are empty. The Olson livestock has dwindled to three cats and a frisky ten-year-old spaniel named Skipper, a good rabbiter but

*Christina Olson died January 27, 1968 at the age of seventy-four, a few weeks after her brother Alvaro. The contents of the Hathorne Farm were auctioned off the following summer, and the farm has since been sold.

getting old, so that his hind legs sometimes give out on him. "Like me," comments Al, his only allusion to his own arthritis.

From the kitchen window they can look across their sixty acres down the Georges River to where it meets the Atlantic Ocean. On a clear day they can see Manana and on a foggy day they hear its fog horn. They see only reflections of light from Monhegan because Burnt Island looms in the line of vision.

There is no hurry any more. They go to bed and get up when they please, watch television in the evening, and read a daily newspaper and an assortment of magazines. Neighbors and relatives drop in to chat, and in the summertime curious tourists flit around the premises snapping camera shutters, sometimes furtively, sometimes stopping in to say "hello."

A frequent caller during the summer is Andy Wyeth, who has carte blanche to roam around the Olson premises at will, and has found inspiration all over the farm for his paintings. The barn was the scene for "Hay Ledge" — Alvaro's dory stored in the loft amid cobwebs and hay — and "The Stall," executed while a family of playful kittens purred and rubbed around and batted at Andy's brushes.

"Dry Well" and "Alvaro's Hayrack" are two of the exterior farm scenes that tell poignant Wyeth stories of Maine. "Geraniums" — on Christina's kitchen window sill — are spotlighted by the sun to the outside viewer. "Weather Side," a tall tempera of the rear of the house, is Wyeth's latest artistic tribute to the Olson home.

Christina enjoys posing for Andy, which provides stimulating occasions for eager conversation between the two mutually admiring friends. Although Alvaro doesn't like to pose, he appears in Wyeth's first Olson work, a tempera entitled "The Oil Lamp." And "Al's Bedroom," a water color of light streaming through a paned window over a patchwork-quilted bed, was shown recently at the Farnsworth Museum in Rockland.

What is the magnetism that draws Andrew Wyeth as an artist back again and again to Christina and her world? To people who admire the Olsons — either as Cushing neighbors, or as unforgettable figures in Wyeth paintings, the answer seems obvious. Christina and Alvaro represent the indestructible core of early Maine families — people who made do with what they had, and met life with dignity on its own sometimes harsh terms. They expected to struggle, and did so with pride beholden to nobody. This philosophy, frequently encountered among the older generation in the State of Maine, is sometimes difficult for people from away to understand. But it is the Maine art of living and, unpretentious though it is, it is an ennobling way of life either to follow or to behold. This is the vital truth which artist Andy Wyeth — with great sensitivity — perceives and appreciates. And he has poignantly immortalized it in his paintings of such neighbors as Christina Olson.

THE INCREDIBLE LUCY FARNSWORTH

BY HERBERT EDWARDS

THE PUBLICITY that Lucy Farnsworth so carefully avoided all her life has come to her in full measure since her death. Lucy made the front pages of the nation's leading newspapers when the Farnsworth Art Museum of Rockland, Maine bought an Andrew Wyeth for $65,000 — the highest price ever paid by an art gallery for a painting by a living American artist.

Many of the visitors to the handsome museum built in 1948 will cross the yard and enter the Farnsworth house next door, where Lucy lived for all but a few of her ninety-five years. When they do, they will enter another era, for everything in the house has been preserved intact, just as Lucy's father left it when he died in 1876. Lucy was thirty-seven then — a confirmed old maid, and already settling into a seclusive way of life that was to deepen with the years.

Some visitors to the house may stop to look at the large painting of Lucy and her brother made by some itinerant artist when Lucy was about ten years old. There is nothing very remarkable about the boy's face, but there is character in Lucy's. Her mouth is a thin, straight line, indicative of a strong will; her forehead is high and broad, and her eyes keen and penetrating. There are no suggestions of future feminine charm in either her face or figure; rather there is a masculine strength and decisiveness. She is not a tomboy, for she is too serious, and certainly there is no girlish frivolity about her.

As a girl Lucy Farnsworth admired her father, even though his favorite among the six children was his beautiful little daughter Fanny. The father was a big, bearded, jovial man who drove one of the finest teams of fast horses in town. Lucy loved to go with him when he drove out to his limestone quarries, or down to the waterfront where his enormous kilns belched forth thick clouds of acrid smoke, burning limestone into the valuable quicklime. Sometimes they would board one of the fast ships that carried the barrels of lime to New York or Boston or New Orleans. Lucy would go with him to the big wooden building on Main Street at the head of Sea Street, where he would give orders to the chief clerk, and then they might drive far out into the country where the lime barrels were made. One day as they were driving back to town William Farnsworth remarked that he now paid twenty cents each for lime barrels that had cost him fourteen cents in 1845, and Lucy replied, after a few seconds of thought, that his cost had risen forty-three percent.

William Farnsworth was no longer amazed at the girl's adeptness in arithmetic, her memory for facts and figures. And the day came when he was to admit that her knowledge of the fundamentals and details of the business was much greater than that of his two sons, James and William. He found himself discussing the business with her, its prospects and profits. The lime business was booming, not only at Rockland, but at Rockport and at Thomaston. As the kilns along the waterfront increased in number and size, over a hundred four-horse teams replaced the slower oxen hauling the limestone from the

quarries. In the 1850s over 800,000 barrels of lime were shipped, and in the 1860s over 900,000. As many as sixty ships
were in the harbor at one time, and over twenty of these were
owned in Rockland.

Lucy reached the age when she must go away to finishing
school. She protested that she could see no sense in the smat-
tering of art, literature and music that girls acquired at finishing schools. But her father insisted. Did he hope that Lucy
might acquire some feminine graces — and thereby, perhaps,
a beau? So far, she had shown no interest in young men; had,
in fact, brusquely repulsed the only young man who had had
the courage to approach her. Lucy obeyed her father and left
for the finishing school near Boston. At the school it was characteristic of her that she would pounce on the one subject that
was well taught there — art — and study it intensively. She
studied John Ruskin's *Modern Painters*, and in those five great
volumes learned as much about art as if she had been one of
Ruskin's students at Oxford. Her enthusiasm even extended
to such little known painters as Rowlandson. Perhaps she fore-
saw the day when Rowlandson would be recognized as a great
water colorist. Lucy was gifted with amazing foresight.

It is interesting to speculate how large a fortune she would
have amassed if, later, she had invested in paintings instead of
stocks. As everyone knows, the purchase of good paintings is
one of the best investments and one of the surest hedges against
inflation. But it was in the stock market that Lucy was to make
the fortune that established her art gallery.

Lucy came home to a booming Rockland. Her brothers were
in the business now, and the money was rolling in. But her
father's health was failing and his hair and beard turning
white. Lucy was reading the New York and Boston papers ever
more carefully. Was she one of the first in Rockland to learn
about the new method of lime burning that required coal for
fuel, and to realize that Rockland could never compete in the
lime market if it had to import coal from Norfolk? Did she
realize, too, that Rockland's ship builders, whose world-famous

clipper ship *Red Jacket* had sailed from New York to Liverpool in thirteen days, one hour, and twenty-five minutes, must soon lose out to steam? Was it Lucy who advised her father to spread his investments before it was too late? Had Lucy, before her father's death in 1876, become his trusted investment counselor? It is possible, for at his death he left $250,000, a good-sized fortune in those days.

Then a malign fate seemed to lay its cold hand on the Farnsworth family. As the years fled swiftly, all the children, except Lucy, died one after the other, and they died childless. Lucy inherited their share of the estate, and she invested it with an astuteness that has had few equals among women investors playing a lone hand. For Lucy asked no one's advice. She studied the newspapers for new discoveries and new developments, and relied on her own financial sagacity.

What caused her gradual withdrawal from the life of the town after her mother's death in 1910 no one can say for certain. There were rumors that she hated her mother and that her mother hated her, but none of these were ever proved. Actually, her withdrawal was a slow process extending over many years. Lucy continued to make forays into the town when necessity demanded. Since her holdings in local real estate were always extensive, and since her attitude towards tenants, mortgagees and leaseholders was uncompromising, there were occasional lawsuits. In court she acted as her own lawyer and amazed lawyers and judges alike by her extensive knowledge of real estate law and court procedure. Lawyers regarded her as a formidable opponent who won most of her cases.

Stories about Lucy are still recalled in Rockland. Mrs. Ruth Wiley, whose grandfather's back door faced that of the Farnsworth house, had an uncle who wanted to put a lunch wagon on her grandfather's lot. But when the wagon was hauled to its location, the uncle was dismayed to find that its rear wheels protruded six inches onto the Farnsworth land. Lucy had no objections — provided she was paid a land rental of $10 a month. Yet when Mrs. Wiley's grandfather suffered a serious illness, Lucy came to the back door one day and announced abruptly: "I want to do anything I can for this good neighbor of mine. If you need money — any amount of it, or anything else — just let me know."

There was the time in 1915 when the town of Rockland needed $20,000 immediately, and no money was available until the next tax collection months ahead. It could be borrowed from banks, but the selectmen felt they could not afford the interest rates. They got $15,000 from the large business firms, but no others seemed willing to lend money without interest. Then one of the selectmen thought of sending the tax collector, Oliver Lovejoy, to Lucy Farnsworth. The other selectmen were skeptical. But in less than an hour Lovejoy returned with a check for $5000. Lucy had been characteristically brief, he reported. When he had stated his request, she asked him to come in. Then she had gone directly to her desk and had written out the check. Lucy did not believe in wasting words.

Oliver Lovejoy was less surprised than others when, after Lucy's death, her enormous benefaction to her native town was revealed. He felt that Lucy, deprived by a cruel fate of a husband or a child, loved Rockland. And he had noted the prominent place in the front room that Lucy had given to the easel supporting her father's portrait.

In all the ordinary, everyday aspects of life she grew more eccentric as the years passed. After the aged family coachman died, the single remaining horse was sold, and Lucy walked on her errands about town. When she went out to the post office, the grocery or the bank, she wore old, long, black dresses and coats that had long ago gone out of style. When the last of the household servants died, no one was hired to replace her. People wondered how she kept the big place clean. She didn't, it was later discovered.

The great depression of 1929 came. Did Lucy foresee it, sell stocks in 1928 when they were at their peak, and buy them back in 1930 when some of the best were far down in price? Later evidence seemed to indicate that Lucy had turned the depression to her own advantage. Had Lucy read the prediction of the stock market crash by wise old Bernard Baruch, or had she simply followed her own infallible intuitions? No one will ever know.

Then came the morning of October 15, 1935 when the milkman in the dark gray dawn flashed his light on the doorstep of the Farnsworth house and saw that all the milk he had delivered that week was still there. He drove down the street and called the town marshal. They found Lucy dead in her bed. The coroner was summoned, and then other officials. Everything in the house was thickly covered with dust except the dining room table which was piled high with brokers' statements, bank books and stock market reports. A china bowl was overflowing with money and checks — recent rent money from her town properties. The bureau drawers were filled with neatly stacked stocks and bonds, all of which, it was later discovered, had greatly appreciated in value since Lucy bought them.

Later, the Boston Safe Deposit and Trust Company, named executor by Lucy in her will, found that the estate totaled over $1,500,000. And all of it was to be devoted to establishing and maintaining the William A. Farnsworth Library and Art Museum, including the Farnsworth house.

Lucy would be pleased if she knew that her last investment was one of the best she ever made, that her museum's Wyeths alone are worth probably $200,000 in today's market, and that every year adds to their value. She would approve the plan which Director Wendell S. Hadlock has followed consistently since coming to the museum: "to acquire works of art by American artists of top quality which we hope will lead to a great, conservative American collection."

WRITTEN IN HILL DUST

BY A. E. McINNIS

GOLDENROD, tarnished with track dust, stood beside the race track at the West Pembroke fairgrounds, down east in Maine. It was September 14, 1966, and during the last race on the card, hooves thundered down the home stretch. From the high stand the judges peered at the flaring nostrils of the horses crossing the finish line.

One of the older judges gripped the rail and leaned over for a closer look at the winner, pacing to a halt and still surrounded by an aura of dust. Recognizing the driver, the old judge wiped the perspiration from his forehead and remarked to a younger man beside him, "For a minute I could have sworn that was Alex Bush and Stout Signal, back in '49."

Alexander Bush will be in mind for as long as there are people to remember. He lies in the spruce-pointed hills of Robbinston, Maine, beside his father and mother, sister and two of his brothers. Alex's grandparents, Tom Bush and his wife, came to Robbinston Ridge early in the 19th century. Alex's father James — but called Ed — trudged over the road with them all the way from Nova Scotia, following a family named Griffin. The two families settled near one another. Ed had good reason to be glad he followed his parents to Maine. He married Annie Griffin and they built for themselves a small farmhouse set back from the old Machias Stage Road.

Their first child, Alexander, born in 1874, was followed by William, John Charles and Louise — the only girl — each child a light in the lives of Ed and Annie Bush. From the beginning the Bush family lived in relentless poverty. The children went to the Ridge school and brought home books and lessons from which Ed and Annie Bush learned to read and write along with their sons and daughter.

The children grew rapidly. Charlie went away to Boston to find a measure of success. Louise worked in various homes, going as far away as Dennysville and Eastport and sending most of her wages home. Alex and Billy and John stayed on the farm, helping their father grub a living from the stony acres.

The Bushes were all active in church work, and any extra money went into the church on the Ridge. Billy was popular at the many dances held in the area. But if another family had sickness, it was Alex who organized a bee to get that household's wood in; if a barn burned, Alex got the men of the neighborhood together for a barn-raising bee. In politics Alex was undefeatable. He argued, laughed, cajoled and even carried voters to the polls in the old farm buggy.

Once while taking a load of farm produce to a stricken neighbor, Alex was stopped by one of the more prosperous farmers. Eyeing Alex's clean but ragged clothes, the farmer asked why he didn't make an effort to sell the produce instead of giving most of it away. "Well, now, Mister," said Alex, who never swore, "the world's just full of people nowheres near as well off as I am."

The farmer went into his house and returned with some eggs, and a large, home-cured ham. "Here Alex," he said, "take these up to those folks along with the things you're bringing them."

In his middle years, Billy contracted that grim disease of the very poor, TB — then known as consumption — and soon Louise also was its victim. Alex had to begin to sell farm produce in earnest, and once a week he made the long trip into Eastport with his four-cylinder Model T Ford truck loaded with fresh food.

When I was very young my folks bought vegetables and one gallon of buttermilk each week from Alex Bush. On Saturday morning my mother would have me wait at the corner of Kilby and Washington Streets. When Alex's little truck huffed into view at the top of Washington Street hill, I would run for Mother and she would come to meet Alex, to save him turning up our street.

One day as I waited, I saw Alex's little truck coming down hill much faster than it should have. Fascinated, I watched it clatter by, and saw Alex's face strained with panic. Tugging at the hand brake, he cast a beseeching look at me as the truck roared past out of control. I saw Dad's buttermilk balanced precariously upon a crate of red astrakhan apples. The truck leaped towards the sharp post office corner, where Washington Street meets Water Street, Eastport's main thoroughfare. Before my horrified eyes the truck veered, and with a pavement-shaking crash tipped over on its side.

The overturned truck lay against a green fire hydrant out of which water spouted against a store window. Vegetables were scattered among the dressed fowl, and broken eggs. Alex lay dazed upon the pavement, an empty turnip crate upon his neck.

People helped Alex to his feet and he sorrowfully surveyed the damage. I felt a nudge and saw that Dad and Mother had joined me. A man with wonder on his face called attention to a minor miracle by holding up the jug of buttermilk, which had somersaulted through the air to land upon its cork, safe and intact. Dad took the jug from the man, saying quietly, "That's the buttermilk I ordered."

Dad handed Alex a sum of money far in excess of the value of the buttermilk. At once, women filled shopping bags with vegetables and fowl, while their husbands paid Alex. It seemed no time until the street was cleared of everything but the stain of egg yolks. It will never be known how much Alex received for his produce that day, but his expressive eyes brimmed as he said, "That's the first time I ever unloaded and sold all my produce at one stop!" Years later, I discovered that Alex's accident was not all profit. In a cobwebby cigar box, I found a receipt stating, "Paid Eastport Water Company $5.20 for damage to water hydrant, November 26, 1927. Alex Bush."

Whatever this tall man did was the act of a gentleman, and always, lurking in his deep brown eyes, there was a waifish, elusive, unforgettable humor. Alex Bush seemed to love all humanity. His second love was for horses and harness racing. His fame as a man possessed of a miraculous way with animals spread through the region. It made no difference to Alex whether it were day or night, if a sick animal whimpered and he knew of it, he would go at once. Many a horse was made well again by his loving, understanding hands.

With summer work on the farm and winter work in the woods, Alex found little time for harness racing. The family demanded most of his free time. His mother and father died and then John, leaving Alex with Billy and Louise to care for. Soon there was only Billy and finally, in 1947 in his birth month of June, Billy followed Louise into the hard red earth of Robbinston Ridge. At the age of seventy-three Alex was left alone.

Instead of accepting defeat and a seat on the warm side of the kitchen stove, Alex embraced his lifelong joy in harness racing. Thereafter, during the racing season, the aging man lived on the Maine harness circuit, returning for the winters to the old Ridge farm. At the start of the racing season Alex drove his sulky behind the dashing Stout Signal over the long road, deep in hill dust, to West Pembroke to the fairgrounds stables.

A man in Pembroke recalled one season's first race: "It was the Fourth of July, and it was a race as tight as a pair of Sunday school pants. Alex got so excited he rammed his pipe into his coat pocket. The coat caught fire. It made quite a sight — the smoke and flame streaming behind Alex as he slammed down the home stretch a winner. Some claimed it was illegal to use rocket power to win a horse race — but Alex was such a gentleman, and everyone liked him and was glad that he won."

At one of Alex's races it was remarked, "There goes a hundred years. Alex is seventy-nine and his horse is twenty-one." It was during this race that he had a tangle with another sulky, extensively damaging his own. Some one in the crowd circulated a feed bucket, then gave it, half-filled with coins, to Alex. It made everyone feel good all over. The tall man accepted with graciousness — the same quality he displayed when he was the giver.

That fall when Alex returned to the old farm to winter, he found the house so badly in need of repairs that he contemplated moving into the barn. The silent, proud people along the Ridge road organized a bee, as Alex himself had done so many times in the past. The old Bush home was moved off-foundation, and a sturdier house was found and moved onto its place. The following spring Alex's old truck caught fire and was a complete loss, and people still remember the enormous supper that was held in the old Robbinston Ridge church, with the entire proceeds going to buy Alex another truck.

As Alex grew older, he became even more loved. One day he found that he had reached an age beyond which the judges were obliged to interpret literally Section 6 of the racing rules and disqualify him from entering any more races. So fellow drivers replaced the name of Alex Bush on racing cards by another name, but it was Alex who lined up and raced in that spot. As summer waned, and the season began to draw to a close at the Cherryfield Fair races, the drivers went to West Pembroke fairgrounds for a final contest.

All of the races that day were close, well driven and very fast. For the last race on the card, Alex lined his sulky up with the others. He had told fellow drivers that he was tired, but all he needed was one more close race. Several of the drivers glanced frequently at the old man, hunched over the reins, for he never had used a whip or snapper. Then the starter shouted "GO!"

Alex got off to a slow start but followed close. At the turn into the home stretch, the drivers bunched — only for an instant, but long enough for Alex to take advantage. Before anyone was aware of what had happened, Alex and Stout Signal surged ahead and across the finish line. And on that wonderful day in September 1958, the drivers whom Alex had beaten cheered him with a heartiness seldom felt by losers of a race.

That night the tired old man and horse arrived at the West Pembroke fairground stables, and Alex remarked to Hal Rose, as each turned in for the night, "This is right where I want to be, with my horse. Good Lord, Hal, did you ever see a night seem so bright and full of stars?"

Shooting stars were still trailing across the sky when, in the predawn, Hal Rose awakened. He noted heavy dew on the grass and the horses bunched in a far corner, as he went to arouse Alex. "It's going to rain for sure," Hal said to himself. Then he stepped into the room, full of leather and horse smell, where the old driver slept, and found that Alex had driven his last race.

The church on top of Robbinston's highest hill overflowed for Alex's funeral. The moving eulogy already had been written deeply in the hearts of the friends and neighbors present, who were eased at hearing what they had felt for Alex put into words. There is little traffic where the Bush family lies beside the Ridge road, but sometimes a horse clops by, its hoofbeats sounding like heartbeats.

When I had occasion to look up Alex's birth certificate, I was startled for a moment at seeing recorded a fact long forgotten, because it was something that no one who knew him ever thought about: "Alexander Bush, born February 18, 1874; Color, Dark."

THE UNSINKABLE STANLEY
BOYS

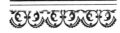

BY LEW DIETZ

No one has yet come up with a satisfactory explanation for the burgeoning of inventive genius in 19th century Maine. It's unlikely that anyone will attempt to understand why this rural society, which accepted the horse as man's best friend, should produce a pair of farm boys who would devote the most fertile years of their lives to the development of an instrument to replace the beast.

In the case of Francis E. and Freeland O. Stanley, who were destined to develop the most successful steam automobile of its day, it would appear that they had nothing in particular against horses, except that horses didn't go fast enough to suit them. Some observers have suggested that Maine's golden age of invention was spurred by the dearth of hard money and the plethora of stony soil; it required ingenuity merely to survive.

This thesis might go a long way toward explaining the inventive climate of the time, but the forces that fanned native talent into a hot flame were a fierce competitive spirit and a pride that was satisfied with no less than the best. One Stanley would have been hard enough to put down; two Stanleys, working in tandem, were unsinkable. Identical twins, who were, like the Smith Brothers of cough drop fame, to dress alike, trim their beards alike and remain inseparable in the public image, each needed the other for complete fulfillment.

The Stanley boys were born in Kingfield, Maine, in 1849. They were in their middle years and already laden with laurels before the idea of building the steam car that was to make them world-famous ever entered their heads. It was no more than happenstance that took them in 1896 to the fair at Brockton, Massachusetts, where they witnessed a demonstration advertised as "the wonder of the day." A steam automobile was to go twice around the racetrack without external aid. The "wonder" went halfway around and stalled.

Legend has it that the twins exchanged glances, then announced to the boys around them, "We'd say we could do better than that."

That they did do better than that is an historic fact. It was barely a year later that the first Stanley Steamer made its debut in Newton, Massachusetts. A photograph which immortalized the stirring event shows two thin, prim gentlemen, bearded and bowler-hatted, sitting stiffly in a rig which was certainly no more nor less than a horseless carriage; indeed, it looked very much as if the horse had run off and stranded them.

But the danged thing went; moreover it went, to employ the quaint phrase of the day, "like sixty." The price of that initial model was $700. That same buggy today is worth $7000. And thereby hangs another tale.

Currently, across this fair land there exists a lively, indomitable and growing clan of "steam nuts" whose members honor these twin Maine tinkerers by spending all their spare time, and some that isn't so spare, collecting, caressing and firing up brave little Stanley relics, and tooting around the countryside with all the gay insouciance of Knights of the Round Table.

Wrote one of the more sober of these quixotic pilgrims recently, "these birds really believe steam is about to make a dramatic comeback, and when a group of them starts talking they sound like a bunch of ex-nobility waiting for the czar to return. If one of them gets wind of some rusty old relic of a Stanley, the cloak and dagger stuff gets even thicker than it does when some sports car character hears about a 57SC Bugatti about to go for $200."

The State of Maine may pride itself on harboring one such steamer buff in the person of L. Maynard Leighton, of Winthrop. Moreover, he is one of perhaps two in the whole state who might be classified as a qualified steam auto mechanic. Fussing around with steam cars is his hobby, let it be added, and a rather expensive one when you consider that owning one antique Stanley for the pleasure of firing it up once or twice a year is much like buying a new Lincoln Continental to use on an annual picnic. Leighton, a lumber dealer, owns eighteen antique cars of which six are Stanley Steamers and one a Mobile, a steam offspring of the Stanley.

Maynard Leighton's love affair with these steam-pressure propelled vehicles goes back to his growing years. To begin with, his father owned a 1916 Stanley. "Mostly," he recalls, "it stood in the yard because my father wasn't much good at running it. He just had no feeling for mechanics. I had to check him everytime he went out of the drive to see if there was oil and water in the thing."

Leighton bought his first antique Stanley when he was fifteen. "Antique" wasn't quite the right word, perhaps: it was a wreck he found on a farm in the country. It took something of the genius and the dogged persistence of the Stanley twins themselves to put the thing together and make it run.

Leighton began collecting antique cars seriously in the early 1950s when he acquired a 1908 Stanley Model EX. The next acquisition was a Stanley Model 750B, and after that the virus had taken hold in good shape and he was beyond curing. As with any breed of collector, swapping often takes the place of coin of the realm. He got his 1918 Stanley 735 in exchange for two Maxwells.

Maynard Leighton has a decided advantage over many old car buffs in that he can take the bones of some ancient vehicle and restore it to all but pristine condition in the garage behind his white New England home. A quiet, modest fellow, with no trace of a mad gleam in his eyes, he seems satisfied that there was a time and place for those stout little steamers and has no dream that some ghost of the Stanley will one day appear on earth to replace the air-polluting, over-complicated, woman-oriented internal combustion gasoline engine. However, there is little doubt where his heart lies.

"The Stanley was, and always will be, a man's car," he said recently, with just a hint of private satisfaction. "There were four systems to watch. First there was the fuel system, then the oil, water and air. A pressure air system was necessary to vaporize the fuel much the way a modern camp-stove functions. Another complication was that a Stanley couldn't be towed, at least not very far. There was no clutch so the engine turned with the wheels and, once the engine stopped, the oil system stopped functioning, too. It was never true, as some of the car's detractors suggest, that a man needed a steam engineer's license to drive a Stanley; but it was a challenge and it's still the challenge that makes owning a steamer fun."

Clearly, it was the challenge that charged the Stanley boys that day at the Brockton Fair. The whole story of the Stanley Steamer had a Maine beginning; indeed it is a Maine story from the beginning to its tragic end.

Of the two brothers it was F.E. Stanley who was the incorrigible tinkerer and all-round mechanic genius. F.O. (it was always F.E. and F.O.) was more of the bookish type. Neither one was exposed to any advanced education, although F.O. did have a brief fling at college but, finding it dull, he packed up and came home. F.O.'s private passion was whittling violins. In fact, he was the first American to produce violins commercially. He taught school for a spell and, after his marriage, went into the business of manufacturing school supplies in Mechanic Falls. The building on Pine Street, which housed his living quarters as well as his shop, went up in flames one night. That was the end of that. The townspeople held a "pound party" to collect food and clothing for the destitute Stanleys. The necessity of accepting charity was something he was never to forget.

Brother F.E. was doing a lot better for himself. He had set up a little business in Lewiston, directing his talents toward developing a photographic dry plate. Starting with a stake of $500, he had succeeded so well that he had built up a capital of $50,000 and was ready to expand. It was at this point that the brothers joined hands. Together, they moved to Newton, Massachusetts and established the Stanley Brothers Dry Plate Manufacturing Company. Once yoked, the two heads proved better than one. The firm succeeded so well that the Stanleys were soon approached by the Eastman Kodak Company with an offer that was too good to refuse.

So there they were in Newton without an enterprise and with nothing but money to beguile the hours. Not that the Stanley brothers despised money; on the contrary, they enjoyed acquiring it and had a Yankee disinclination to part with it. Money, however, was not enough. That aborted demonstration of the steam car at the Brockton Fair came just at the right time. In a wink they were off and running again.

They were the first to admit when they sat down at drawing boards that fall of 1896 that they knew little about steam engines and even less about steam boilers. They set about correcting that deficiency. This was a time when the internal combustion gasoline engine was being plagued with bugs and frustrating problems. What appealed to the Stanley brothers was the utter simplicity of the steam engine. They promptly figured out that their first requirement was a light two-cylinder, double-acting steam engine. They took their specifications

to the Mason Regulator Company only to be dismayed when
the delivered engine weighed around 400 pounds, very nearly
the estimated weight of the complete car.

It was at this juncture that Maine came back into the picture. The Stanley brothers took their problem to the machine
shop of J. W. Penney & Sons in Mechanic Falls. S. R. Penney,
a mechanical genius of sorts himself, allowed as how he might
find the answer, given a little time. The three rolled up their
sleeves and went to work. And they didn't stop working until
they had designed a steam engine that weighed a mere 35
pounds, which together with a boiler, trimmed down to less
than 100 pounds and made a power package not only equal to
the job but far superior to anything thus far developed. In
little more than a year from the day they had made their
boast to the Brockton Fair grounds, the delicate and gleaming
little pilot model was unveiled and ready to astonish the waiting world.

The Stanleys built three more cars that fall and winter of
1897-8, two two-passenger cars and a four-passenger surrey. By
the following year the shop was really rolling, turning out an
incredible 200 cars per year.

These were the years when the derisive cry "get a horse" was
heard in the land. That summer of 1899 F.O. Stanley effect-
ively stilled such taunts by packing himself and his wife aboard
his spidery contraption and driving the rocky, unpaved road
to the top of Mt. Washington in two hours and ten minutes.
It was 1903 before a gas buggy accomplished the feat. F.O.,
never one to ignore a challenge, climbed aboard the latest
Stanley steam model and dismayed the opposition by achieving
the summit in twenty-seven minutes flat.

Although the brothers Stanley steadfastly refused to adver-
tise their product until almost the bitter end, they seldom lost
an opportunity to gain free promotion. They liked to think
that performance and word of mouth sold cars and they proved
their point by being flooded with more orders than they could
fill. This happy situation was not lost on others with risk

capital to invest. The Stanley brothers began to be besieged by offers to buy in or buy them out.

It was with the idea of getting rid of one particularly persistent petitioner that the Stanleys named the fantastic price of $250,000 for their business. Instead of blinking and quietly backing out, the fellow wrote out a check. In a glimmering they discovered they had sold out to what became the Locomobile Company and were out of business once more.

There were those who insisted that the Stanley boys were sharp. The more benevolent suggested that they simply couldn't forget their steamer and were plagued with feelings of guilt for having forsaken their brainchild. In any event, they began once again to tinker, now directing their genius to the delicate task of designing a steamer to circumvent their own patents. They succeeded to their own satisfaction at least. However, when the "new" Stanley appeared a cry went up from the Locomobile people that could be heard halfway around the world. The Locomobile Company contended they were using a small part of the chain tensioning device protected by the original patents. The brothers, faced with a lawsuit, prudently retreated and set about designing a whole new transmission system.

As it turned out, they needn't have bothered. The powers at the Locomobile Company, faced with the bitter truth that it was impossible to outflank the Stanley boys, tossed in the sponge. They sold back all the patents for peanuts and threw in their lot with the gas buggy.

The conservatism that marked the Stanleys in their money spending habits was not apparent in the matter of speed. They were incurable hot-rods long before the term was coined. It was a common sight to see the sedate pair, goggled and dustered, careening wildly over New England highways, frequently with a cop in full cry. At times they would set forth in separate and identical cars; while one brother was getting a ticket the other would tear by, a gambit that never failed to drive the minions of the law crazy.

This love of speed, coupled with a keen sense of the value of publicity, led the twins early into the field of racing. In these more serious tests they employed the legendary Fred Marriot and built for him a special steam racer called the Stanley Rocket. Marriot proceeded to break five world's records at Ormond Beach, Florida, reaching in 1906 the then incredible speed of 127.6 miles per hour. Still not satisfied, Marriot tried again the next year, pushing the pressure up to 1300 pounds per square inch. The car had reached the unprecedented speed of 197 m.p.h. when something went wrong. The car took off into the air and rolled over, the boiler going off on its own another mile down the track. Marriot was thrown clear. He survived, but the Stanleys never tried for another record after that. (As there were no speedometers in those days the speed of 197 m.p.h. was no more than a guess. Later authorities estimated the speed to be nearer 150 m.p.h.)

The Stanley boys stated early in their automotive career that a practical steam carriage could be made without the necessity of appropriating any patents or inventions. It was their firm belief that the common sense use of known principles was all that was required. They were particularly vehement in this conviction when it was someone else who controlled the patents they wanted. A fellow in Lewiston named Whitney had designed a burner that seemed a little better than the one they were using in their early model steamers. They simply copied it. When the improved boiler appeared as standard equipment on the new models, Whitney threatened to sue. The Stanleys, Yankees from their bowlers to the fringes of their dusters, knew how to handle the situation. Mindful of the irresistible attraction of cash money, they changed $500 into fives and tens and, stalking into Whitney's shop, flourished the bundle before his eyes.

"Take it or leave it," F.O. said. "If you don't take it, we'll spend $50,000 fighting your lawsuit." Whitney took it.

In the heyday of the Stanley Steamer, which spanned the first decade of the new century, the cars were selling at a steady rate of 1000 a year. But already there were clear indications that steam was losing ground in its battle with the gasoline engine. Not even the Stanleys with their passionate conviction of the superiority of steam failed to see the writing on the wall. It could only have been out of desperation that the company surrendered to the trend and placed a commercial advertisement. In 1916, a rare Stanley ad trumpeted the virtues of the steamer and damned the opposition with biting sarcasm. "The Stanley uses no clutches, gear-shifts, flywheels, carburetors, magnetos, sparkplugs, distributors, self-starters, or any of the marvelously ingenious complications with which inventors have had to overcome the difficulties inherent in the explosive engine. That is why 90 per cent of Stanley owners drive their cars without the assistance of trained chauffeurs."

This was the truth; it was also the swan song of the Stanley Steamer. The following year the firm suspended production of its vehicles. A year later F.E. Stanley, returning from a trip to his beloved Maine, met his death on the Newburyport Turnpike. Ironically, it was a horse that was his undoing. He turned off the road to avoid hitting a dawdling farm wagon and ended up in a ditch in the wreckage of his Stanley Steamer.

Brother F.O., having no heart to continue the business, sold out to a group headed by Prescott Warren. The end of the brave age of the steam auto was delayed but briefly. The last Stanley Steamer slipped silently from the factory in 1925.

Gone with gaslights and moustache cups is the stout little Maine-bred steamer, but thanks to the likes of Maynard Leighton this endearing brainchild of the brothers Stanley is not forgotten. In the little over a quarter of a century that the Stanley Steamer was in production, less than 20,000 cars rolled out of the plant. What defeated the Stanleys in the end was their refusal to hurry and their steadfast insistence upon meticulous Yankee craftsmanship.

The Stanley boys themselves would have asked no more than to be remembered for this admirable failing.

A MAGALLOWAY
SCHOOLMARM
NEVER GOES HOME

BY GERTRUDE ALLINSON BENNETT

As a young student at the end of the college year in 1916, I needed money to further my education, so I embarked upon a teaching career at a one-room, all-grade school in Magalloway.

I left the little town in Maine where I had been educated, and by a circuitous route on the railroad arrived in Berlin, New Hampshire. Here I learned that a stage would transport me up into the Magalloway 45 miles farther on and back into Maine again. Looking toward the mountains that separated me from my destination, I thought the journey would be up and down them and my heart sank within me.

The next morning I boarded the Model T Ford which served as the stage. Another teacher occupied the back seat with me, and a woodsman sat in front with the driver. Our first stop was eight miles away at Milan, New Hampshire, where bags of mail were received at the post office to be distributed along the way to every house and lumber operation. Here, too, the other teacher left, as she was engaged by the Milan school.

The stage continued on to Errol, New Hampshire, through the Thirteen Mile Woods, unbroken except for a few lumber camps on one side and the Androscoggin River on the other. At the Errol post office, another exchange of mail bags was made and here, the driver informed me, was the end of the day's trip. The fifteen remaining miles would be covered the next day when he could continue on to pick up the mail in Magalloway.

"Oh, but you can't leave me here now," I told him; "school starts in the morning and I must be there."

After a little bargaining about payment for his extra effort, the Model T chugged on. The woodsman had left the stage in Errol, so the driver asked me to sit in front with him. As we bounced along over the rough road, he plied me with information. "Well," he drawled, "I've been bringing schoolmarms up to these parts for years and never yet have I taken one back."

"How do they get back?" I asked.

"They never do get back," he replied. "The woods are full of rugged men who lay in wait for each new teacher as soon as she enters their territory, and a new schoolmarm never has a chance."

"Here's one you'll take back," I told him. "I have no intention of staying up here — not for all the men in the country! Not me!"

He gave a knowing chuckle and favored me with a few recent case histories. One teacher riding in on the stage — then a horse-drawn buckboard — came to a place where the river had crested and inundated the road. The water came up to the seat of the buckboard, so a woodsman, riding as passenger, picked her up and held her on his knee to keep her dry. This gallantry culminated in a wedding. Another teacher from Massachusetts, one of my contemporaries, was traveling into Magalloway with an ever-present woodsman as traveling com-

panion on the stage. As she glanced at the cemetery they were
then passing, the woodsman said, "Pick your lot now, Schoolmarm, because that is where you'll be buried." (And there
she rests today, having married the same year as I did and
raised six husky children to adulthood.)

We were riding along the Magalloway River, which flows
into Umbagog Lake and emerges as the Androscoggin. It was
late in the afternoon on a rainy day early in September, and
the journey had taken almost all of the day. The mountains I
had dreaded didn't present the up-and-down problem I had
feared, since we followed the river valley. But through a short
stretch of woods, a bear and two cubs crossed the road in front
of us, giving me more reason than ever to realize how wild a
country I was in. When we entered Wilson's Mills, a point
where Maine juts out into New Hampshire, I was back in my
native state again.

The stage driver had told me so many stories of schoolmarms
being swallowed up in this human vortex that I expected some
rugged individual might snatch me off the stage and carry me
off before I even had a chance to teach school. This didn't
happen, but at the first house in the hamlet a young fellow
dashed out to stop the stage. "There he is now, waiting for
you," prophesied the driver.

"Just want a lift to the post office," the young man said,
boarding the stage.

"I've got the new schoolmarm with me," the driver remarked. "Do you know where she is to board?"

"Yes, over to Hart's," the new passenger informed us.

I was to learn that in Magalloway a teacher always was
spoken of and addressed as "Schoolmarm," never as "Miss."
The occasional male who was hired received the title of
"Schoolpa," but women were preferred. There always was and
still is a dearth of women in Magalloway, despite the continuous supply of schoolmarms imported into the region.

The stage driver deposited me on the steps of the Hart family home, where I was greeted and taken in. After traveling for

two days by so circuitous a route, I felt that I had reached the proverbial jumping-off place, and indeed I had. The road ran on for only two miles farther and jumped off into a lake fifteen miles long, so there was no way out but to journey back.

Next morning the school conveyance with several pupils already aboard stopped to pick up the teacher and two Hart children. The vehicle, drawn by two heavy horses, was a buckboard which changed during the winter to a sled bearing a piano box affair with seats along the sides and a back opening covered by a curtain.

The schoolhouse room had a small platform for the teacher. Near the platform was a huge box stove and a pile of wood, regularly replenished from the shed by one of the bigger boys, who acted as janitor.

When I organized my classes, I found that there were no pupils for two of the eight grades. However, the school board informed me that two boys, who had finished eighth grade the year before, would like to take first year high studies, so I found time to fit them into my schedule. After all, I was being paid more than many teachers — $12 a week, out of which I dispensed only $4 for my room and board. Moreover, the town reimbursed my traveling expenses, but with no provision for a return trip.

The school went along very smoothly, except for the box stove, which presented a problem every few weeks. A pipe rose from the stove at the front of the room to the ceiling, where it ran along to enter the chimney at the rear. The long stove pipe would fill with soot, causing so much smoke as to make our eyes smart and burn. At that point, school activities were adjourned while the janitor disassembled the stove pipe and separated it into sections. Each child took a section outdoors, and tamped it on the ground to remove the soot; then the pipe was reassembled, put back onto its supporting wires and classes were resumed.

The buckboard which brought us to school in the morning called for us again at night. Lessons were arranged so that pupils living beyond the schoolhouse could leave early, enabling the empty vehicle to return at the closing hour for those of us going in the opposite direction.

Instead of crossing Abbot Brook Bridge on the home journey, the horses would leave the road and take us down over the bank into the brook, while we all gasped and grabbed whatever supports the seats afforded. When the horses had drunk all they wanted of the clear, cold brook water, they would pull us over the opposite bank into the road again. Although we knew this would happen on every homeward trip, it always gave us a thrill.

Autumn progressed into winter and the Nasons, who operated a sporting camp up the lake, closed up and came down to swell the Hart household, of which Mrs. Nason was a daughter. They brought along a Nason brother who was about my age, and all together they made the winter more interesting.

It was my first Christmas away from home, since it would take several weeks' pay to make the trip back and I was saving every penny to resume college next year. However, it was a happy occasion. In addition to the house where we were living, the Harts owned a smaller house which was vacant at the time. The Nasons gave orders that everyone except themselves was to stay away from the little house while they prepared it for Christmas. When they had completed their "surprise," we all went to the brightly-decorated little house to be regaled with haunches of venison, chicken, and partridges, wild berries put up during the summer, and other delicacies.

One evening Mr. Nason turned to his brother and said, "Well, Cliff, the ice is getting pretty thick and we must go back to camp to fill the icehouse and get a supply of wood for next summer." I looked aghast at Cliff and, although he must have been expecting this assignment, he looked benumbed at me. This meant the end of our walks together through the snow and the companionship we had enjoyed.

The next morning when they set out with their provisions on a horse-drawn sled, Mrs. Nason and I accompanied them to the edge of the woods. While George gave Jennie a fond fare-well, Cliff exacted my promise to wait for his return. O, the fickleness of women! He returned to find me waiting, but not for him.

One day Jennie looked through the window to see her cousin driving by alone in his sleigh. She jumped to the door and called to him, "The schoolmarm wants a ride in your sleigh."

"Not now," he replied. "Tell her a skunk got into the car-riage shed and scented up this whole rig. I'll give her a ride another time."

Despite my remonstrances, every time Jennie saw her cousin driving by, she made the same demand, several times getting the same response. One day she saw him coming with a pair of horses drawing a load of ice. "Now the skunk hasn't been near *that* outfit," she said, "so you give the schoolmarm a ride."

This time he was unable to think up an excuse. Jennie ran back into the house, pulled me out of my chair, bundled me willy-nilly into my outdoor clothes and shoved me through the door. I had no alternative. Neither did he. He took off his coat, spread it on the ice, reached down and pulled me up to sit beside him. We had never met before, so this constituted our introduction. His name, I learned, was Leon. He took me to his home for supper with his parents, and later in the eve-ning he brought me back in the sleigh about which the odor of skunk still lingered.

Thus began a ripening friendship. Every Friday night we would go fifteen miles to a dance in Errol. Since the horse never hurried, it took a long time en route, and we would return in the early morning to find Mrs. Hart kindling the fire for breakfast.

When spring came and the roads once more were clear of snow, the few people who had autos took them off the jacks where they had been all winter and put them back in opera-tion. One evening Leon arrived in a brand new Buick. He jumped out and surveyed the car with pride. "What do you think of her?" he asked.

"Pretty special," I replied.

"Well," he said, "she's all mine, and I hope soon she will be all ours."

This I recognized as a proposal.

My plans and resolutions to come to Magalloway to earn enough money to return to college became less and less firm. We finally decided on a September wedding. The day was celebrated all over the United States because it happened to be Labor Day, but for added measure to me, it was my twenty-first birthday.

The only evidence that I ever taught school in Magalloway is in a sort of monument. During my year of teaching the wooden flagpole in the schoolyard often was blown down in the wintry gales, so the town voted to erect a steel one. On a spring day a crew arrived with various sections of a new flagpole to be set into a large square of concrete. After the pole was assembled the schoolmarm was invited out to admire the result. "Now," said one of the men, "write your name and ours in the cement and the date when the pole was put up." So I did that and, although forty-eight years have elapsed, my prints as schoolmarm at Magalloway are still visible.

(Editor: Mrs. Gertrude Allinson Bennett, who wrote these reminiscences at her home in Magalloway, passed away there on April 30, 1965 and is buried in the cemetery mentioned in her story. "Thus," her son, Russell Bennett informed us, "she fulfilled the prophecy of nearly fifty years ago that 'A Magalloway Schoolmarm Never Goes Home.' ")

ELIJAH KELLOGG
OF ELM ISLAND

BY ANNE MOLLOY

SIX MILES BROAD OFF TO SEA between Bailey Island and Cape Small Point lies Ragged Island. On its westerly side the Devil's Wall stands off the breakers; on the east great boulders form a natural barrier to the sea. A cleft in the rocks opens into a small haven for boats. Ragged is only a small island, perhaps not more than a mile long nor more than half a mile wide, yet over the years it has been more familiar to young American readers than any other in fiction, except Treasure Island and Robinson Crusoe's. For Ragged was the island that Elijah Kellogg made the heart of his Elm Island series of books which were so eagerly read by both boys and tomboys.

Some claim other islands on this stretch of coast as the model for Elm Island. They are correct in doing so, for Kellogg took an artist's privilege in borrowing some of Birch Island, some of the Elm Islands and possibly some snips of the mainland when he put together his ideal Elm Island. His mixture became the perfect spot for the cultivation of the pioneer virtues which he so admired. Then he settled his fictional island with hardy folk and endowed them with the proper attributes — industry, courage, wisdom and humor — that they would need to prosper there.

This did not mean that the true inhabitants of Ragged Island — the Skolfield family — were in any way unworthy by Kellogg's yardstick, but that so many others rightfully clamored to be included in his enthusiastic accounts of coastal life. The author was fifty years old when he first sat down to write. In that time he had met many admirable figures between Casco Bay and Gloucester.

The manner in which Elijah Kellogg first found Ragged Island is a story in itself. Born, as he was proud to admit, with webbed feet, he found an outlet from studies and work when he was a student at Bowdoin College between 1836 and 1840 by sailing his catboat, *Cadet*, among the Casco Bay islands. He was a sociable young man and soon made friends among the seagoing farmers of Harpswell Neck and the offshore islands. He went to services in the old Harpswell meeting house. When he let its members know that he had decided to become, like his father, a Congregational minister, they promised to build him a new church if he would settle among them. Both parties kept the bargain. In 1844, after his ordination, he preached from the pulpit of the promised new church. He liked to say of his parishioners that "There is not a house in the parish in which the roar of the surf may not be heard, and in many of them the Atlantic flings its spray upon the door-stone." Needless to say, he made his pastoral calls as often by sea as by land.

One day as he skimmed over the bay on such a mission, he was hailed from another boat. The voice was that of Tom Skolfield, who had bought the farthest-out island, Ragged, and was raising a growing family there. To Tom, life at such a spot lacked nothing, but his wife missed her church. When Tom saw the amphibious parson, he thought of a way to save himself the twelve-mile trip on a Sunday. He invited the minister to visit his wife.

Kellogg accepted the shouted invitation, went ashore and held an impromptu prayer service for the Skolfield family. Afterwards he explored Ragged Island. It fitted in every way his conception of a proper setting for a family with all the pioneer virtues. Over the years he often went back. He was thought to have bought some of the island, perhaps even a half, but in the days of desperate poverty that came to him, he lost his holdings there. Even so, in a sense the whole island belonged to him from the moment it took hold of his imagination. By making it the greater part of his fictional "Elm Island" he made Ragged Island his own forever.

He began this literary work when he was the minister of a Boston parish and homesick for the Maine coast and its people. Into his stories he put his grandparents' tales of frontier days in Gorham, Maine, the people of his salt water parish and his own experiences.

The first of these had been shipping out before the mast when he was fifteen. No one, least of all his parents, was surprised when he did so. Elijah Kellogg Sr. was minister of the Portland Second Parish and the family lived in the old Bedlow house at 345 Cumberland Avenue. Young Elijah was surrounded by salt water temptations. Behind the house was the Back Cove where he sailed a wooden sugar box with his shirt for a sail; before it was a web of tarry rigging above the Fore Street wharves. The boy listened to sailors' tales here and was badly sea-struck — so much so that his worried parents considered sending him to stay with a family in Gorham in exchange for boarding their daughter whom they wanted to go to a school in Portland. The scheme failed. Reluctantly, the Kelloggs gave their consent to the boy's shipping out. For three years he was a sailor.

In some accounts we are told that he served aboard East India clippers. His stories give little evidence of this. They give details only of voyages aboard West India schooners. He knew the "sugar islands" so well that there is little doubt of his having visited them. Cuba, Martinique, Dominica — he describes them all. Some one aboard the vessels in which the boy sailed saw to it that he learned navigation. Later, in his book *The Ark of Elm Island,* he tells in such detail of the voyage of a strange vessel, virtually a lumber raft with sails, that his story could almost be used as a coast pilot to certain Caribbean waters. As for what he learned of the economy of the sugar islands, their agriculture and the lot of their Negro slaves, no one taught him that. He used his active mind and his observing eyes no matter where he went. In spite of his great interest in these tropical places, he found life in them far inferior to the one he was born into in the still-new North American Republic. Although he gave up the sea as a career, the three years he spent on it strongly influenced the rest of his life.

Once ashore for good, he went to Gorham to learn the business of farming. One of his maternal McLellan cousins took him in as an apprentice. He endeared himself to the whole family. He pleased his master because he applied himself so energetically. He delighted others because, being intensely sociable, he loved what he called "skylarking" and all sorts of high jinks. But his serious side pleased, too. His elderly grandparents told him stories of pioneer days in Maine when their parents, by their good sense and understanding of the Indians, survived the attacks that killed their neighbors. And they remembered even earlier family tales of Scotch-Irish ancestors who lived behind stockades because of their fear of the native Irish.

The young apprentice enjoyed farming and although he was not a large person he was able and willing. But as he hoed and plowed, cut wood and manufactured it, he began to think that something was missing in his life. He decided that it was education. He went to Gorham Academy and, after graduation from that school in 1836, to Bowdoin College. By that time he was twenty-four years old. Surprisingly, six of his thirty classmates were at least his age.

In those days there were few scholarships. A boy without means needed to have his tuition money earned and in hand when he entered college and, once there, to work at odd jobs during the school year to pay for his lodging. Kellogg could receive no help from home and was glad to be so proficient with an axe. He worked on the college woodpile and was chosen to repair the college fence when it needed mending. This was more often than would be suspected; in those days of few outside activities, students let off steam by attacking the fence and making soul-satisfying bonfires. Then Kellogg and his axe would be called in to replace the rails. He admitted in later years that when his purse was empty he tided himself along with a few private bonfires.

He worked hard and he studied hard. In spite of this, he never lost his active sense of fun. Kellogg's name became a by-word for pranks. Since the college president, Dr. William Allen, was a pompous, humorless man, he afforded the student body a natural target for their jokes. Kellogg, like others, took advantage of it. Once when a levee was going on at the president's house, he thrust a goose, its head tied up in a lady's calash bonnet, through an open window and among the guests. Another and more famous of his exploits was that of Dr. Allen's "wicker work" hat.

When Kellogg heard that two other students had stolen Dr. Allen's hat, he volunteered to set it at the top of the church steeple that night. And so he did, in spite of a sharp electrical storm. To make the climb with only a lightning rod to cling to took nerve and agility. It would also seem to bear out those who claim he served on clippers during his years at sea. Who but a "royals boy," steeled to go aloft in dirty weather, could perform such a feat? The next morning Dr. Allen vowed to have the headgear down before chapel time. But to the pranksters' satisfaction it took several men and ladders and the whole forenoon before the doctor got his hat back.

When Elijah Kellogg wrote the Whispering Pines series, he was describing Bowdoin College as it was in his student days. The books give a better picture of the college than an official history could. Although he started work on the series more than twenty-five years after his graduation, his memories of student days were sharp. And the college was always in his mind. He went back often. The boys were as glad to see him and hear him speak as were the professors.

From Bowdoin, Kellogg went to Andover Theological Seminary in Andover, Massachusetts. It was during his studies here that he wrote the declamation that made his name a household word. In those days of highly-admired pulpit oratory, the seminarians were required to write and deliver declamations as part of a rhetoric course. For Kellogg, this was an ordeal. He resolved to write a piece so dramatic that his listeners would forget him under the spell of his words. With his "Spartacus to the Gladiators" he more than succeeded. The fame of its dramatic situation, its ringing, rounded phrases traveled beyond the seminary. Epes Sargent included it in his *Standard Speaker*. After its appearance in this universally used book, more than a generation of school boys chose the declamation for prize-speaking days. There must have been few schools that did not ring with the words, "Hark! Hear ye yon lion roaring in his den? 'Tis three days since he tasted meat; but tomorrow he shall break his fast upon your flesh . . ."

When Kellogg finished at the seminary, he kept his promise to the Harpswell people of whom he said, "it was a love match at the beginning and so it continued." And the people kept their part of the bargain, too. Even before he had finished his courses they had the timber for the new church piled at its site. In September of 1843 the building was dedicated, and its pastor was ordained the following June.

The structure is a fine one. The unknown designer combined a Greek Revival building with touches of "Carpenter

Gothic" in a surprisingly successful way. The exuberant curves of its beautiful doorway stand out in strong contrast to the smooth matched boarding of the facade. We do know who made the doorway: Moses Bailey of West Harpswell, a joiner. As for the steeple, that was the young minister's particular delight. In the poem he wrote for the church's dedication he said,

> Its spire shall be the last to meet
> The parting seaman's lingering eye;
> The first his homeward gaze to greet,
> And point him to a home on high.

At the beginning of his ministry Kellogg "boarded around." Then, after his mother became a widow, he needed to make a home for her. He bought sixty-five acres of land that ran down to the shore of Middle Bay, and decided to place his home on the site of a tumbledown block house. He cut the timber for it and carried it to the sawmill and back by himself. On the day he planned to start building he had a pleasant surprise. From neighboring shipyards seventy-five carpenters brought their tools to help. The work flew along. By sunset of the first day, the men had hewn every stick for the heavy house frame and fitted most of it together. On the next day they raised it, then boarded and roofed it. It is not likely that the energetic preacher stood idly by. Nor is it likely that the carpenters, used to a rum ration to get them through their rugged day's work, accomplished all they did on spring water.

This house was always home for Kellogg, even during his years away, and he died there in 1901. Now the old building is like the block house it superseded — tumbling down, too. It is a prey of vandals and looters.

"The neighbors took to Ma'am and Ma'am to them," her son said of Mrs. Kellogg Senior. But her time among them was short. After her death the parishioners suggested that he take a wife. This step was not one that he had considered but he was game about it. He took their recommendation for a bride and went off to Syracuse to court her. She was someone he had known in Gorham, Hannah Pomeroy, a minister's daughter.

"Smart as a whip," her advocates said, and a school teacher.
She accepted, and although her suitor may have been diffident,
the marriage was a good one. They had a son, Frank, and a
daughter, Mary.

The Harpswell minister believed in the dignity of labor. In
fact, he prescribed "essence of hoe handle" as the best remedy
for persons afflicted with "nerves." He took large doses of the
medicine himself. He pitched hay, chopped wood, pulled rockweed for dressing his fields, ploughed, did everything that
his farming parishioners did. Their response to this and to his
preaching was to fill his church for the services.

When he saw work for others to be done, he did this, too.
One Sunday morning notice that he read from the pulpit is
typical of his attitude both to his ministry and to labor. "Widow Jones's grass," he read, "needs mowing. I shall be in her
field tomorrow morning at half-past four with scythe, rake, and
pitchfork. I shall be glad to see all of you there who wish to
come and help." He was there, and a large crew of men and
boys as well. One of them, a giant of a man, told Kellogg, "Parson, I am going to cut your corners this morning." Before noon,
however, the wiry parson had set him such a pace with his
scythe that the man had to drop exhausted beneath a tree to
rest.

So great was the response of boys and young men to Kellogg's sympathetic interest that soon another task was added
to his others. Bowdoin College sent some of their students who
had gotten into scrapes or become heavy drinkers to live with
him for a few weeks. They called this benevolent practice
"rusticating." More plainly, it was being straightened out by
the minister. He was successful, as far as we know. In his book,
The Hardscrabble of Elm Island, he describes how he went
about such an assignment. His character, James Welch, a lik-
able, intelligent young man, well on his way to being an al-
coholic, is shipped to the island as a last resort. Lion Ben treats
him with understanding and keeps him occupied outdoors.
When he paddles to the mainland in the birch and backslides,

Uncle Isaac, whom James admires, gives him the "quicksilver treatment," some very straight talk. The cure was a success and the methods used sound much like some in use today.

It was Kellogg's concern for seamen with James Welch's problem that persuaded him to leave his Harpswell pastorate after eleven years. He could remember from his life at sea how often sailors, dumped dead drunk aboard of a vessel at sailing time, became "when the alcohol was out of their system," invaluable seamen. When the Mariners' Church in Boston called him to be their pastor, he accepted. To leave his amphibious parish must have been a hard decision for him to make. His justification for the Boston work he put as vividly as anyone could. The church was connected with a Sailors' Home and he described the need for the hostel this way. "Suppose," he said, "twenty-five seamen from Calcutta, with beard and hair of 130 days' growth, hammocks, canvas bags, sheath knives, chests lashed up with tarred rigging, redolent of bilge water, with a monkey or two, and three or four parrots, should drive up to the Revere House in a North End wagon and say, 'We want to stop here; our money is as good as anybody's.' Would they stop here? I trow not." He knew that these men, potential parishioners, would have nowhere but a dive to go to unless the Sailors' Home existed.

At the time he went to Boston, 1855, the American merchant fleet was a large one and the port was extremely busy. He worked with vigor among merchant seamen. Many signed the temperance pledge for "Father" Kellogg and he even had the satisfaction of some of these here-today-and-gone-tomorrow men returning to him. But as the years went by, the Civil War cut down on the amount of shipping. Many American vessels were sold to other flags. The Fort Hill section of Boston was becoming more a resort of businessmen than sailors. The seamen's hostel on Purchase Street in that section was less needed. This gave Kellogg an incentive for making a drastic change. In 1865 he embarked wholly on a writing career.

He went at this new career as vigorously as he had the others.

His working stint was fifteen hours a day. He walked from the rooming house at 99 Pinckney Street, where the Kelloggs had quarters, to the Boston Athenaeum library. Here, although he "sweated his brain," as he liked to say, for such long periods with his pen, he enjoyed the sociability of the place. Others working there found his humor an addition to their lives.

His books poured out. Twenty-eight were published in an eighteen-year period. The first were so enthusiastically received that he felt justified in keeping on with them. He knew that he was reaching a larger audience than ever before. His ideas and enthusiasms were traveling across the country in the pages of his books.

The Elm Island series, the Pleasant Cove series, the Whispering Pine stories flowed continuously from his pen. In fact, the Elm Island series is in reality one long book lopped off at conventional volume lengths. He was not interested in plotting or building his stories and the bridges he built to link the lopped-off parts of a series are very rough. And no editorial pencil interrupted his long digressions; if he wanted to stop and build a birch canoe or a log cabin, snare a bear, or grow willow sallies and weave them into baskets, this he did before the eyes of the reader, no matter what drama might be going on in the lives of his characters. If he wanted to moralize, he did. The nearest he came to sugar-coating his moral pills was to have his little sermons spoken by admirable frontier characters.

He peopled his stories with characters drawn from life. Many, like those of Hugh and Elizabeth McLellan, his maternal grandparents, were straight from life. None of them spoke stilted story-book speech. His prose had the cadence as well as the vocabulary of down east talk. The author's ear was sensitive and his memory good. He used the rich figures of speech, many going back to Elizabethan England, that he heard his friends using.

In two quite different characters in the Elm Island series, he gives a picture of the two Elijah Kelloggs. His *Parson Goodhue* shows him as the kindly shepherd of his coastal flock. In *Charlie Bell,* the "waif" of Elm Island, he gives us his own eternally boyish side. We see his enthusiasm for "contriving" and not being "balked" by difficulties, and his terrific response to the wonders and beauties of the world around him. In Charlie, as in Kellogg, joy and thanksgiving were always breaking out. The minister could never, like many of his colleagues, preach grimly and fearfully of retribution.

Perhaps this was why he felt so much sympathy with the Indian characters in his books. Like them he had a strong sense of place. Under a particular giant tree or beside a certain stream he experienced a compelling religious feeling that was almost pagan. He describes Indian life in peaceful times almost with envy. As for their wartime atrocities, he was too honest and too dramatic to omit them, but he insisted that the natives were the victims and tools of European policies.

Although he was a great believer in the American creed of prosperity, he demanded that wealth be won in morally respectable ways. Best of all was to have money the by-product of some good deed, as when his Elm Island people sail to a sugar island to rescue a Negro cook caught as a slave, and make a prosperous voyage of it as well.

As for his own affairs, they never prospered. Just when he had reached the point of expecting royalties from his books to assure a comfortable old age, his publishers, Lee and Shepherd, failed. He lost the copyrights to all his books except one. No doubt a better businessman than he would have either salvaged something from the crash or protected himself from going down with the firm, but not Kellogg. He was crushed by it. His wife had become an invalid and the Harpswell house was already mortgaged.

Soon after, his journal, always written with more candor than care for periods and commas, contains the following entry for May 29, 1882: "I have been called by the Church to go to Harpswell. I dare not refuse to go at the same time I do not see how I can go I am in debt to persons there whom I cannot

meet without paying I must cut my hay which I cannot do
without a Horse and I am not able to buy 1 * * am in the
greatest distress & Perplexity possible * * I have this day endeavored to cast my burdens on the Lord feeling that as he
has sent me to Harpswell he will provide me with a way . . ."

This faith was rewarded. A friend gave (or loaned) him
money for his debts. He went to Harpswell and at once planted
peas and potatoes. Later, with more financial help, he bought
a horse. Of his first Sunday service after the return he wrote in
his diary, "The people seemed to make much effort to get to
meeting and seemed I thought very tender."

From 1883 to 1889 he took over the pulpit in the Topsham
church. The salary was small and he carried on his farming in
Harpswell during the week. Although he could supply most of
his needs in this way — he manufactured his own firewood, grew
grain, vegetables and fruit, produced butter and milk — life was
pretty much a hand-to-mouth affair.

Often he hitched up a rig and traded eggs and butter for
sugar or oil at the local store, or carried produce to Brunswick for sale. On these selling trips he must have looked "a
sight" to the prim, who had the notion that parsons should
always wear black broadcloth. He wore a denim frock and
tucked his trousers into cowhide boots. For a period, after he
lost his horse and he could not buy another, he yoked the
family cow with a steer and walked beside them to Brunswick.

As the lean years passed, his hearing, that had gradually
been failing, deserted him. He was no longer able to manage
the "social meetings" for the Topsham church. The Harpswell parish called him to preach at $8 a Sunday. When the
summer people requested one of his often repeated sermons
such as "The Anchor of Hope" or "The Prodigal Son," the
Harpswell folk admired him enough to sit patiently through it,
although they admitted knowing it off by heart.

They were proud, too, of his saintlike generosity and liked
to tell about it. One of their favorite stories was that in which
he went St. Martin — who divided his cloak with a beggar —

two better. One very cold day the minister set out wearing a warm coat which had just been given him. He met a thinly-clad neighbor on the road, and unsolicited, peeled off the coat, forced it onto the shivering man, and went on his own way coatless.

"No more appreciation of money than a child two years old," his people liked to say. To insure his having certain necessities, they held a yearly donation party for him. "He was tickled to death to have us come and take possession of his house," one neighbor said, "but he doesn't care a snap for the things we bring." In fact, they warned the housekeeper (his wife had died in 1890) that she must hide their gifts. Otherwise the minister would give them to someone needier than he

His economic struggles went on to the very end. Fortunately, he was able to stay active. Well into his eighties, he was still climbing up into his apple trees. In 1901, shortly before his death, he wrote in his journal, "I went to God and He sent a man to buy my apples find the barrells & haul them off & this morning sent me money & I have just paid my housekeeper Betsy Randall for 4 Weeks Work."

He never became bitter, and indeed had many satisfactions. His people were "gentle" towards him. He was a favorite son of his alma mater. At Bowdoin's centennial observances in 1894 he was a speaker in the distinguished company of a chief justice, a general and several professors. The applause given the others was nothing to the tumultuous approval he received. Part of it may have been for his spunky admission that he was too deaf to hear any words of those before him save the name of Bowdoin. One of his last tributes was the gratifying throng that turned out to hear him in Merrymeeting Park outside Brunswick. His old voice stood up to the test of speaking outdoors. And his topic, "Say Not That Former Days Were Better Than These," shows that his spirit had not become crabbed.

Over the years that his books were published they never brought him much money, but he received many letters from grateful readers. This told him that he was still an influence on another generation, and that his enthusiasms were still being shared.

And he must have been happy that the sailors among his people found his writing seaworthy. One of them said, "He always gets everything right when he writes about the sea. When he tells about working a ship in a storm or about managing a dory in a squall, you can use what he wrote for a sailor's guide. I have read Clark Russell and Marryatt and Dana's *Before the Mast* but I must say Uncle Kellogg gets it nearer from a sailor's point of view than any of the others."

Uncle Kellogg "got it nearer" from many points of view.

MAINE TALENT

Maine has produced a goodly share of writers,
artists, figures of the theatre
and people deft with their hands.
All share the same characteristic:
they see beauty in the commonplace
and are determined
to share it.

THE DERMOT SISTERS
OF ROCKLAND, MAINE

BY DIANA FORBES-ROBERTSON

IT WAS NOT SO VERY RARE to be born a beauty in the last quarter of the nineteenth century and in the State of Maine. Mrs. Louis Wardwell of Camden said that she could name at least a dozen women of the 1880s-90s, living in the small area between Thomaston and Camden, who could have claimed fame as international beauties if they had wanted to.

Only one, however, did seize upon her beauty, transport it out of Rockland, show it upon the stage and, as soon as she could manage, make it her passport into the world of international society. She was Jessie Dermot — born March 5th, 1868 in Rockland — who changed her name to Maxine Elliott, a name which blazed in lights on Broadway and above every theatre throughout the United States, and then became known to all of London society. Like a mighty vessel she ploughed ahead through the rough waters of her career, while behind her for a while bobbed a little boat in tow — her younger sister,

May Gertrude Dermot, also born in Rockland (December 14th, 1874).

The Dermot girls were very beautiful, children of a handsome Irish immigrant father, Captain Thomas Dermot, and his Rockland-born wife, Adelaide Hall Dermot, also a renowned beauty. Jessie (Maxine) was six and a half years older than her little sister, more vividly remembered in Rockland because her school days were shared at McLain's Grammar School with Rockland boys and girls till her fourteenth year, whereas May Gertrude's childhood in Rockland was cut short by the premature death of their mother and the removal of their father to Oakland, California.

Jessie's contemporaries saw little remarkable in her, except for her unusually dark, gypsy-like looks, enormous eyes, a bulky and awkward body and some tomboyish traits which made her seem slightly different (and at a disadvantage) compared to other dainty-waisted girls of her class. She had the reputation of a "loner," but she was generally liked, a friendly girl, a good sport who romped with the boys rather than flirted with them. Nothing suggested a future actress; in fact, she was markedly self-conscious in school recitations and ducked them whenever she could.

Inside Jessie's good-humored exterior, there burned ambition. Perhaps an incident in her childhood, when she was about ten years old, awakened it. A fair had set up its tents on the outskirts of Rockland and one of the main attractions was a gypsy fortune-teller. A group of girls gathered round eagerly, with many giggles, and among them was Jessie Dermot, clutching the piece of silver which her father Captain Tom, always lavish in his gestures, had given her. Her turn arrived. The gypsy, whose takings so far had consisted of frugally donated pennies, tucked the silver away and exclaimed in dramatic amazement, "Here is a young lady who will grow up to know kings and queens, and to have as much money as any of them. All the world will know of her and admire her."

Undoubtedly there was some laughter and the suggestion

that Captain Tom's silver had produced this rosy picture. Jessie did not like to be laughed at. She was also almost simple and literal about things she wished to believe. She may have forgotten this incident in later years, but it could have set in motion the driving and highly practical ambition that sent Jessie on her way to fame and fortune.

Her career did not begin auspiciously, however. She was taken out of school in Rockland at fourteen, when an involvement with a local boy was thought unfortunate and premature, and her father sailed off with her to South America while Jessie studied her school books and practiced her piano on board the little 578-ton bark, *Will W. Case.* By sixteen she had married a city marshal in New York, George MacDermott, a flashy, shallow man, involved in shady politics, the race-track and too much drink. By 1888, before Jessie was 21, she had fled from this miserable marriage. She was alone again, more beautiful, bitterly experienced and just as ambitious. She knew she was beautiful; therefore all that early self-consciousness must be conquered and she would go on the stage.

The playwright-actor-director, Dion Boucicault, who also was head of an acting school, gave her some instruction and helped her invent her new name. In response to his suggestion that she find the grandest name she knew, she told him that Maximilius, the name of a school-friend's father, struck her as splendid. They played with it and evolved Maxine. It was a brand-new name, coined that very moment, and any Maxine today owes her name to Maxine Elliott. Elliott was added from a family name occurring among her mother's Tolman forbears. It was pleasing to Mr. Boucicault to see that Maxine with the "x" dropped out spelled Maine, and the initials ME were the same as her native state's abbreviated form.

For six years Maxine Elliott slogged her way through supporting roles, spending many months "on the road," touring the length and breadth of the United States. In 1894 the little sister, May Gertrude Dermot, was whisked from the schoolroom (now Hunter College, New York City) onto the stage at Saratoga Springs and became Gertrude Elliott. Maxine was much photographed as a "stage beauty" — the 1890s version of the pin-up girl — but her acting ability was seldom mentioned by critics. She rose a little in critical and public esteem when she joined the great company of Augustin Daly and gave some creditable performances in Shakespearean roles, but her way to leading lady status was blocked by Ada Rehan, the star of Daly's company. Meanwhile little Gertrude was piling up fine reviews.

It was not until the comedian and ex-vaudevillian, Nat C. Goodwin, became associated with Maxine that she began to rise to the top of the billing. He made her his leading lady and then his third wife (with two more to follow her). Their acting partnership acquired a devoted following, made a great deal of money and lasted seven years. At its dissolution, Maxine soared into stardom alone. From then on she played light comedies with such forgotten names as *Her Own Way, Her Great Match, Myself — Bettina, The Chaperon.* By 1908 she built and opened her own theatre — The Maxine Elliott Theatre on Broadway and 39th Street in New York City.

But she had never liked acting and her goal was not the perfecting of her art; rather her ambition was to accrue enough money to leave the theatre forever and live opulently and independently as a woman of society. On visits to England — first with the Daly company, then with Nat Goodwin — she became passionately attracted to the world of London society, the lavish world of Edwardian England. She and Nat, before their marriage collapsed, entertained at a country estate, and soon the lords and ladies began to rile the freewheeling Nat, but Maxine went on alone from house party to house party. Around her the rumors grew; her name began to be coupled with great names in English and American society, and the public became far more interested in her legend than in her status as an actress. It was whispered that J. P. Morgan had made the building of her theatre possible; it was shouted that King Edward VII called her "the most beautiful woman in the world"; she was mentioned as being devotedly admired by a member of the Widener family, a member of the English Rothschild family, by Winston Churchill, by Lord Birkenhead ("F.E." Smith, brilliant attorney and Lord Chancellor under Prime Minister Bonar Law), and by the Duke of Rutland. Two brilliant marriages were offered her and turned down; one with Lord Curzon, ex-Viceroy of India; the other with Lord Rosebery, ex-Prime Minister of England. Maxine Elliott, however, had already realized her ambition to be a member of society on her own terms and under her own (invented) name, and needed no man, however great his titles and estates.

The shy little sister had tagged in her wake until three years after Maxine's marriage to Nat Goodwin. Gertrude was in the Goodwin-Elliott company, playing small parts and frequently stealing the show. Then she was engaged by the English classical and romantic actor, Johnston Forbes-Robertson, to be his leading lady, and after two months they were married. As Maxine played smart drawing room comedies, piling up her money through tireless work and brilliant investments, Gertrude soared to heights in her art by the side of her husband, and shared with him the final honor given his work in the theatre, when he received a knighthood from the King. Thus Maxine, who had an obvious weakness for English titles, found herself sister to Lady Forbes-Robertson. But she continued as "big sister" always, bossing Gertrude unmercifully, as well as Gertrude's four daughters, of whom the writer of this article is one. We called her "Auntie Dettie," a distortion of Jessie made by Gertrude when she was an infant; so, all unknowing, in our childhood we were harking back to Maxine Elliott's early Rockland days and name, while faced with the formidable Aunt Maxine.

Maxine's final stage was the French Riviera, where she built an enormous white villa at the water's edge and entertained a constant stream of people. Her own interpretation of this glittering life was given in an interview to the press when she briefly returned to the United States in 1933: "People will probably think me stupid when I admit that peace is the principal thing in life. I have my lovely home, an ample income, a pet monkey, a few dear friends to crony with . . . My idea is to sneak into a little corner and never see my name in print again." When Maxine's loyal sister Gertrude pleadingly persuaded her daughters to go and share the splendors of Auntie Dettie's Chateau de l'Horizon, it hardly seemed to us "a little corner" into which we could "sneak." We would much rather have stayed in the peaceful village on the English Channel which was Gertrude's home after Forbes-Robertson retired from the theatre. Gertrude enjoyed the Chateau de l'Horizon visits no better than her daughters did, and I knew, when Mother and I were there together, that she would never venture down to face all the card-playing groups around the swimming pool without me to back her up.

These two sisters were astonishingly unlike except in looks: both with coal-black hair, enormous eyes and classic features. The difference between them was created not only by inherent characteristics but also by circumstance. Maxine early became mother-and-father to Gertrude, with their own mother dead and their father away at sea for months at a time. Maxine had the strong, practical nature of Captain Tom; she had a man's mind for organizing and leadership while the brilliance of her financial dealings seemed astonishing in a woman. Gertrude was like an adorable shy young girl, always a little unsure of herself and looking up to her older sister as all-knowing. She had much of the gentleness and nervous anxiety of their sweet mother Adelaide, also a person much in need of support, who crumpled under the long absences of her husband.

The sisters' paths diverged as sharply as their basic attitudes towards life: Maxine the "loner," Gertrude the wife and mother; Maxine the disciplined worker — who forced herself through thirty years in the theatre for the money and subsequent liberty it would bring her; Gertrude the actress — who loved her work and wholeheartedly shared her husband's sense of duty in presenting only the noblest and most poetic in dramatic art. Yet, both women were ruled by the powerful influence of Rockland, Maine.

In Maxine it might seem hard to recognize. But surely it was from Rockland that she acquired her strong do-it-yourself attitude. No matter how many millions of dollars she possessed, she preferred a homemade dress to any couturiere's creations, and spent the periods between guest-filled weekends absorbed in making clothes for herself, her sister and her nieces. The attention that she gave to the last detail of a house might have stemmed from memory of her father's meticulous care with the building of the *Will W. Case* in Starrett's shipyard, Rockland, when she was only ten. Like all independent Mainers, she refused to be beholden, preferring to entertain the noble lords she acquired in England rather than to enter society under their wings. She also had the Maine trait of keeping her counsel, and thus became the trusted friend of men in power, who appreciated her gift for keeping her mouth shut. She was willing to take any risks herself, but she chaperoned and watched and guided her family with a savage Puritanism, utterly bewildering to us in her gossipy circle, amid the shining diamonds, the splashing pool, the endless food and the raffish tone of high society.

Her sister Gertrude openly admitted that her early Maine influences were with her forever. "Oh dear," she would say, when faced with some awkward decision, "a New England conscience really is rather uncomfortable sometimes." She was fortuitously pushed into the part of the young Cleopatra in *Caesar and Cleopatra*, which G. B. Shaw had written originally for Forbes-Robertson and his former leading lady, Mrs. Patrick Campbell. The play had been shelved and when Forbes-Robertson decided to present it, Gertrude had become his wife as well as his leading lady. Shyly, Gertrude started rehearsals of the vixenish Egyptian. And in the cold, partially-lit theatre Mr. Shaw walked down to the front of the orchestra stalls and called up to the stage, begging her to give more abandon to her performance: "Remember, Miss Elliott, you are Cleo-

patra, Queen of Egypt." "Yes, Mr. Shaw," Gertrude replied,
"but born in Rockland, Maine." Shaw collapsed in laughter
and the following day Gertrude received one of his inimitable
postal-cards which said, "Cleopatra shall be forgiven her virtue
for the sake of her beauty."

Both Rockland-born girls, who had traveled so far and so
wide, ended their days by the side of the sea. The sweep of the
Bay of Cannes with its offshore islands, les Iles de Lerins, is
not unlike Rockland Harbor (but not so beautiful). At Gertrude's home, St. Margaret's Bay, Kent, on the English Channel, there is the constant sound of gulls and the hoots and
whistles from the busy sea-lane when fog encloses it, while on
clear nights the lightships and light houses flash their beams
across the bedroom windows.

Maxine sat amid her myriad guests constantly playing cards,
eating chocolate cake and getting fatter and fatter. She wore a
visored cap and as her jawline grew heavier she became more
and more like her sea-captain father. She never spoke of Rockland; she was the kind who shut the door on each phase of her
life and did not look back. Gertrude walked with her family
along the heights that are called the White Cliffs of Dover, her
Aberdeen dog at her heels, and at home kept up a never broken
correspondence with cousins in Rockland — Perrys, Brewers,
Halls, Chattos.

It may be presumptuous for someone of a younger generation to sum up the lives of those gone before, but it seems to
this niece of Maxine and daughter of Gertrude that the life of
the former was a triumph and of the latter a fulfillment.

THE CAMDEN GIRLHOOD OF EDNA ST. VINCENT MILLAY

BY ISABEL CURRIER

IT WOULD HAVE BEEN DIFFICULT, during the past fifty years, to find anyone of pronounced English literary tastes who never had heard of Camden, Maine. A summer resort with the well-merited slogan of "the prettiest town in Maine," Camden formed the background for an eighteen-year-old girl's immortal poem, "Renascence." The "three long mountains and a wood" and "three islands in a bay" lure many literary pilgrims, who occasionally are horrified to find that some residents of the town know nothing of either the poem or its author, Edna St. Vincent Millay. Such a visitor last summer — from Finland — remarked, "If so great a poet had grown up in a village in my country, there would be a statue of her in the public square."

A memorial plaque to honor the Camden poet was embedded in a boulder atop Mount Battie in 1968; it was donated to the State Park Department by Mr. and Mrs. Harold B. Dondis of Boston. There is a Millay Memorial Room at Whitehall Inn, where "Renascence" was first publicly recited by the poet herself in 1912, and another "Millay Room" at the Hathaway-Cushing-Tufts house at 31 Chestnut Street, once the home of family friends with whom the Millays often visited. The "Millay Scrapbook" at Camden Public Library was compiled by local librarians, including "the other redhead" in the poet's high school class of 1909, Miss Corinne Sawyer, who began as a schoolgirl to collect evidences of her friend's genius and always thought her worthy of Edmund Wilson's later tribute as "the spokesman for the human spirit."

Miss Sawyer is one of a dwindling number of contemporaries who remember Edna St. Vincent Millay vividly as a pixyish schoolgirl of sixty years ago. Inevitably, each person's memories of Vincent — as she was called by family and friends in her youth — reflects his own personality, so that a few former schoolmates are frank in saying that they "never understood her poetry or cared much about it." Still other childhood acquaintances, not of the Millays' immediate circle, base many of their recollections upon hearsay; hence, their memorabilia of a greatly gifted girl — who became a legendary literary figure in her twenties and would be only in the late seventies if she still were living — are significant of the smalltown Maine culture of which Millay was a valiant product and remains — sad to say — also a victim. Unfortunately, both Millay myths and outright inventions have been perpetuated in several published versions of her girlhood in Camden.

In the summer of 1904 Mrs. Cora Buzzell Millay and her three daughters moved into a house — no longer standing — in the Millville section of Camden. Several years earlier she had divorced her husband, Henry Millay, a popular teacher and superintendent of schools in nearby Union because, it was whispered, "he gambled." There never was a hint of moral impropriety in the family life of the Millays but, among those who measured worth by income or status rather than by talents and graces, even their conformities were subject to criticism.

For instance, they were faithful members of the Congregational Church, where they were censured for arriving in a breathless group each Sunday — often a few minutes after the service had started. The mother's cultivation — especially her accomplishments as a musician and a poet — were thought unbecoming in one who had to support her daughters by practical nursing and the weaving of hair switches for that era's women of fashion. In fact, all of the resentment of the Millays seems to have been directed at their most shining qualities: their well-bred indifference both to limited means and to malice, their boundless admiration for each other, and their joyous pursuit of tastes and ambitions beyond the cultural horizon of their detractors. As Vincent described that period later, "We had all of the luxuries of life, but few of the necessities."

Actually, the family quickly found its place among the intellectuals of the town, and early appreciation of the Millays by perceptive friends presents a truer picture. "The Millays weren't *poor*," says Miss Corinne Sawyer, "they simply never thought anything about what they didn't have. They had infinite riches in talent and hope and goodness and generosity of mind and spirit, and they were lavish in sharing them. Few families ever know the sheer happiness of the Millays. And the word for Vincent was 'radiant'."

Vincent's radiance sometimes was obscured by her more serious qualities. "She was small and frail for a twelve-year-old," recalls Mrs. Jesse (Emma Harrington) Bradstreet of Rockland, then a young teacher of eighth and ninth grades at Camden's Elm Street School, where Vincent enrolled in September of 1904. "Her mane of red hair and enormous gray-green eyes added to the impression of frailty, and her stubborn mouth and chin made her seem austere, almost to the point of grimness. When I read her first composition, it was so mature that I kept her after school to try to find out if someone had helped her with it. I was trying to say tactfully that I wondered if, perhaps, her mother had seen her excellent composition, when the child interrupted me. 'Excuse me, Miss Harrington,' she said, 'but I can tell that you think I didn't write that composition. Well, I did! But the only way I can prove it will be to write the next one you assign right here, in front of you. And I promise it will be as good as this one, and maybe better.' "

Mrs. Bradstreet was absent, due to illness, during the winter of 1905-1906 when Vincent — then in ninth grade — clashed literally head-on with the Elm Street School principal, Frank Wilbur. A quick-tempered man, albeit a gifted teacher, Mr. Wilbur's method of coping with Vincent's disconcerting habit of questioning the points her teachers made in class was to misconstrue her given name, which apparently he considered outlandish.

Vincent — born on February 22, 1892 in Rockland — owed the unusual portion of her prophetically lyrical name to her mother's whimsical tribute to a hospital, which had nursed a relative back to health. It became the habitual whimsy of Mr. Wilbur, teacher of history as well as principal of the school, to address the girl always as Violet, Veronica, Vivien, Valerie — any name beginning with a V — rather than Vincent. With her poise unshaken, Vincent would respond, "Yes, Mr. Wilbur, but my name is Vincent." However, Vincent so valued Mr. Wilbur that she once wrote a poem for him, and presented it to him on his birthday.

One day Mr. Wilbur erupted at some student-teacher exchange, and shouted at Vincent. "You have run this school long enough!" At the same time he threw a book at her head. Vincent picked up the book, took it to his desk, walked out of the classroom and school, and went home. Mrs. Millay promptly went to ask the school principal the reason for his behavior and, in trying to avoid the interview, Mr. Wilbur closed his door, pushing her away from it so that she nearly fell down the stairs.

Having been married to a superintendent of schools, that was the official to whom Mrs. Millay went next for action. He agreed with her that her oldest daughter should not go back to Elm Street, and that she probably was a sufficiently able student to transfer directly to the high school on merit. This was immediately arranged. Vincent Millay entered the future Camden High School Class of 1909, midway of its first year, as "The Newest Freshman" — the title of her first composition to be published in the high school periodical, *Megunticook*.

The clash with Mr. Wilbur added, of course, to the community interest in the Millay family, whose carefree ways of adapting to difficult circumstances were "eccentric" to some citizens, admirable to others, and universally enchanting to children. For instance, during the first summers in Camden Vincent and her sisters undertook to teach themselves to swim in the Megunticook River. Lacking waterwings, they snatched pillowcases from the house and "blew them up" to serve the purpose.

They were adept at making good use of unexpected windfalls. During one unusually cold winter night the kitchen fire went out, and the water pipes burst, flooding the kitchen and dining room which, by morning, had a solid floor of ice. On arising and descending to the lower floor, the girls greeted their calamity with glee. One started the fire, one started breakfast, and the other brought their skates, and when Mrs. Millay dropped in from a nursing case to see how her girls were faring, she found them skating merrily about on the lower floor. After her initial astonishment she joined her laughter with theirs and postponed her call to the plumber.

Mrs. Millay had once studied for an operatic career, and had taught her daughters to sing and to play an old melodeon. Norma had the finest voice, and later sang on the professional stage, while Kathleen and Vincent — the latter a contralto — held strong parts in the operas which the family delighted to perform. Vincent was particularly talented at the piano and — until finances made it possible for her to receive a piano of her own on her thirteenth birthday — used the old organ to improvise compositions, for which she also created the lyrics. During her first year in Camden, she put *Mother Goose* into operatic form.

At that period Mrs. Millay was caring for the wife of Professor John Wheeler Tufts, a distinguished composer and piano teacher, retired from the New England Conservatory of Music. One day Vincent called there to wait for her mother, who was to have a few hours off duty. From the hallway of the gracious Tufts home, she saw an open grand piano in the next room. Impulsively, she went to sound its keys, then burst into a spirited rendition of one of her own compositions. She was interrupted by her mother's shocked entrance into the room, followed by Professor Tufts, who applauded, "Bravo! Encore!"

While she played other pieces at his request, Professor Tufts begged Mrs. Millay to allow him to take Vincent — without fee — as an advanced pupil. For a time, thereafter, Vincent had hopes of developing as a concert pianist — an ambition ultimately thwarted by the fact that her hands never grew large enough to span an octave comfortably. But the friendship with the Tufts became an enduring and precious relationship to both families. Professor Tufts' sight was failing and, as blindness overtook him, Vincent had the thoughtfulness to call daily and read aloud to him. In later years Mrs. Tufts, widowed and living in the family home with her sister, Miss Cushing, suffered ruinous financial reverses, and confided her plight to her faithful correspondent, Edna St. Vincent Millay. A close friend of the ladies relates that Miss Cushing and Mrs. Tufts lived out their years on a monthly allowance that arrived regularly from Vincent, to whom in loyal gratitude and love, Mrs. Tufts bequeathed the home at 31 Chestnut Street. Vincent never lived there as owner of the house. Shortly after inheriting the property in 1945, she sold it to its present owners — Messrs. Edwin Sears and Vincent Short — who converted the library into a Millay Room, in which books and pictures, once belonging both to the poet and to her mother, may be seen.

Vincent's girlhood was enriched by other friendships with appreciative adults. One of these was her Sunday School teacher, Miss Abbie Evans, daughter of the Congregational minister, and herself a poet. Another was a lawyer, Job Montgomery, also a poet and, one year, Vincent's vacationtime employer. Still a third was Miss Jessie Hosmer, whose enduring friendship with Vincent was formed through her church group, and who now recalls Vincent as "the life of the party, wherever she went. Miss Evans often remarked — and I was one of the many friends who agreed — that Vincent Millay was one of the nicest girls — as well as one of the most gifted — to grow up in Camden."

This opinion was shared by Vincent's high school teachers, despite her exasperating tendency to question and to probe during classroom discussions. And she was overwhelmingly popular with the girls in her class who, separately and collectively, contributed to the improvement of her slapdash housekeeping, a skill she never really mastered although, during Mrs. Millay's enforced absences, Vincent was responsible for the home life of her younger sisters.

"We used to do our homework at the Millays'," recalled the late Mrs. Stella Derry Lenfest. "Vincent was a whiz at languages and geometry, but weak in algebra, and my talents were the reverse. The first time I was invited to supper, Vincent vaguely produced a date pie from the bakery — and nothing else. I was hungry, so I offered to make potato stew as a first course." The concoction of salt pork, onions, potatoes and milk (often called poor man's stew) was hailed as a miracle of cuisine by the Millay girls, and the making of it became Mrs. Lenfest's regular contribution to their friendship.

As a housekeeper, Vincent was inclined to leave all dishes unwashed until no clean ones remained — or until her mother was expected home. Then she would organize her sisters and schoolmates into a dishwashing brigade. Everyone pitched in and cleaned up, singing Vincent's composition, "Down Where the Dishpan River Flows." Since the impresario played the

piano accompaniment, she was unable to join in the dishwashing, but no one felt that she was shirking.

"My mother used to ask me why I liked washing dishes and
making potato stew at the Millays' when I hated to do these
things at home," Mrs. Lenfest said. "It was because Vincent
made everything wonderful fun. She was always making up
songs and games, and on walks through the woods and up the
mountains, she would make birds and plants and wild flowers
as fascinating as people. But she would never discuss people,
and wouldn't listen if others did, and she could be a spitfire
if she thought something wasn't fair. No one ever heard a word
of gossip from Vincent, or a swear word — not even slang."

Vincent's contagious gayety and generosity weren't confined to
her immediate circle. "I think I'd have failed Latin if Vincent
Millay — younger than I (she was youngest of her class) and
behind me in school — hadn't explained sentence construction
to me," recalls Mrs. Eleanor Gould Hutchins, class of 1908.
"She could read Latin — translating from the textbook — as
easily as English. She also taught me to waltz. She was a marvelous dancer, and would give up her recess to teach dance
steps to us older girls and to help us with our lessons."

Corinne Sawyer seems to have been one of the few schoolmates to pay much attention to Vincent's gift for making words
dance and sing in poetry. Vincent had begun in 1906 to submit poems to *St. Nicholas Magazine*, and her first published
effort, "Forest Trees," appeared with St. Nicholas League contributions in October of that year. In March, 1907 she received
the St. Nicholas League's gold badge for "The Land of Romance"; in July "After the Celebration" was published, and
"Vacation Song" appeared in August. She was class correspondent and, eventually, editor-in-chief of the school publication,
Megunticook, copies of which, containing her verses, are now
collectors' items. Her talents extended to the theater; she took
part in class plays, wrote a Hallowe'en play which her classmates performed, and obtained several summer "bit" parts in
stock companies playing in Camden. Her social life, however,

was limited to girls' clubs such as Genothod (Sunday School), the S. A. T. (Saturday Afternoon Tea) Club of six girls, who took nature walks before teatime at each other's homes, and a reading group called The Huckleberry Finners.

Despite her extreme popularity with girls, Vincent had few boy friends in Camden, and seemed disinterested in them. Oddly, too, in view of her translucent beauty, which so enchanted young men later in her life, Camden youths seemed not to find her attractive. The late Dr. Raymond Tibbetts (DOWN EAST, JULY 1962) recalled, as a member of the Camden High School Class of 1907, the viewpoint of some local boys at that period. "I remember Vincent as a scrawny girl — not nearly as attractive as her pretty sister, Norma — and too smart for most of us. We had no frame of reference for appreciating her genius, and she hadn't learned — as many brilliant women do — to conceal her superior gifts from young male clods."

Her particular Nemesis was George Frohock, son of the local Baptist minister, and perhaps the most popular boy in their class, whose leadership of the entire group might have been unquestioned had not Vincent's stardom among the girls shone so obviously. Frohock was credited with organizing the thirteen boys in their high school class into a gang dedicated to "taking Vincent down a peg," a gallant purpose which called for laughter and mimicry of her at morning exercises and for outright warfare at all class meetings. The peak of malice was reached when class elections were held in the senior year. Vincent — whose every attempt to speak inspired the thirteen heroes to stamp and catcall until she subsided — was nominated as class poet, but withdrew when one of the boys nominated Henry H. Hall, with the evident intention of steam-rollering his election.

The honor of being class poet had seemed assured for Vincent — the only resident of Camden to have achieved national poetic recognition. (*Current Literature* had reprinted "The Land of Romance" with the comment that it was "phenomenal . . . its author — whether boy or girl we do not know — is but

fourteen years of age," and *The Camden Herald* had taken
note of this tribute.) Furthermore, Vincent had been so certain of being elected class poet that she had already begun to
write "La Joie de Vivre." But she met this humiliation with
the restraint and poise that was a lifelong part of her personality. On her mother's advice, she decided to finish the poem
and submit it as the essay required from each graduate.

Those who were present at the Camden High School graduation of 1909 barely recall that an embarrassed boy — for
Henry Hall had not coveted the role — recited a pedestrian
class poem. But several remember Vincent Millay, a tiny girl
in a homemade white dress with ruffles, whose dramatically
trained voice held her hearers spellbound through a magnificent ode to youth, with the glorious quatrain that bespoke her
own soaring spirit: *The world and I are young! Never on lips
of man, Never since time began, Has gladder song been sung!**

Before graduating exercises ended, the listening school committee awarded Vincent Millay the $10 prize for the best essay
to be presented by a member of the class of 1909. Ever generous
in triumph, as in defeat, Vincent quietly accepted her prize
and with it took a vacation journey to visit relatives in Newburyport.

The thought of going to college — a rarity in those days —
probably never occurred to Vincent, so eminently equipped to
do so in everything except financial means. During that summer of 1909, she gave a piano recital in Camden, which few
seem to remember. She also worked for six weeks in The Village Shop, owned by her friend Jessie Hosmer and still flourishing in partnership with Miss Bertha Clason. "She couldn't
bear the monotony of store routine." Miss Hosmer says: "She
liked action and variety."

So, Vincent remained at home, still in charge during her
mother's absences. Home had been a succession of addresses
after 100 Washington Street: 40 Chestnut Street, 82 Washing-

*From *Collected Poems*, Harper & Row. Copyright 1912, 1940 by Edna
St. Vincent Millay. By permission of Norma Millay Ellis.

ton Street, 12 Limerock Street. There Vincent wrote to her mother, then working in Rockland, that she "felt so sorry and ashamed" — at her inability to be a wage-earner and her inadequacies at housekeeping. Her safety valve seemed to be the new poems singing in her mind and, once on paper, laboriously taking the flawless shape of perfectionism. But now she had no market for her poems because, at eighteen, she could no longer contribute to St. Nicholas League; her swansong, "Friends," received a $5 prize, with which she bought a coveted copy of Browning.

None of the Millays had limitations in each other's loyal eyes, and her mother and sisters unstintingly applauded the poems she produced. Although her life was rich in simple pleasures, with many friends to share her love for her spectacular natural surroundings, she began to have something to say about the choking boundaries of her life.

She had begun the long poem, attesting a religiously fervent love of life for its own grandeur rather than its circumstances, which was later to electrify the literary world as "Renascence." Then her father fell ill and Vincent went, early in 1912, to Kingman, Maine (where he was superintendent of schools and first selectman) to administer to his comfort. There she evidently basked in a Maine town's cordiality towards the daughter of one of its most prominent citizens.

During Vincent's absence Mrs. Millay, keeping a nightlong vigil with a sick person, found a discarded magazine, several months old, in which contributions from American poets were solicited for a volume to be called *The Lyric Year*. In great excitement, Mrs. Millay wrote to her daughter, urging her to return to Camden at once so as to complete and submit the long poem she had begun the previous year. Vincent complied and, with the manuscript of "Renascence," she also submitted "Interim," which she herself considered a finer poem.

The result is well-known in literary history. Ferdinand Earle, editor of *The Lyric Year,* and a friend, Professor Donner, were wading through fully 10,000 submissions — mostly of

mediocre poems — in an effort to select the 100 best ones for
the volume. Donner happened to open the Millay submission,
chuckled and cast the manuscript into the wastebasket. When
Earle asked what was so amusing, Donner retrieved the manuscript, chanted the first four lines in a mocking voice, and
again discarded it. "Hey, that sounds good!" Earle protested.
Donner again fished it out, read the closing passages, turned
back and read the entire poem aloud twice. Both men agreed
that it was by far the "find" of the competition. In his enthusiasm Mr. Earle immediately wrote "E. St. Vincent Millay, Esq.,"
informing the "gentleman" that the poem was expected to
win *The Lyric Year's* first prize of $500.

Vincent had been picking blueberries when she came home
to find her mother flourishing the letter. The delight with which
the Millay quartette received the great news — carrying with it
the promise of a small fortune — must have been boundless.
Close friends were promptly informed and they, in turn, joy-
ously passed the word along through the town. But Mr. Earle
hadn't consulted his fellow judges — William Stanley Braith-
waite, poetry editor of *The Boston Transcript*, and Edward J.
Wheeler, president of the new Poetry Society of America and
the very critic who, five years earlier, had called 14-year-old
Millay's "The Road to Romance" phenomenal!

Whether through honest judgment or offended egos, these
two gentlemen repudiated Mr. Earle's opinion that "Renascence" should win first prize in *The Lyric Year*; they went
a step further, denying it a prize altogether and assigning it
to fourth place. Of the several disappointments and public
humiliations that had dogged Millay's footsteps throughout
her young life, this must have been the most bitter, although
she valiantly insisted that it was a miracle simply that her
poem "would appear in the book."

At this point her sister Norma, working as a summer wait-
ress at Whitehall Inn, invited Vincent to be her guest at a
masquerade "for the help," planned by the hotel's summer
patrons. Listlesssly for her, Vincent argued that Norma should

.invite some boy friend. But Norma insisted, having a scheme in mind to lift her sister's spirits and, to please her, Vincent went, attired as Pierrette.

It was a triumphant evening for the Millays. Norma won first prize for a waltz and Vincent the prize for the best costume. After the planned festivities ended, Norma asked a third person to suggest that Vincent play some of her piano compositions. The impromptu program was warmly applauded and, during repeated requests for encores, Norma again coached a friend to ask Vincent to "tell her new poem." Swinging around on the piano stool, Vincent recited "Renascence" with the quiet passion which still thrills owners of her recording of this and other poems. One of her listeners, Miss Caroline B. Dow, was so moved by this revelation of genius that she later arranged a scholarship to Vassar College. Its president, Dr. H. N. McCracken, wrote of Miss Millay, class of 1917, "There were few students who had done more for the college than this young poet."

With the publication in November, 1912, of *The Lyric Year*, Vincent became the center of a literary storm. Scholars the world over protested that the *only* remarkable poem in the long-awaited book was "Renascence," and other poets and editors clamored to know more of the work and identity of E. St. Vincent Millay of Camden, Maine. One of the winners of the two $250 prizes announced that his check rightfully belonged to her, and she might claim it if she wished. Orrick Johns, winner of the first prize, so agreed with spontaneous public opinion favoring "Renascence" that he refused to attend the award dinner as guest of honor.

Following her legendary years at Vassar, Vincent's mother and sisters shared her life in New York, and individually earned recognition of their own considerable talents. Kathleen was sent to Vassar and Vincent took her mother on a European tour. Norma had a notable stage career, both as actress and singer, and was married young to actor-artist Charles Ellis, with whom she still lives happily at Steepletop, the home inherited from her older sister, whose literary executor she has become.

Mrs. Millay, who also published a volume of her poems, always wished to return to Camden, and the daughters bought a summer cottage for her on Howe's Hill, overlooking the Megunticook River and the mountains. Mrs. Millay died in Camden on February 5, 1931, and Vincent and Norma came to move her remains for burial at Steepletop, Vincent's home estate in Austerlitz, New York. Kathleen could not be there, although her sisters were in touch with her in Europe. There was no funeral service in Maine so, as a farewell to the town in which they had lived so happily together, the daughters, with their husbands, followed the black van bearing their mother down the streets that had been home to them, before the Millays as a family left Camden forever.

Kathleen was the first of the daughters to leave their beloved world. She had married before finishing at Vassar and had also won literary recognition as the author of two novels and several volumes of excellent poetry. Later she separated from her husband, fell into ill health, and died suddenly in New York City in 1943. Norma and Charles Ellis represented her family, Vincent being ill. Following Kathleen's wishes, her gravestone is in Rose Lawn Cemetery at Pompton Lake, New Jersey, an area in which she had lived for some years. All of the Millay girls remained childless.

Vincent's spectacular career as "The High Priestess of Modern American Poetry," ending with her untimely death on October 19, 1950, is not pertinent to her life in Camden. This might be said to have ended when she recited "Renascence" at Whitehall Inn, where the Millay Room fittingly contains — among books, photographs and other papers — a facsimile of the original manuscript.

After her marriage to Eugen Boissevain, Vincent spent many summers in Maine, but they had purchased Ragged Island in Casco Bay, which they preferred to Camden. On the occasions when she returned to Camden to visit her mother or Mrs. Tufts, few of her girlhood friends saw her. Most of them say that they felt shy at seeking her out, fearing that so great a celebrity might not find much in common with them any more. It seems likely that Millay — always painfully shy — shared their diffidence.

In *Letters of Edna St. Vincent Millay*, edited by Alan Ross MacDougall, a letter to her mother comments wryly that, although she had paid all family debts through her earnings on reading tours, it was a pity this was accomplished after her marriage to a rich man. She felt that Camden critics never would credit her with having vindicated the family honor through her own efforts. There are other indications in her letters that the devil-may-care indifference she had maintained, through the endless mortifications of limited means in an income-conscious era, was merely the facade for a desperate sensitivity.

As one old friend remarked, "Those who couldn't understand why Vincent's feet never touched the ground sometimes made mean remarks to try to bring her down to earth." And incredibly — although Camden knew Vincent Millay as an exemplary young girl, too modest to parade her towering achievements before her defamers — one may still hear occasionally sixty years later, "All the Millays had was what their mother earned, but you'd never suspect it from the airs they gave themselves."

It is possible that these differing standards of judgment among her fellow citizens so sharpened Edna St. Vincent Millay's perceptions as to enable her to write, in "Renascence": *The world stands out on either side, No wider than the heart is wide. Above the world is stretched the sky, No higher than the soul is high!** Had these lines never been written, the literary world — which honors Camden, Maine as the scene of their inspiration — would be infinitely the poorer.

THE TOUCH OF SWEETGRASS

BY A. E. McINNIS

As far back as I can remember I would pick up my mother's sewing basket and, holding it close to my nose, breathe the summery scent of the old sweetgrass braids. I could not ever get enough of its smell. What I loved in the smell was Indian, for I thought Indian, played Indian, read Indian, until I almost believed I was an Indian.

As I grew, my love for sweetgrass remained. I watched Maine's sweetgrass Indians — the Passamaquoddies — gathering it, their hands darting like birds. Finally they would lift great scented shags of sweetgrass and walk home to the Pleasant Point Reservation at Perry, Maine. They walked beside the road slowly, the grass rounded over their backs, covering them with a glistening, olive-green coat that left the air redolent long after they had passed from my sight. But when I went into the salt marsh to the exact place where they had been, I could not find a single blade of sweetgrass!

The sweetgrass that stirs a boy's senses and imagination with delight is not exclusive to Maine. Our sweetgrass, *Hierochole borealis*, is one of eight species found only in northern Europe and North America. Its common names other than sweetgrass are vanilla grass, Seneca grass and holy grass. It is found from Newfoundland to Alaska, south to New Jersey and west to Colorado.

In northern Europe in olden days peasants sold bunches of sweetgrass to be hung in bedrooms because it was believed to have a mysterious power of inducing sleep. On religious festivals, Europeans scattered sweetgrass before churches and placed scented sheaves of it on the paths leading to shrines of the saints — hence its name of holy grass. In the ancient Scottish marriage rite of handfasting, a couple sat before their friends with the right hand of the man tied to the left hand of the woman with sweetgrass.

Here in Maine sweetgrass has so long a history that stone knives excavated from Indian sites sometimes glisten on the cutting edge. This polish has been determined to be an overlay of silica granules — the substance which strengthens and hardens the stems of grass — deposited, perhaps 1000 years ago, on the stone knives used by Maine Indians for cutting sweetgrass.

In my growing years I came of an age to seek people as friends, and so it was that I discovered Joe Nicolas. Joe is many things. He has been delegate to the State Legislature, organizer and director of the revival of the old Passamaquoddy dances. He is a barber in the nearby city of Eastport. But first, last and always, Joe is a Passamaquoddy with a strong pride in his race and love for its traditions. Joe's personality is made whole by a unique and refreshing sense of humor. In our joking back and forth, I prodded Joe many times, "If you are Indian, show me some real live sweetgrass growing. I think there is no such thing. It's just part of the Indian hocus-pocus, another joke upon his brother white man!"

Joe always grinned. "You wait," he promised. "When the right time comes, I'll show you some sweetgrass growing."

Our two families, Joe's and mine, had a picnic we shall not forget out on the beautiful salt water point near the reversing falls in West Pembroke. After our meal I again needled Joe, asking for a showdown concerning sweetgrass. Instead of joking back, Joe and his son Steve indicated that I was to follow them. We walked from the picnic area and approached a grassy swale beside the falls, now roaring with the incoming tide. Father and son stopped at an especially thick growth of grass. Joe asked softly, "Can you see it?"

I could not see anything but a lot of grass that I had seen many times before. Steve Nicolas spoke in the musical way that all young Indians have, "See it shining?"

It was as if the scales fell from my eyes! I could see it shining as no other grass ever could: olive-green ripples of satiny grass blades, showing the way of the seawind upon erect stems about 20 inches tall! I knew why Joe and Steve remained so quiet, because I, too, had a feeling of revelation. One by one, I picked my first sweetgrass blades, grasping at their shell-pink bases and pulling quickly. July stained the farthest corners of the salt meadow with blue, and swelled beginning bayberries with a deeper green than ever could be imagined. The world was all braided together with bird-sound, the heavy-footed sea roaring down the incline of the salt water falls in thundering majesty and spray, and the air was heavy with the glorious scent of my growing hank of sweetgrass.

Joe quietly jogged me with a reminder of the time, and also that we should go to have our sweetgrass combed. We went to the small home of Mitchell Francis, aged ninety-six, who lived with his affable son, Louis, then the Lieutenant-Governor of Pleasant Point. Joe explained to me that Mitchell was one of the last men among the Passamaquoddies to occupy himself exclusively with gathering sweetgrass. Now only a few men and children gather it sporadically.

I found Mitchell, a small man with very few wrinkles creasing a complexion the amber of weak tea. His old, old eyes were beautiful and wise, with depths for dreaming and remembering. Mitchell's son, Louis, found the old man's sweetgrass comb.

Sweetgrass combs are rare. Made of hardwood, they are used to comb down through hanks of sweetgrass to remove weak culms, spikelets and roots. Mitchell's comb, I noticed, had no whole teeth — only stubs, polished by years of combing until they shone and smelled of sweetgrass. I recognized the same deposit of silica upon the comb that I had seen on stone knives found at some of the Indian sites near Pleasant Point.

Louis guided his father as if he were handling the greatest of treasures, and together we went outside where Mitchell sat upon the wooden steps. The old man looked about him a moment, and I wondered what thoughts he thought. He gazed out upon the poured blue of St. Andrew's Bay, then turned and smiled as he took the comb from my hand.

With wonderful quick motions, the old man of the tribe pulled the comb energetically towards him through the sweetgrass, trimming it until the whole became silky smooth, ready to be braided. As he combed, Mitchell explained that sweetgrass leaves a waxy stain upon the fingers; this touch of the sweetgrass causes the fingers to be soft and fragrant for a long time.

"No matter how old and dry the grass," he added, "just wet it with water and the aroma comes back strong, even on the oldest baskets."

He had gone about the combing so quickly that I had to ask, with considerable embarrassment, if he would kindly comb the grass again so that I could take a photo. As he obliged, he smiled with pleasure and told me that no one had ever taken his picture before. He thanked me, and because he was cold in the summer wind, went back inside to sit with a lingering smile that made me glad I had found sweetgrass.

During my search for any information to do with the grass, I learned that our early Maine farmers knew that hay cut from salt water meadows sometimes contained a certain amount of sweetgrass, which gave the hay a wonderful fragrance. At one time the farmers theorized that if sweetgrass were fed to cattle it might improve the flavor of milk and butter, but the idea was not one to catch hold and develop. Sweetgrass is propagated by roots and grows interspersed with many other varieties of marsh grass. This is the reason why it is so difficult to find and, once found, must be picked individually. Also, it seems to prefer the company of salt marsh hay, which is greedily eaten by cattle, but possesses a strong rancid smell that affects the breath of cattle and is said to give an off-taste to milk and butter. Finally and positively, sweetgrass prefers the wetlands of a salt water marsh in a peaty soil upon clay, which would make it highly impractical insofar as the use of farm machinery to harvest it is concerned.

However, the question haunted me as to whether cows eat and enjoy sweetgrass. Books failed to give me an answer, so I sought a farmer having cows that grazed a wetland containing sweetgrass. A dairyman long in business in Perry and Eastport considered my question, rocking to and fro in a Boston rocker. "Do my cows eat sweetgrass and do they like it?" he repeated. "I don't know. I never asked them."

It was quite a while before I asked another farmer. Bill is a Katahdin of a man, who paused in the middle of haying to send me "to the house to talk to my father . . . I really don't know." Resurrected from a midsummer's day nap, the eighty-five-year-old father peered at me through dim eyes, repeated my question and said, "Best thing for you to do is to get some sweetgrass down at the Indian Village and try it on a cow."

I was determined to try one last time. Another farmer paused the daily round of his labor and pondered my question. His nose quivered slightly as he answered. "Known cows for sixty-five years, but sweetgrass? Wouldn't know it if I fell in it!"

Interrupting the Perry farmers no more, I picked my own sweetgrass, and when everyone had left their hayfields for the Fourth of July parade, I self-consciously sidled up to a contented cow. Extending my sweet-scented offering to the cow, I held my breath as she stopped chewing upon her cud. The cow sniffed once, twice, then sneezed a great gust of meadow and my handful of sweetgrass all over me.

I have found sweetgrass most abundantly out in the marshes on points where white men first settled. Later their descendants fled away over single team roads: the isolation, the harshness, the grubbing existence was not for them. Alders and gray birch quickly closed the roads behind them. Farm buildings became mounds in the grass. Orchards prospered for deer. The white man's roses escaped the foundation stones and ran down hill to meet and mingle with Indian sweetgrass. Responding, the sweetgrass climbed the hill to merge with the roses about the cellar holes of abandoned salt water farms. I like to listen to sweetgrass. Wrapped about the old foundation stones, sweetgrass is a trembling sound — a silken rustle as it comes alive in the seawind.

It is possible that a time will come when one will no longer see hanks of sweetgrass drying upon clothes lines at the Pleasant Point Passamaquoddy Reservation, or at the Peter Dana Point Reservation, in Princeton. Competing imported baskets have forced the price of Maine Indian baskets down, until now only a few of the older people find it economically feasible to make them of sweetgrass.

But the sweetgrass is a part of Passamaquoddy poetry, repeated through countless generations, as sentient fingers wove graceful baskets that mysteriously held the smells and sound and feel of summer as long as the cords of sweetgrass endured. The Indians cling to their sweetgrass legend as tenaciously as its touch lingers on their fingers: no matter how long and cold the winters may be, summer will come again as long as sweetgrass shines and spreads its fragrance over the marshes beside Passamaquoddy Bay.

AN ARTIST CALLED JAMIE

BY MARGE COOK

JAMIE WYETH seldom takes a day off, but he likes to disappear on his birthdays. On July 6th, 1967, he collected some friends, hired a boat, and went sailing off the coast of Maine to celebrate the day on which he became twenty-one.

Most of Jamie's summer birthdays have been spent in Maine, where he and his brother Nicky have sailed since they were knee-high to an oarlock. Jamie, the second son of the Andrew Wyeths, already had come of age as a recognized artist with an impressive portfolio at a time when most young men still are trying to decide on their life's work. Six months before his twenty-first birthday a one-man show of James Wyeth's oils and watercolors was displayed in New York City at the 57th Street gallery of M. Knoedler & Company. In a foreword to the catalog, which listed the show's forty-one paintings, Mr. Lincoln Kirstein — whose portrait by Jamie furnished the frontispiece —

unequivocally stated, "He is the finest American portrait painter since John Singer Sargent."

The world of art first was introduced to James Browning
Wyeth in a 1952 dry-brush by his father, Andrew Wyeth, entitled "Faraway." Five-year-old Jamie was shown in faded dun-
garees, a Davy Crockett coonskin cap, and a pair of metal-
tipped boots which had been worn by a boy before the Civil
War; he sat in a field of winter-browned grass, lost in dreams.
A quiet, introspective child, he used to peek into his father's
studio, ask a question which would be answered quietly, then
go away.

"I used to go to the movies and come back and make draw-
ings of the characters — merely pencil and paper," Jamie says.
"It was there; it was natural; I just evolved into it."

Jamie has been surrounded since birth by a family of artists.
His maternal grandfather, the late Merle James of Cushing,
Maine, was an artist of merit, as is his mother's sister, Gwen-
dolyn James Cook, who lives at Mosquito Harbor in Martins-
ville. In addition to his paternal grandfather, the famous illus-
trator, Newell Convers Wyeth (DOWN EAST, April 1964) and
his father, Andrew, three Wyeth aunts are well-established
artists. They are Carolyn Wyeth, Ann Wyeth McCoy and Hen-
riette Wyeth Hurd. To complicate this family Who's Who
further, the latter two are married to distinguished artists:
John W. McCoy of Chadds Ford, Pennsylvania and Wheeler
Bay, Maine and the much-in-the-news Peter Hurd, whose com-
missioned portrait of Lyndon B. Johnson was turned down by
the President as "the ugliest thing I ever saw."

With his older brother, Nicky, Jamie played on the rocks
and in the woods bordering the Georges River in Cushing,
Maine, where the Wyeths' summer home was built during
Jamie's first year of life. (It is the living room of this house
that Andrew Wyeth immortalized in his tempera, "Her Room,"
which was purchased by the Farnsworth Museum in Rockland, Maine for $65,000, the highest price ever paid for a paint-

ing by a living American artist.) One autumn, when the Wyeth family remained in Maine late in the season, Jamie and Nicky went to school in Cushing. Jamie remembers "sitting down near the front on the left, and all the grades in one room."

Back in Chadds Ford, Pennsylvania during the winter months, the boys formed a Robin Hood outlaw band and terrorized the countryside, burning down the camp of a rival group called the Tree Hackers. Following the Wyeth tradition of dressing up, they borrowed from their father's store of costumes dating from Revolutionary War days, and pretended that they were living in another era.

To allow Jamie more time with the art which absorbed him, he was taken out of public school after the sixth grade and privately tutored. He studied the usual subjects, but didn't like math, so dropped it after awhile. In his early teens his Aunt Carolyn took him in command and made him draw forms, such as circles and cubes, for a whole year.

"I wanted to do other things, but she said, 'Just draw in black-and-white.' It was tiresome, but a good background. She has had as much influence on my work, really, as has my father. She's terrific with the basic things, color and what-not."

To get a thorough knowledge of anatomy, Jamie worked in a morgue, dissecting cadavers under the watchful eyes of a top-flight surgeon. He usually asks a sitter to take off his shirt to allow examination of the structure of bones and muscle, and he will often feel of a subject's face as he paints.

More "James" than "Wyeth" in looks and mannerisms, the quiet little boy has grown into a six-foot-plus good-looking young man, polite, poised, still introspective. He answers questions easily, elaborating knowledgeably in dramatic detail or expertly parrying, always charming. The crisp curls which are a Wyeth family trait have been tempered in this third generation to silky-fine locks, worn moderately mod. The eyes, which appraise and absorb every detail, are strange in color: light brown with a hint of green edging the irises. His nose still shows where it was broken when a speeding car smashed into his Corvette at a bend in the road in Cushing a few years ago. He dresses casually and comfortably, often in dun-colored corduroy slacks and heavy, hand-knit sweaters.

The early discipline instilled into Jamie has stayed with him.

"Many times I make myself go to the studio. The idea that people work only when they're inspired is ridiculous. There are many things that pull you away. You're exposed to many types of life. It gets interesting, and you want to go into this or that. I think I create time for myself, pushing things that should be done, trying everything as fast as possible. Getting things down and expressing as much as possible at an early age seems terribly important. Also to be free to jump from one thing to another — not to get set in a certain way.

"I hate to sound like a work horse — work, work, work. I'm not a great worker, but I suppose I have the best time when I do work, when I get interested in something. It becomes intoxicating and I want to get back to it, you know, or I go sort of stir-crazy. And yet, when I'm not working, I don't particularly like talking about painting. I've seen so much of this — young painters in New York who stay up all night talking about what they're doing and what they're going to do, and who have no energy left the next day to do it. I never want to get into that sort of thing. There's a great group of them in Greenwich Village. They look on me as some sort of oddity."

He paints in oil and in watercolors, about evenly divided between the two media. He has tried tempera, but the quality that his father likes — the dryness — is exactly what he doesn't like. Jamie likes the moist, transparent quality of oil which he uses in his portraits, although he confesses to some impatience with its slowness in drying. Once he stuck some of his finished paintings in ovens to hasten the drying process and a couple of them burned up.

He doesn't care that people compare his work with that of his famous father. But he welcomes criticism of his work from his dad.

"We're two different types. I think that most of the similarity comes in subject matter. Both living in the same area, I think we tend to work on the same sort of things."

Jamie describes himself as a slow painter, and destroys much of what he paints in an effort to be more selective as he gets better known, "I look at some of my old stuff and think, 'Jeez, how could I ever have done *that?*'" Nevertheless, his output is amazing. And the selling prices, determined by Knoedler's, are steadily climbing. A year ago a watercolor brought as much as $1500 and people were willing to pay $20,000 for an oil by Jamie Wyeth.

Like all painters, Jamie constantly gets suggestions for subject matter. He thinks everyone is paintable but tries to steer away from "characters." He often depicts things that people walk by without seeing — a white-wash bucket or an abandoned capstan. This past summer he was fascinated by a kettle on the back porch of a Maine residence. He saw it every day and it was always covered with flies and he wondered what was inside. So he painted it, flies and all; he paints things as they are.

But it is in portraiture that he shines. He has painted his young friends, forgotten old men, society matrons, governors, movie stars and the military. He would rather not paint on commission, because he insists on painting his way and does not like to be answering questions constantly as he paints — it "breaks the mood." For this reason he has painted mostly people with whom he is acquainted. He so thoroughly studies the personality of whomever he is painting that some of his subjects are startled to see themselves as they look to others.

He loses himself in his work and is oblivious to all else. During a recent summer's marathon fog, he worked right next to the Manana Island fog bell without hearing its loud clanging. He even forgot lunch while he worked until Manana's hermit reminded him.

He recalls a girl who was posing for him when a huge plate glass window let go in the wind and crashed all around them.

The girl fled, but Jamie kept on painting. And one day he was lying on his stomach across some railroad ties, working away, when he felt the ties moving under him but didn't hear the train which was a few yards away. He threw his paints over the side and jumped after them as the train rumbled by.

Because much time away from painting, like piano playing, makes one lose his touch, service in the National Guard Ready Reserves in the State of Delaware has been an ideal solution to Jamie in fulfilling his military obligations. He reports for duty on Friday and Saturday of the first weekend of every month.

As a member of the Air Guard, Jamie became acquainted with Brig. Gen. William W. Spruance, winner of the Congressional Medal of Honor, who miraculously escaped from a burning jet and then spent four years of recuperation in a hospital. Jamie had been offered the opportunity to go to Vietnam to paint whatever he wished, so he made a date one Sunday to discuss it with the general.

"When I got down there he said, 'We're going to take a little flight in a plane,' and here was this huge, six-engine, experimental jet that the general was testing for the Pentagon. We wore oxygen masks and he flew it with one hand, put it into spins, and obviously was trying to break some kind of record. I've never been so terrified in my life. But it was terrific to do because I was painting him at the time, and this is part of *his* life."

In identifying himself with the subject he is painting, Jamie's most challenging and longest involvement lasted over a year, when he painted a posthumous portrait of President John F. Kennedy.

First approached to do the Kennedy portrait on commission, Jamie said, "No." Working from photographs had no appeal. Then, because he always had been interested in President Kennedy, he thought, "Why not?" and was given full cooperation by the Kennedy family to do it his way. "If it turns out, fine — and if it doesn't turn out, fine."

As is his wont when painting a portrait, Jamie lived the same kind of life as his subject. He lived with members of the Kennedy family, campaigned with Ted, who most resembled his brother Jack, and learned the true story of the man behind the public myth.

"My greatest fear with the portrait was that it would look dead, like a photograph, so I used Ted a lot, just to get life into it. I immersed myself in films and thousands of photographs and recordings until John Kennedy was so imprinted on my mind, the way he moved and everything, that I could move him any way I wanted — visually, you know. It was interesting to sit down and put him in a position on paper and see how he'd look in it."

The result is very different from any published likeness of President Kennedy. It is pensive and serious. Mrs. Kennedy likes it. Caroline Kennedy observed, "It looks like Daddy in conference."

Nowadays, Jamie spends as much time as possible in Maine, and has a special fondness for Monhegan Island, which he and Nicky reach in Nicky's supercharged speed boat from their Cushing home in less than twenty minutes. Recently, Jamie purchased a piece of Monhegan, next door to artist William Hekking. He plans to build a house there, "definitely *not* a split level."

"I like cold weather, hate the heat. Most of the people I know on Monhegan live there the year round."

Whether or not he ever elects to become a Maine year-rounder, Maine and its people already share lavishly in the brilliant work of a young artist called Jamie, who has both the individuality and the industry of one of their own.

THE ISLANDS

There are some people, natives and summer visitors,
who would never consider themselves truly content
unless living on an island.
Fortunately, we have islands a-many
to choose from.
And not only do people prefer islands.
So do puffins!

MATINICUS ISLAND

BY HAZEL YOUNG

BACK IN THE YEARS when sail boats were the only means of communication between Maine's outlying islands and the mainland, it was often many days before a message could reach inshore. Tradition has it that at one period a flock of carrier pigeons was kept on Matinicus and once when a death occurred on the island during a rugged spell of weather, birds were released carrying the news to Rockland. When the storm subsided, the funeral paraphernalia plus the minister were brought to the island and the service and burial took place. Now Matinicus is linked to the rest of the world by microwave telephone and it is a common-place occurrence to talk with Boston, San Francisco and places between. One boy recently called his mother from Greenland and talked with her as successfully as if face to face.

Matinicus lies twenty miles straight out to sea from Rockland. It is the largest of a small cluster of islands which guard the entrance to Penobscot Bay. Beside Matinicus, this group consists of Criehaven (called in the old days Ragged Island, a corruption of *Racketash*, the Indian name), Wooden Ball, Matinicus Rock, Tenpound, Seal, Noman's Land, Twobush and numerous smaller ledges and rocks.

A staunch little mailboat may carry you out to Matinicus, with trips three times a week in summer but only twice in winter. Of course you may take a Piper Cub in Rockland and land on the island in only a matter of a few minutes. On a "pretty" day, the sail to the island is delightful. From the water as you leave Rockland, the little city seems snugged down along the shore of Penobscot Bay. Back of it rise the Camden hills, and off to the west, the twin plumes of smoke that mark the cement plant at Thomaston. As you chug across the harbor, the scores of windows in the huge Samoset Hotel blink in the early morning sunlight. You pass picturesque Owl's Head Light, peering out from among the spruces, then out to the open sea by Monroe Island and the mouth of Mussel Ridge Channel. Soon a shadow along the horizon becomes land and you are approaching Matinicus.

You skirt the wooded end of the island by Marky's beach (named for a crusty old character of a bygone day) and round the point into the little harbor where dories are bobbing at the moorings while their owners are out in their power boats to haul their traps. For here on Matinicus lobstering is a big business, and practically all males — from youngsters in their early teens to old men in their eighties — have their strings of traps.

On a slope facing the harbor are a hodgepodge of buildings: fish houses and bait sheds in faded greens, yellow and reds, and hanging on them lobster buoys of every shape and shade. The island store, a business operated continuously since 1851 by a Young, and the Centennial building, built of course in 1876, dominate the scene.

Unlike the custom on many of Maine's coastal islands, the principal dwellings on Matinicus are found some distance from the harbor. But distances are short on Matinicus, as its total area covers slightly over 700 acres. Its length is approximately two miles and nowhere is it more than a mile wide. The interior of the island is well elevated, with occasional bogs and marshes, but the shores are mostly rocky, rising in places to high cliffs against which the waves dash to incredible heights. At both the north and south ends of the island appear unexpectedly delightful little sandy beaches where bathing may be enjoyed by those who can stand the frigid water.

From the north end almost to Southern Point, the road runs straight through the center of the island. The air is clear and salty and in late June fragrant with the scent of wild strawberries. The houses on either side of the road are trim and well kept and the fields are gay with buttercups and daisies and wild roses against a backdrop of green spruces. Toward the north end is the church and beyond it the oldest house on the island, built in 1800 by Joseph Young and still occupied by a Young. The white Cape Cod houses at the southern end of the island all look out across the water to Criehaven, the Bennett's Island of Elisabeth Ogilvie's delightful novels: *High Tide at Noon, The Ebbing Tide,* and *Storm Tide.* Five miles or so beyond looms up the great mass of Matinicus Rock, a famous breeding place for sea birds and the site of one of the most remote lighthouses along the entire coast.

In the old days there were prosperous little farms on Matinicus, but now the farms are "run out" with the woods always creeping closer and closer. Several of the places on the island have been bought by "folks from away" and for two months in the summer these houses take a new lease on life. But from Labor Day through lovely September and October and through the months of winter and spring, they are lonely and deserted.

As on most islands along the coast, the population of Matinicus has shrunk during the past century. According to the census of 1869 and 1870, there were 276 and 277 people respectively on Matinicus. These years marked the highpoint in the number of inhabitants. Today, a century later, the winter population

numbers approximately 150 permanent residents. Many of the
young people, after years away at school or in the service, have
chosen to return to the island to make their homes. This has
kept the population much higher than on most of Maine's offshore islands. And today several of this younger generation still
bear the old family names: Ames, Young, Philbrook.

Little is known about the very early history of Matinicus;
probably it was sighted by some of the earliest explorers, and
it is believed that it was occupied for a time in the 16th
century by French fishermen. For untold ages, Indians from the
mainland visited the island, fishing or sealing or taking sea
fowl and their eggs for food.

It wasn't until the middle of the 18th century that Matinicus
had a permanent white settler, Ebenezer Hall, who came
around 1750 with his wife, stepson and four small children to
make his home. From the very first, Hall had trouble with the
Indians. In June 1757, his house was attacked. In the fracas
Hall was killed and scalped, and the house pillaged and burned.
The stepson, Joseph Green, escaped and hid on the western
shore until the Indians left the island. He finally attracted the
attention of a passing vessel and was taken to the mainland.
He later married and eventually settled on what is known as
Green's Island. Mrs. Hall, Ebenezer's wife, and children were
taken by the Indians, the mother and children being separated. The children were never heard of again. Mrs. Hall,
suffering many hardships, was taken through the wilderness to
Quebec. From there she went to England, then to New York
and finally is said to have made the trip from New York back
to Maine on foot. Here she remarried and lived to the ripe old
age of 89.

On a bronze tablet, not far from the Matinicus post office
and on the spot where Ebenezer Hall's log house stood is this
inscription:

Ebenezer Hall

The First White Settler

of Matinicus Isle, Maine —

Killed by the Indians
June 6 1757

Fortunately for the many Hall descendants, Ebenezer Junior, a son by a previous marriage, was away on the mainland at the time of the tragedy and so escaped. Some years later young Hall returned to the island with his wife and children and established his home. A few years later the first of the Youngs arrived — Abraham, who had married Mrs. Hall's sister. This was the beginning of the Young regime, which continues to the present day.

Another early settler was John Crie, a British soldier in the Revolution, stationed for nearly five years at Fort George, now Castine. At the end of the war, young Crie was given the choice of returning to his native Glasgow or of staying on in America. In the words of Charles A. E. Long in his delightful *Matinicus Isle, Its Story and Its People*: "John Crie, a native of Scotland, in his travels happened upon Matinicus. He and Mary, a daughter of Ebenezer Hall Junior, became mutually attracted. They were married in 1786, and their union marked the beginning of the next prominent family on Matinicus."

Matinicus islanders have always been a gregarious lot and still are. Even though the island road is only a couple of miles long, there are plenty of rather ancient automobiles in service and some of them clock up a surprisingly high mileage.

There are no hotels, no inns, no gift shoppes in this lovely remote spot, far from the crowded tourist circuit. Nor is there an art colony here, but occasional artists do visit the island. Years ago George Bellows did some of his best pictures here on Matinicus.

Recently several comfortable rental cottages have been built, and at times a Matinicus housewife may take a few boarders for the summer months. Island women have always been good cooks. Nowhere can you get such lobsters as you get on Matinicus; the lobster stew is something to dream about. And the berry pies! An island cook follows the berries from June, when the fields are red with wild strawberries, through the

blueberry and raspberry season when she and the gulls compete to see who can harvest the most. In the fall, she goes after
the tiny red cranberries that gleam crimson in the swampy
spots along the shore.

On a lovely summer day with the sky a deep, deep blue and
in the distance the muted sound of the bell-buoy, you can
pick your way along a rough path through the woods and
finally come out on the rugged back shore. The waves break
against the rocks below and the only living things are the gulls
circling overhead and a lobsterman a few hundred feet offshore hauling his traps. Off on the distant horizon are Green
Island and Metinic — and farthest of all, the gray blue that is
Monhegan Island, eighteen miles away.

TRAP DAY ON MONHEGAN

BY ALTA ASHLEY

IT WAS DECEMBER 31ST — the morning before the traditional New Year's Day opening of the lobstering season on Monhegan Island. A handful of voyagers, en route to the only New Year's observance of its kind in the world, gathered on the *Laura B.*, the mail boat which plies three days a week during the winter between Monhegan and the mainland. Spirits were high among the passengers, whose only topic of conversation was Trap Day and the worrisome question, "Will the lobstermen set· tomorrow?"

Since 1909, in the interest of conservation, Monhegan has had a closed season on lobstering from sunset on June 25th to sunrise on January 1st of the following year. All summer long the homes of the islanders display piles of lobster traps, buoys and toggles, with lobster cars hauled up on the beach and nearby lawns. The islanders busy themselves with hospitable tasks related to the summer colony of artists, cot-

tagers and tourists. But after Labor Day, as the summer people depart, Monhegan dwellers turn their attention to their
fishing gear. Boats are scraped and painted; moorings checked
and replaced as necessary; pots are built and repaired; knitted
potheads are tacked into place, and pot buoys are painted in
bright colors individual to each owner.

At least one day is set aside for "rocking." Dry lobster
traps tend to float; hence a flat rock must be placed in each
trap to weight it. Since flat rocks are almost impossible to find
on Monhegan, the men go to the mainland shores to gather
suitable stones, which they bring home and pile in readiness
beside their lobstering gear.

Once the pots are ready, the painted buoys dry and the toggles assembled, rope up to sixty-five fathoms long is measured
for each trap, the buoys and toggles attached, and the warp
coiled with nautical neatness inside the pot. A mark is made
to indicate the depth for setting, and the pot is ready. By the
middle of December, great piles of finished pots may be seen
around the fishhouses and workshops of the fishermen, but not
until the last week of December may they be brought to
the dock.

Last December 31st, in a little more than an hour after we
had pulled away from the wharf at Port Clyde, the dock at
Monhegan came into view. Lobster traps seemed to cover its
entire surface. After we had tied up and stepped ashore, we
found only a narrow path open between rows of traps piled
eight-high from the ship to the shore. Each trap contained
its neatly coiled warp, buoy and toggle, lending blobs of bright
color to the picturesque scene. Several off-islanders were wan-
dering about in hip boots which identified them as "helpers,"
brought to Monhegan to work with the fishermen during the
setting.

By early afternoon lobster boats began to come to the dock
to be loaded with the owners' traps and bait, and as evening
fell the harbor was crowded with fishing craft, waiting for

New Year's Day to dawn. Even the lobster cars were in place at their moorings, ready to receive the first catch.

The wind began to freshen as evening deepened into night. High winds were forecast, and everyone worried that traps might be blown overboard or that the setting date might have to be postponed. Despite the wind, however, there was no thought of welcoming the New Year with midnight merriment. By eleven o'clock, everyone on the island was in bed and asleep, ready for the hard day's work ahead.

Sometime in the night the wind "let go" a little, and those who felt the change slept more peacefully in the knowledge that the threat of a storm was easing up. About an hour before dawn the island began to come to life. Lights appeared in homes throughout the village. But as daybreak approached the wind began to increase again and by dawn, which came shortly after seven o'clock, the seas were racing into the harbor, casting plumes of surf on Casket Rock at the southwest end, by the tip of Manana.

Gradually fishermen and their helpers began to gather in little groups along the Fish Beach. One could see an anxious face lifted to the sky, a head shake. Men wandered from group to group, from fishhouse to shore and back. We women, peering from our windows, could only guess as to what was being said, although we knew well the gist of the conversation. We were almost resigned to Trap Day's postponement until the southerly should pass when, just at ten o'clock, the cry went out, "Let's go!"

The men dashed to their fishhouses to don their "yellows," dragged their skiffs to the water's edge and were off to their waiting boats, tugging at the moorings in the harbor. Soon the sound of motors could be heard, blue-white smoke rose from one exhaust after another, lines were cast off and the boats began to move through the harbor. Almost instantly a lobster trap slipped over a gunwale, warp unwound, and a bright buoy and toggle bobbed in the water. The first trap had been set; the season so long prepared for had begun.

After the first boats returned to the dock for second loads
of traps, the women went home to fetch great baskets of sandwiches and goodies, with thermos bottles of hot coffee. These
were put aboard the boats on their return trips, and passed
out to the men and boys who were helping to load the boats
from the dock.

As long as daylight lasted the boats plied between the dock
and the setting grounds. Men on the dock worked unceasingly,
unerringly sliding the right traps into position for the right
boat. The cooperation of the land workers was geared to the
high spirit of competition among the boat crews, each trying
to reach the best fishing grounds before another claimed them.
Despite the open competition — a part of the holiday excitement of Trap Day — the overriding spirit between the fishing crews was one of comradeship and mutual concern. As the
boats gathered at the dock for traps, weighting stones, buckets of bait and gasoline, the crews bantered each other and
passed the word along about amusing happenings during the
relay race out of sight of the landsmen.

By nightfall the piles of traps on the dock which had greeted
us the day before were more than half gone, and the stacks
along the road, a familiar sight to summer people, had practically disappeared. Setting was over for the day, and the boats
lay at their moorings. But the day's work was not yet done.
By the light of cabin lamps, the men prepared and baited traps
for the following day, then climbed wearily into their skiffs
and rowed ashore, bone tired and ready for supper and a good
night's sleep.

On January 2nd, as soon as there was sufficient light, both
lobstermen and dock crew were working swiftly again to load
the waiting boats. All day the island throbbed with the sound
of boat and truck motors, as the few traps remaining along the
road, at workshops and fishhouses, were brought to the dock
for loading. That evening only one pile of traps still waited
to be loaded and set. It belonged to one of the younger men
who, according to his friendly rivals, had set too high a goal

for his first season. Soon those too, would be gone, and the dock at Monhegan would revert to its usual uncluttered state.

That night nearly every household on Monhegan Island feasted on the first catch of the year.

LIGHTHOUSE GIRLHOOD

BY MAIZIE FREEMAN ANDERSON

(Dedicated to my parents, James and Iva Freeman, and to
all the lightkeepers of the old lighthouse days.)

THE FIRST HOME that I remember was Petit Manan Island in
Frenchman's Bay, off the coast of Maine, where my father was
an assistant lighthouse keeper for twelve years. I had been born
on Plum Island, Massachusetts, my father's first lighthouse station after his discharge from the Navy following World War
I. And my first two years of life were spent on Isles of Shoals
off New Hampshire. But when I think of my childhood home,
I see Petit Manan, which I grew to love with all my heart.

Petit Manan has one of the strongest lights on the entire
coast. The tower itself is 120 feet high. Circular iron steps take
you to the top. If you aren't squeamish, you can go out upon
an iron balcony, completely circling the tower, with a hand
rail and open framework.

The beacon at Petit Manan was run by oil at that time.

The lamp was enclosed in a large, round glass lens which could be entered easily by the keepers. The lens, revolving around the light, sent the flashing beam far out to sea. The whistle house held the fog signal. Gigantic iron wheels stood in an upright position, attached to the engines, which were powered by steam. The wheels turned at such speed that you could not see the spokes, only a blurred area of gray. The noise inside was deafening, yet I have seen the keepers sit there rocking, calmly reading a book, not at all disturbed. The mournful sound of the signal was our lullaby during all of our childhood. After awhile, you didn't hear the horn blasting away, but if you were sleeping and it stopped, you would awaken immediately.

No trees grew in the shallow soil of Petit Manan, but there were patches of grass and a few hardy wild flowers grew in abundance, even among the rocks — sweet pea, buttercups and others. We had a small cranberry bog yielding berries to can each year. We tried putting in a vegetable garden, using seaweed for fertilizer, but we gave it up as hopeless. We also tried keeping a cow, because fresh milk was a rarity. I shall never forget getting her there; you've never lived until you've shared a rowboat with a cow! But she ate oil-soaked grass one day and passed on to greener pastures.

Every building on the island was painted white and kept in tiptop condition by the keepers. At the top of the island stood our beautiful duplex home, which housed the first and second assistant keepers and their families. Each side had six rooms with beautiful hardwood floors. The kitchen had a government issued stove. It was the mark of a good wife to keep this black monster in shining condition. My mother sat on the floor, papers spread all around, polishing and cleaning, and the stove was a thing of beauty when she finished. The other furniture was ours.

We collected our water in large cement cisterns located in our basements. Gutters ran to them from the roofs. When the rains were far spaced, we would call the district office and the tender *Ilex* or *Hibiscus* would come out with a supply, carrying massive hoses ashore to fill our cisterns. There was no electricity at that time, so we used kerosene lamps. We didn't have sanitary facilities either, but each family had a small out-house, also painted white with a lattice-work enclosure.

The head keeper had a single house. It included a small room for our well-stocked medical supplies, and a good sized library.

The boathouse held a government issued dory and a larger craft — an awkward boat called "Old Liz," a sturdy means of transportation to the mainland. A double slip, kept greased with a thick yellow substance, extended from the boathouse to the water's edge. A machine inside the boathouse with a hook and rope device pulled Old Liz up the slip when we made our landings. To launch her the procedure was reversed. The hardiest of us entered the boat before her descent, then rode faster and faster down the slip until we hit the sea with a resounding splash. A section of railroad track, which carried a four-foot-long car, ran from the wharf to our homes. It was a constant sport of the island children to push the car to the top of the hill and go flying down to the wharf. This was dis-couraged by our parents, because we stopped our descent by dragging our feet — not only hard on the shoes, but there was always the possibility that we would not be able to stop and would have toppled over the end of the wharf.

When a son was born to my mother in 1930 and another in 1932, my joy knew no bounds. I was four years old when the first arrived. My mother went ashore for each birth and re-turned when the baby was a month old. An older sister lived on the mainland with grandparents most of the time, so I welcomed these brothers as playmates.

The dangers of our island must have been taught us early. We weren't allowed to go to the top of the tower unless Dad went too. We never could go into the whistle house when the signal was running. The giant wheels of the engine could easily have torn an arm off had we ventured too close. We were also never allowed to go in the boathouse, since curious young hands might loosen the lines holding the boat on the greased ways. But we often followed our father around as he went about his duties. By the time we were ten years old we could have started any engine on the island or lighted the beacon, but our knowledge never was tested.

When playing we usually kept to the top part of the shore. The section below the tide line was covered with seaweed and very slippery. None of us could swim. There was really no place to learn in the open, frigid Atlantic. We did have a small pool, almost six feet in diameter and about three feet deep, left in a shallow spot when the tide went down. We waited for the sun to warm it, then went in and paddled around. Once I found a complete set of false teeth, which I treasured highly and kept on my dresser to admire. They disappeared one day, probably because Mother hadn't shared my enthusiasm.

With the higher tides of spring, the water often came up to the grass edge. One day we got word from headquarters to expect an unusually high tide. We carried everything that was movable to the second floor and Dad brought his new rowboat up near the house and secured it. Later we all went to the tower, from which we watched the tide's slow progress. At its peak the entire island was under a foot of water. Our chicken coops were afloat in the low cranberry bog. Three days later the tides had resumed their normal pattern.

During the summer months, tourists came out to see the island. The tourists asked us children many silly questions and we gave them equally silly answers. We often caught my brothers telling how hard it was to do without candy, which always produced chocolate from various pockets. These people didn't know that all lighthouse keepers have large stores of groceries. Candy was bought by the box, but rationed for obvious reasons.

Among our regular visitors was the Maine Seacoast Missionary Society's clergyman aboard the *Sunbeam*, who gave us reli-

gious instruction in the manner of a regular Sunday School.
But it was my parents who taught us the Bible. They quoted
from it often, and perhaps we knew the Bible better than most
children do.

When I turned six it was decided I should go ashore and
live with my grandparents each winter to be educated. There
was a small, fully equipped school on the island; the Lighthouse Service used to supply a teacher, but either they ran out
of money or no one cared to take the job. September and the
day of separation came all too soon. My mother had been crying all morning and Dad often wiped his eyes. We went ashore
in the new power boat my father had purchased for his own
use, but the ride held no thrill for me that day. We went by
car to Jonesboro, where my grandparents lived. Of course,
we had visited these dear people before, but this was different.
My heart was heavy as Dad hurried away to get back to the
island before dark.

Next morning I went to the little white school with my
cousins. I got through the first hour, but suddenly the home-
sickness was more than I could bear. I put my head down on
my desk and sobbed. Miss Foss, the teacher, was a very understanding person who knew that I couldn't remain away from
home. My father was contacted and said he would come for
me that afternoon. Someone drove me to Pigeon Hill to wait
on the beach for my father. The lovely white boat came into
the harbor. He tied her up and started toward shore in the
rowboat. I could hold back no longer. I ran into the sea —
shoes and all — to meet him. The sun was setting as we started
home, and the ocean picked up the rays. Up ahead was my
island, and I watched the tower for the light. Soon it came,
sending its beam out over the ocean as if to say, "Welcome
home." Dad stood by the wheel, head thrown back, singing
an off-key song that sounded beautiful. Tall as a man should
be was my father, with snapping brown eyes and black curly
hair. His skin was deeply tanned from years of sea duty. He

was a gentle man, who thought children were the most precious things in life.

Holidays never were overlooked on the island. Christmas was observed just as it was on the mainland. Fourth of July, too, was made a big day for us with fireworks, cases of pop, and usually a clam bake or a lobster broil on the beach. The children gathered the driftwood and the men started the fire. We would let it burn down to bright red coals, then seaweed was spread over it. Buckets of clams were spread over that and more seaweed was put on top. After a half hour we would remove the top layer of seaweed and there the clams lay, nestling in their shells, yellow and delicious. We children often picked periwinkles off the rocks down near the sea. We cooked them on the shore in a little pot, picked them from their shells with a large safety pin and when the pin was full of the tiny meat, dipped them in butter or vinegar. Mussels were cooked in the same manner.

Every summer the keepers would set out a trawl. Great coils of heavy line were made ready, with large hooks every foot along the line. The hooks were baited and the trawl taken far out to sea to be dropped overboard, with a buoy to mark the spot. A day or two later, the men hauled in the trawl and when the boat returned everyone ran to the slip to see the catch. Dozens and dozens of fish of all kinds — cod, bass, haddock, pollock, even halibut. Sharp knives were brought and everyone turned to cleaning the fish by the sea, tossing the bodies into a pool of water. The tongues and cheeks would be removed from the heads for supper, then the discards were tossed into the sea. Sea gulls would have a feast that day. The fish were then salted down in wooden kegs. Some were left for later use, but the smaller ones were taken out after a day or two and placed on drying racks out in the sun. A week or more passed before they were completely dry. Then we would eat them as they were or have them boiled.

We had our share of excitement on Petit Manan. One day

in 1937 our parents called us to see the dirigible *Hindenburg* going over our island. She crashed in New Jersey soon after.

Dad announced on another occasion that President Franklin D. Roosevelt would be sailing past our island in a few hours on his way to his summer home on Campobello. We went out in our boat to salute him. The escort vessels soon appeared, and we tooted our horn madly and waved. It was exciting to bob up and down in the wake made by these large ships. Someone in the group signaled; my young brother believed it to be the President himself. Jim tossed his cap high in the excitement and the wind carried it out to sea. For months after that he believed that the President had retrieved the cap and kept it. Jim was quite put out about it.

At low tide a bar came out of the water, and you could walk from Petit Manan to an even smaller island. It was here that we got our clams and speared our flounder. We were permitted to cross the bar to the other island provided we returned before the tide started to change. The summer when I was ten I took my six-year-old brother and two visiting children on an exploring trip. We hunted gull's eggs, dug for clams, and I kept one eye on the tide. I wanted the fun of being marooned. Soon it was too late to return; the children didn't seem to mind. They had found an old, weather-beaten skiff on the shore. For awhile they tossed rocks at it; then my brother found an abandoned oar and climbed in the boat. Another child pushed the boat off before I realized what was happening. The tide was coming in fast and the current was peculiar around that island. We were in a cove, but beyond lay the open sea and the day was not calm. The boat was warped and not at all safe. My brother could row, even at six, but not with one oar. I was nearly out of my mind. My carelessness might very well cost him his life.

Forgetting that I couldn't swim, I plunged into the sea, yelling for him to sit quiet. I paddled out a few feet, then went under. Somehow I turned myself around and floundered back to shore. I screamed and screamed. During this time we had been missed and they were looking for us from the tower with binoculars. When my mother heard me scream, she fainted. The father of the other two children who were with me ran to the wharf and launched a boat to come for us. Meanwhile, my brother's boat was taking on water and being swirled around by the current. I could not help him — I could only yell encouragement and warn him to sit still. He was accustomed to taking orders from me and he did not panic. It saved his life. The other boat finally got there and towed him safely to shore.

We all started home — a very wet, frightened foursome. My big-eyed brother huddled in the boat behind me. As we neared the island, the boat started in toward some dangerous ledges, half hidden by the water. My father, seeing our new danger, hurriedly launched his boat to come for us, should we capsize. Back in the window my mother couldn't see my brother behind me in the boat. When she saw Dad leave the slip, she thought he must be going after my brother's body. She fainted again. Needless to say, my heart ached as well as other parts of my body before that evening was over. The horror stayed with me for months. I'd wake up at night, thinking my brother was drowned, and I'd run to his room to make certain he was safe.

Financially, we were very secure. Our living quarters and fuel were free. The government supplied our soap, brooms, paint and medical supplies. We had a telephone connected to the mainland by an underwater cable. We seldom left our island, so my father's $105 monthly wage was sufficient in those days. We took much of our food from the sea. We read no newspapers, but we did subscribe to a good many magazines and we had our radio. We had a car on the mainland, a good-sized boat and a paradise to live in.

When I was fourteen years old, my father was offered a head keeper's job at higher pay on Great Duck Island off Southwest Harbor, twelve miles from the nearest land. We were very distressed and had hoped he'd refuse it, but the tower was much shorter on Great Duck; Dad was not getting any younger and the long climb to the top of Petit Manan's tower was beginning to affect his legs. Also, the painting of the structure would be easier and less dangerous on Great Duck. When the Petit Manan tower was painted the keepers had to work from a large wooden cage, lowered from the top of the tower by means of block and tackle.

In the summer of 1940 we said goodbye to Petit Manan with heavy hearts. Great Duck Island was very large — a mile long, half a mile wide. It stood very high out of the water and steep cliffs surrounded most of it. Great Duck had large areas of woodland, and the government reservation took up only one small end of the island. Three single homes were here, all in a row, with a small white tower that looked very puny to me. The largeness of the island bothered me. Parts of it were restricted, and I couldn't get acquainted with it unless I had free access.

There were lots of scrubby trees on Great Duck near the shore. Years of rugged weather had beat at them until the tops were matted and flat. We would walk around on them and jump from tree to tree without falling through.

Far beyond our home area was a wall of steep cliffs at least twenty feet high. Below were jagged rocks and the sea. Sometimes I would escape my brothers and go to that spot. I had discovered cracks in the cliffs and by lowering myself down carefully, could get my toes into the openings. Holding to the ground above, I could inch my way across the face of the cliff, a stunt which took a good half hour. There was a fascination in looking down at the sea tossing waves up at me and knowing that a slip meant certain death.

One day I was engaging in this fine sport when I heard giggles behind me. When I looked around and saw my brothers, my heart pounded. I could not order them to go back. They might get stubborn and insist on coming on. So I pretended I was tired of the game and suggested that we leave and return another day. They finally accepted that and made their way back, during the longest ten minutes in my life. Once

I had them safe I turned each over my knee and paddled him soundly. I threatened all sorts of disaster if they ever went there again or told our parents. I gave up cliff climbing forever that day.

A year after we moved to Great Duck, Mother became very ill one stormy night. We did our best with what we had, but it was obvious it was not enough. We called several doctors before we found one who would come out. The Coast Guard brought him and his nurse to us from Bar Harbor. All night they worked over Mother and her life was saved, but she never was strong after that.

The U. S. Coast Guard took over the Lighthouse Service in the early forties and the old keepers were gradually replaced by young Coast Guardsmen, but Dad was informed that he could stay on until he retired. Mother died in '43 at the age of thirty-nine and Dad left the island soon after. He was only forty-six, but he was aging fast. He was kept on the government payroll and given land duty, but he had been a seaman for twenty-eight years and he soon became restless. He got a new assignment, repairing the engines on the lighthouses up and down the coast until his retirement about two years later. His legs had given out and his heart was tired. He bought a house near the sea and the government pensioned him very well. He died at the age of fifty-six.

I suppose it was inevitable that I should eventually marry a sailor too — a young Coast Guardsman from Michigan who had been a friend of my father. We were stationed on shore for several years. Then in 1948 he came home with news that filled me with joy. He had been transferred to Boston Light, the oldest lighthouse in America. We went there in July with our three children, ages five, four and two.

The island was beautiful: smaller than Petit Manan but very similar in layout. The island had electricity installed a few months after we arrived and was much more convenient. The other families there were young and very nice, but we mostly lived our own lives. I soon taught my children the dangers

and spent many hours on the shore with them. We fished off
the docks and broiled our catch on the beach. I gloried in the
severe storms and the foghorn was music to my ears.

My new baby was expected in December and I was taken
ashore in November to await the birth. The waiting period
extended until well after Christmas. I was very lonely for my
children. My husband had full charge of them, as the other
island women had gone ashore to escape the severe winter.
The day before Christmas, Edward Rowe Snow, the Flying
Santa, flew over the lighthouse and dropped gifts. Also, a
boat went out from the mainland with nearly fifty people, all
generously bearing gifts to the keepers and their families.

Donna Marie finally arrived on January 20th. I was so
lonely that I left the hospital nine days later in spite of my
husband's protest. The Coast Guardsmen were kind as usual
and I was given every comfort on the long, twelve-mile trip
home. The wind buffeted the boat and we could not tie up
at the dock, as it was nearly low tide. We anchored off-shore
and a small boat was lowered for me. My husband came out
from the dock in his rowboat to take off our provisions and
mail. Our boats passed, but we could only give each other a
big smile. His hands were busy rowing and mine were holding
the child. We came to the dock, where there was a wooden
ladder to climb, the rungs covered with ice where the tide had
gone out. The Coast Guardsmen couldn't help me. It took two
of them to steady the boat against the sea. With one hand on
the ladder and the baby cradled in the other arm, I somehow
made it to the top.

Three days later on February 2nd, they brought the Christmas tree up from the basement — brown and falling apart, because they had waited Christmas for me. I cooked a big turkey
dinner and the gifts from Flying Santa, relatives and friends
were opened.

Summer soon came and we delighted in our usual playtime.
One day I discovered my oldest daughter, Carlette, walking
along the top of a seawall. I coaxed her away from it with my

heart in my mouth and watched her every move from then on. Recalling my own escapades at her age, I was usually able to anticipate her.

We kept our oldest daughter out of school until she was seven, teaching her the ABCs and numbers ourselves. We had decided to leave the lighthouse when she started school, because I didn't want my children living away with strangers. It was very sad saying farewell to Boston Light, knowing that I might never enjoy this kind of life again. For seventeen years it had been my way of life, and if there is anything in the world more beautiful than a lighthouse, I have yet to find it.

For several years we lived on Mt. Desert Island, where another son was born. Then we came to my husband's home state so that he could attend a special school. My children speak often of home and the sea and their kinfolk. They frequently look over my albums. The photos of their grandfather, standing tall and proud in the black-and-gold-trimmed uniform of the lighthouse keeper, delight them. We struggle with the usual problems of "civilization" and often wonder at man's determination to outdo his neighbor.

We find our need for solitude is still very strong. Soon we will return to Maine, and once again I will walk the shores of my youth, stand by the sea and savor the taste of salt on my lips. I will live close to the handiwork of God and will feel sad for those who can never know such tranquility.

MEET THE PUFFINS!

BY ANNE FULLER

I HAVE A THEORY that long ago Mother Nature, looking into the future, said to herself, "There's going to come a time when man will need all the laughs he can get. I think I'll just go ahead and evolve some nice creatures to amuse him." So, among other of Nature's oddities, the Puffin came into being. To look at a Puffin is to laugh! It is the feathered clown, the putty-nosed low-comedy character of the bird entertainment world. So fantastic is this winged jest of Nature's that it wouldn't be at all surprising to learn that it laid square eggs.

Both the male and female of our Atlantic Puffin, which are alike, are as unique as they are laugh-provoking. They are only about a foot long but ridiculous in shape like a plump football and they are surmounted by a round head that looks as if it had been borrowed from a far larger bird and stuck in place without taking the trouble to see if it fitted. The head — like a blue-black croquet ball — has large cheek patches which are white in summer and dimmed to a dusty gray in winter. From each of the patches there gleams a large round eye with such a heartbroken expression that the Puffin seems to be struggling to hold back the tears. Above and behind each eye are conical projections, giving the quizzical expression of permanently raised eyebrows. To add to this grotesqueness the eyes are circled by vermillion lids, creating the effect that a Puffin is studying the world through high-style plastic spectacles. Its chunky chest, narrow collar and underparts are snowy white, its broad back a sooty black.

But the incredible thing about any adult Puffin is its beak. No, I cannot belittle it by calling it a beak. For if ever a bird had a nose the Puffin has one. And what a nose! Triangular in shape, it juts from the Puffin's forehead, covers most of the face and is so high-bridged and aristocratic that even the noblest Roman could have pointed to it with pride. But what makes it really unforgettable is its array of colors. Its base, or first ridge, is lemon yellow, the middle section a soft blue. The rest of it is as red as a traffic stop-light.

Puffins are not blessed with this dazzling decoration all year. Only when they are aflame with love in the Spring and when they are proud new parents does their startling facial adornment also flame into full bloom. Actually, it is a mask that covers a serviceable year-round nose and its construction is remarkable. In Spring the soft parts grow out of the original beak and harden into horny substances, marked with characteristic ridges and furrows. When the time comes for the Puffin to unmask, the nose is not shed in one piece, as a Deer sheds its antlers. Instead, the Puffin relinquishes it slowly in nine precise plates, always in the same order. Then it is left with an every-day beak, a smaller bluish-gray replica of its former splendor but still retaining the typical flattened triangular shape and a rosy glow at its tip. In both sexes, young and old, the change of plumage after the moult is barely noticeable.

It is small wonder that Audubon wrote in utmost delight of his first meeting with these appealing personalities. It hap-

pened in 1840 when he found them in countless numbers on
Perroquet Island near Bradore in Canadian Labrador. At that
time he recorded that Puffins bred prolifically also on many sea-
islands off the coast of Maine. Today, Perroquet Island is still
a flourishing breeding ground as are numerous islands from
southern Greenland and Ungava Bay to Nova Scotia, the Bay
of Fundy and the more remote islands in the Gulf of St. Lawrence. But, sad to say, in Maine waters today Puffins are making
their last stand on only two small down east islands. One is
Machias Seal Island. The other is Matinicus Rock. July or early
August is the best time to visit either colony.

Of these two Puffin colonies the one on Machias Sea Island
is the older and much the larger. This is an American island
but is leased to the Canadian government which maintains
the lighthouse, fog-signal station and keepers' houses. Unfortunately getting to Machias Seal Island is difficult. You may
hire a boat at Grand Manan, New Brunswick, or get a lobster
fisherman to take you straight out to sea from the Maine village of Cutler. This is a two-hour trip over often upsettingly
rough water. Also, even if you start on the clearest day you are
apt to become engulfed in fog and have to turn back, because
a fog-bank lurks stubbornly 50 miles offshore and sweeps in
whenever a southeast wind blows, which is often. Either trip
must be made on a calm day or you cannot land, since Machias
Seal has no harbor. But if you are lucky in making a successful
trip you will be richly rewarded. Not only will you see around
500 pairs of nesting Puffins but many Leach's Petrels, Arctic
and Common Terns. If you plan to make an extended visit
you must get permission from the Department of Marine, St.
John, New Brunswick, and be prepared to camp out.

The Puffins of Matinicus Rock are more easily seen. The
mailboat from Rockland goes to Matinicus and returns the
same day. But in order to visit the Puffin colony on Matinicus
Rock you must stay overnight on Matinicus Island. Private
homes will take tourists and a lobster fisherman can be hired
to take you on the five-mile trip to the Rock.

You can visit the Matinicus Rock Puffins also by way of Monhegan Island, going there on the daily mailboat from Port Clyde or on the daily excursion boat, *Balmy Days,* from Boothbay Harbor. The Maine Information Bureau and Maine Audubon Society, Portland, will gladly give you specific information about boat schedules. You will have to spend a night, possibly two, on Monhegan but this is far from being a hardship since you can stay at one of three hotels, pleasant and not expensive, as well as in some private homes. To see the many beauties of that wonderful island with its towering headlands, amazing varieties of birds and wild flowers is an experience you will cherish. From there the hour and a half trip to Matinicus is made in a comfortable boat expertly captained by Sherman Stanley, one of Monhegan's young lobster fishermen. You may join an already planned group or make up your own party. The boat stops at Matinicus long enough for you to explore that interesting island, then goes on to the Rock.

Matinicus Rock is 35 acres of granite, 60 feet high, jutting out of the sea and topped with a picturesque lighthouse. Almost always rough water prevents a landing on that harborless island, but the birds which hover around its rim may readily be watched from a boat circling close to the shore. You will see Leach's Petrels, Great Black-backed and Herring Gulls, Black Guillemots, countless Arctic Terns and lingering flotillas of Eider Ducks. But most exciting of all you will meet face to face the incredible Puffins and have the opportunity to watch their amusing antics and get intimate glimpses of their home life.

Puffin residences are of two kinds. Some, like the majority of Machias Seal Island nesters, are willing to settle for a ready made grotto-like nursery in crevices or under overhanging rocks. The more energetic Matinicus Rock Puffin prefers to dig its own burrow. Papa Puffin does the excavating, which is no small undertaking for that portly gentleman since the burrow often curves inward for an arm's length. You'd think he would use that massive beak of his as a one-bird-power steam shovel, but instead he makes the dirt fly with his big, webbed red feet. The nest itself is a slap-dash affair of grasses and a few feathers casually assembled by Mrs. P.

Once in a while an ambitious Puffin mother will surprise the expectant father with twins. But ordinarily a Puffin couple achieve only one dullish white, brown-splotched egg a year. Both parents take turns incubating and from the way they act they must find this underground vigil an awful bore. When one comes blinking out it will stretch luxuriously, flutter its wings as if happy to get out of that dark nursery into the fresh air, and rubber-neck around to see what the neighbors are up to. But while a Puffin is doing its nest-duty it guards its solitary treasure, both in the egg and afterward, zealously and ferociously. Woe to anyone who goes poking into a burrow and finds the Puffin at home! Then that usually benign comedian will scratch and bite like a cornered bobcat and his false-face beak can mangle any fingers not protected by heavy leather gloves.

As soon as possible after Baby Puffin emerges from its shell its parents urge it up into the light of day at their front door. If you are fortunate enough to see a really young one you have a surprise coming to you! The infant Puffin bears not the slightest resemblance to its delightful parents. It has not even a suggestion of their wonderful beak but only a thin pointed bill like a thorn sticking out of its muffiny face. As for the rest of it, it looks like an oval plastic sack filled with loose jello and smothered in dingy gray down. It is such a blob of fat that its parents have to prod it from one spot to another where it collapses into a heap and stays there until they give it another shove.

You would think that nothing short of a miracle would ever get that roly-poly Puffinette off the launching pad. But Nature sees to it that even the puffiest Puffin babies grow up to look and behave exactly like their parents.

On land they walk upright, shuffling awkwardly along on the entire length of their stumpy legs and splayed feet. Often they will line up in neat rows, standing ram-rod erect as if they were playing soldiers; and when they sit down on land they stick those ridiculous feet straight in front of them so that they appear to be reclining on their round rumps. On the wing they seem to buzz rather than to fly because their wings, shaped almost like pointed flippers, are so small they have to work them at top speed to keep their robust bodies airborne.

Most water-birds are graceful, floating upon their natural element. But not Puffins. They ride high in the water like miniature craft without enough ballast and go rocking along with a motion reminiscent of an old stern-wheel river boat. However, droll as they appear, they swim competently on the surface, and under water they really come into their own. When they are chasing the small fish which are their principal food they are aquatic marvels. Using their wings for paddles and their feet as a rudder they zip by faster than the startled trout. It is a champion fingerling that ever makes a getaway.

When they are bringing these fish ashore to overstuff their perpetually hungry children, Puffins know a trick which scientists have not figured out to this day. They don't waste effort toting home one fish at a time. Sometimes they carry as many as five laid out in a row crosswise in their beaks with heads all facing in the same direction. Without the use of hands how on earth do they manage to keep the first fish from escaping while they catch the others? Maybe this secret is what they keep chuckling about. Their most common call is so nearly like a distant guttural laugh that it is uncanny. If you want to get an idea of how a Puffin sounds try laughing deep in your throat with your lips tightly closed.

One of their more endearing traits is that they show genuine fondness and concern for their neighbors as well as their families. If one is injured in the water his Puffin friends will gather around, making pathetic sounds of distress and nudging him with wings and beaks, trying to help him ashore. On days of deep fog, groups of them will gather, usually on the same chosen ledge or boulder. There they will stand affec-

tionately close to each other, as if they craved the warmth
of companionship to offset the bleakness of the world around
them. When they are in such conclave a human can stand still
a few yards away and they will pay no more attention than
if he were just another lonesome Puffin. Also, they are so in-
quisitive that they will approach a quiet boat to within a dozen
feet and sit there watching to see what it's all about. This, un-
happily, makes the trusting little fellows a perfect target for a
gunner with no conscience and no heart.

Year after year Puffins return to the same nesting sites on
such a rigid schedule you can almost set your calendar by it.
Although they do not have a true migration they leave their
grounds with equal regularity to winter on the open sea, a few
venturing as far south as Massachusetts. By mid-to-late August
the fish on which they depend for food begin to move away.
Then the Puffins go too. A whole colony will precipitately desert their homes completely. It is a puzzling thing that then
they, who have been such conscientious and doting parents,
will callously desert any babies that have hatched late and are
not able to join the exodus. These tragic orphans become the
prey of hawks, ravens and other predators.

But man, more than any other enemy, can be blamed for
the population depletion of these beguiling creatures. For
wherever Puffins were found, man with his heedless greed has
been their persecutor. In by-gone days in Europe devout
church-members annually salted down barrels of tender young
Puffins to add to their Lenten menu. They rationalized this
unorthodox behavior by convincing themselves that although
a Puffin wasn't really a fish it tasted enough like fish so their
consciences needn't twinge when they ate it on days the church
designated as meatless ones. The natives of the coasts and
islands of the far north catch them in nets to use their bodies
for food and their skins as clothing. The skins are tough and,
sewed with the feathers inside, make durable and extremely
cozy parkas. Since Puffin stew is considered a delicacy by those

with a gamier taste, hunters everywhere have done their best toward eliminating these trusting children of the wild.

In Maine, as well as in other localities, Puffin eggs are also greatly relished as food — all the more because they are so rare. The result of this vandalism has been a tragic reduction of the Puffin population.

Puffins are members of the Alcidae family which includes also Auks and Murres. Surprisingly, their closest relatives are Loons and Grebes. The Puffin has many nicknames including Sea Parrot, Labrador Auk, Pope, Bottle Nose, Tammy Norie, Coulternab and Tinker. But by whatever name we choose to call him, we should give thanks that under protective laws Maine today is fortunate enough to have two rugged spume-swept islands where that pompous, lovable buffoon, the Atlantic Puffin, still finds sanctuary.

OUR SUMMER MONTHS

We sometimes jokingly refer to our visitors
as "summer complaints," but we
welcome them back each year
from June to September and
share with them the joys
of summer living
in Maine.

AUGUST TAPESTRY

BY RUTH L. W. DRAPER

AUGUST WAS THE MAGIC MONTH in Dennysville, Maine. All the vacationers who could not be "down home" for the entire summer came in August, and for the visitors from away that was the enchanted month. The sweet early summer days were past, not to be relived until another year, but August was the lush climax of all that had gone before.

With great sagacity, the women of the Ladies Circle planned their annual apron sale and supper to coincide with the August influx — and also with the full moon, so that the horse-and-buggy trade would have a clear bright evening for the homeward drive. Each year everyone marveled that it never had rained on the appointed date for this major event.

Aprons of all sorts, shapes, and sizes, made at Circle meetings through the previous winter, graced the sale. There were also linens, doubtless smuggled in from St. Stephen and so beautifully embroidered they looked as if they had been done in a

convent. All of this handiwork sold for a pittance, but as everything was contributed, it was reckoned as clear gain.

Then came the supper, so modestly named. Quantities of
chickens, donated and roasted by the farm women of the community, were carved and piled on huge platters for each of
the tables, with plenty more in the kitchen to replenish the
serving dishes as they were emptied. There were a number of
baked hams, and if an Atlantic salmon — running twenty
pounds or more — had been caught in the river, the firm, pink
fish was made into salads with stuffed eggs alongside. There
were big pans of hot potato scallop and corn scallop; bowls of
cold potato salad, cabbage salad, fruit salad, tomato aspic with
crisp cucumbers. Plates heaped high with hot Parker House
rolls flanked big pats of country butter, home made pickles and
jellies. For dessert, there were all kinds of pies, layer cakes and
tarts — each cook's specialty being recognized by the patrons
and loudly called for by name. Gallons of strong hot coffee —
as many cups as anyone wished to drink — were served with
cream so thick it had to be spooned from a bowl, because it
would not pour.

The price for this little snack was twenty-five cents — well
worth the drive from the neighboring towns and, as some of
the "outsiders" said, "even worth the fare from Boston." When
the price finally was raised to thirty-five cents, there was a
great hue and cry, especially from those who practically had
emptied a whole platter of chicken onto their own plates.
But as long as the receipts from that gala event approximated
$100, everyone was jubilant about its dizzying financial success.

Our playtime came in August. House-cleaning was over, haying done, and the struggle with the weeds in the garden was
paying delicious dividends.

Those were the days before there were two blights for every
vegetable. The only one prevalent was the potato bug, whose
demise was a source of pocket money to small boys and girls
armed with an old tomato-can of kerosene and a stick. We were

paid five cents a hundred for ridding the potatoes of the bugs and no cheating!

Now we relished Early Rose potatoes, devoured in their jackets with a garnish of salt, pepper and cream; curly lettuce, dressed with sugar and lemon juice, and cucumbers, tomatoes and baby carrots — both for garden nibbling and for the table. The black Mexican and sweet yellow corn was at its best and vines were loaded with Kentucky Wonders and Lowe's Champions.

In leisurely August we held picnics galore at all the favorite spots, and took long afternoon rides in the surrey, with Mother expertly handling the reins. We often went to "The Point," three miles down river at the head of the bay.

Picnics at The Point usually included all the kin, near and distant, who were at hand, as well as any visitors from "outside." The Point had a huge ancient pine, as well as a small pebbly beach with rocks at one end just right for the clambake, and a grove of spruces at its head for shade.

There was a little woods road fragrant with pennyroyal, and jeweled with small crimson Highland cranberries on their lacy vines, which led through a thicket of evergreens to Punch Cove, where we used to find marsh rosemary or sea lavender. It was said that the early mariners used to stop at the cove to mix their punch on their way up river, hence the name. Also Big Dram and Little Dram islands in the bay were purported to have been stops for refreshment, before the sailors reached port, "half-seas over."

Beside the road to the cove were quantities of gaily colored toad-stools, which we used to think formed a fairy ring, and we felt the presence of the "little people" as if they had at that moment taken flight.

We could often see seals as they slithered off the rocks near the cove and lazily swam around, with their sleek black heads and big eyes glistening, while loons laughed crazily — either at the seals or at us. The long-legged blue heron fished in the cove, standing on the edge of the mud flats at low tide until some careless fish came near enough to be speared by the bird's long bill.

Overhead the ospreys hovered watching for fish, ready to drop like plummets to grasp them in their strong talons; above, "Old Baldy," the eagle, soared in majestic circles. Once we saw an osprey dive and get a fish which he took aloft. Old Baldy swooped down on him, so he dropped the fish which promptly was retrieved and immediately eaten by the watchful blue heron. Manna from heaven!

One summer the girls camped out on the point across the cove, and one night the boys came down from town and, from the opposite shore, set off a charge of dynamite. The girls, who were sound asleep, leaped from their beds in fright. One, braver than the rest, demanded, "Where are my corsets?" — as if, encompassed by this coat of armor, the young Brunnhilde then would be equipped to go forth to meet the foe. Having accomplished their dastardly feat, the boys went laughing and whistling back to town, leaving the damsels to regain their composure as best they might, though the desire for sleep had been shattered.

We girls took our bathing suits when we went to The Point, donning them in the little old house up on the hill, where each girl had her private dressing nook in the far from communal "bathhouse." Our bathing suits consisted first of a one-piece garment, something like a baby's romper, comprising a blouse and full bloomers which came well below the knees. The blouse had a high neck and sometimes an added sailor collar, and the long sleeves were buttoned snugly around the wrists. Over this we wore a very full gathered skirt, which came down to the calf of the leg. The suits were made of cotton flannel or some serge-like material. They usually were navy blue and trimmed with white braid. With this daring outfit, we wore long black cotton stockings.

Covering the entire costume with a raincoat, we self-consciously paraded to the beach where our parents, uncles, aunts and elderly cousins sat around visiting. Slipping off the rain-coats behind a convenient bush, we dashed into the water to submerge immediately. Once we were thoroughly water-soaked, it was permissible to remove the stockings — but nothing else.

Leaving the Point in late afternoon for the short ride home, the faint smell of salty rockweed at ebb tide followed us up the hill. We went along the narrow deeply-rutted road through a field brilliant with great clumps of Black-Eyed Susans and Queen Anne's Lace. At "The Opening" we stopped, looking back yearningly at the bay with its wooded shoreline and small islands. Along the woodsy road, dappled with sun and shade, we heard the veery and the hermit thrush singing their twilight songs, and the white-throat whistling, clear and sweet.

In the dank dark of the woods, against a fern-covered ledge, the Indian pipes stood stark and white like tiny ghosts, and along the edge of the road, scarlet bunch-berries reflected the light of the late afternoon sun.

Then, down over Tom Thumb Hill and through Witch Hollow, where cow bells tinkled wistfully at milking time. Home — with woodsmoke curling from the kitchen chimney and swallows twittering and dropping into the unused south chimney, where they nested. Supper was ready, with big bowls of enormous blueberries, brought from The Ridge that afternoon.

Some afternoon the boys would say, "Let's go to the pond." Off we would go, up the dusty road and down to the edge of the pond, to find the skiff under the alder bushes, just where we had left it.

The boys had their lines and hooks and a tin box of worms, and we rowed across to the opposite shore where there was a clay bank, and the cool deep pool at its base was a favorite haunt of the bass.

While the boys fished, we sat there quietly, watching the dragonflies darting among the flowers of that water-garden — pond lilies, cow lilies, and water hyacinths, while along the edge of the pond were tall spikes of cardinal flowers and turtle head.

We watched the dragonflies — we called them "devil's darn-ing needles" — with wary eyes lest they should come and sew up our mouths, as our brothers had warned us they might, if we talked too much.

Going home through the pasture with its pink and white hardhack, and steeplebush, its Joe Pye weed and asters mingled with goldenrod and spicy sweet fern, we carried a string of black bass for supper and arms full of waxen fragrant pond lilies. Some of these were put into great-grandmother's big blue soup tureen on the sitting room table, and the rest were given to less fortunate neighbors, who had not been "up the pond" that afternoon.

One of our most memorable August picnics was an all-day trek to the ocean, to Cutler or West Quoddy, some twenty-five miles away. This meant the three-seater and a pair of horses, and we had to start by seven in the morning to allow time for the four-hour ride each way, the picnic itself and "browsing around" while the horses rested for the long haul home.

At Quoddy there was the life saving station to visit, with its sandy beach, big rocky headlands and pounding surf. It was bordered by "The Heath" and filled with pitcher plants and fringed orchis, and was the home of the white-rumped marsh hawk.

On the beach we once saw a tall, lanky blue heron trying to make a sculpin into an edible delicacy. He shook it; put it down on the sand and held it with his foot while he tried to tear it, then picked it up in his long bill, waded into the surf and swished it back and forth in the incoming waves to wash off the sand. He was still working at it when we left.

A little farther along, on the very tip of the Head, was West Quoddy Light, painted in red-and-white stripes — a giant candy cane on its high bluff, the most easterly point of mainland in the United States. We climbed the narrow spiral stairs to the lantern with kindly Cap'n Ephie, the keeper, whom we all loved, and looked out over the Atlantic, due east. Had we possessed unlimited vision, we could have seen the "Castles in Spain," straight ahead, "as the crow flies."

Cap'n Ephie's eyes were bright and keen and crinkled at the corners from years of scanning the sea. He was weatherwise, without fail, and on that bright, sunny cloudless day, he laconically said, "Land loom — weather breeder — rain tomorrow." We were skeptical — but sure enough, it did!

The granite boulders of the bluff were seamed and ground by the constant motion of the sea, and on the beach below some of the smaller rocks were polished and as round as balls, or oval like petrified eggs. The bell-buoy near Sail Rock in the channel rang its continual warning, while the gulls wheeled and screamed. And in the midst of all this wildness and force of sea, wind and rocks, the fragile little harebells danced lightly up the cliffs — lovely and unafraid.

Then came the long ride home, sunburned and relaxed, old and young playing "carriage cribbage" — counting horses, cows, dogs, and loads of hay, and looking eagerly for the "white cat in the window" which would give one the game. We arrived home at dusk, cramped and tired — and how wonderful to tumble into bed and sleep the clock around, knowing that another adventure would take place tomorrow, in the lovely August of nostalgic memory.

DO I HEAR FIVE?

BY VIRGINIA CHASE

THERE IS NOTHING I would rather do than go to an auction. As soon as the notice of one appears in the county paper, my blood starts stirring. Fatigue disappears. Poison ivy stops itching. Blisters suddenly heal. Though I cannot weed a garden for ten minutes at midday without dizziness, even collapse, I can stay for hours under the blazing sun in some farmyard listening to the compelling voice of a Maine auctioneer.

My family — alas — feels less enthusiasm. While I am making the sandwiches, slapping on the peanut butter, they delay over breakfast, making pointed remarks about the crowded state of our attic and the depleted state of our finances. Dressing, they debate among themselves whether it is better to sit with me and suffer mortification (I being an audible bidder and prone to raise questions) or to sit apart, preserving their dignity, yet leaving me unrestrained.

But when we are about five miles from the site, they, too, catch something of the fever. For the roads are crowded with farm trucks, station wagons, convertibles, even a motorcycle or two, all headed in the same direction. Though (due entirely to my own initiative) we are always early, we can never park as close as we want to, for fully a quarter of a mile from the white flag cars have been left everywhere, even in the ditches.

We fit in where we can and push our way forward, jostling picnic baskets, knitting bags, baby strollers, camp chairs, umbrellas. Women are always in the lead. Perhaps the men are remembering the sideboards or the marble topped commodes tried out in every room in the house and finally stored away in the barn chamber.

When we get there what jumble lies before us! Cut glass. Blown glass. Pressed glass. Milk glass. Sandwich. Hobnail. China dishes, their patterns half obscured by grime. Books with swollen pages and faded loosened covers. Tea pots with chipped or broken noses. A coffee grinder that someone will grab for a lamp base. A bird cage that will ultimately support ivy. A splendid pair of Bristol vases . . .

Felt hats, straw hats, hats with broken, dusty feathers. Sad irons and vinegar jugs by the dozen. One or two conk shells. A heap of shoes with laces that no one could ever untangle. Old clocks, a few still running. Old quilts. A box of patent medicines. A Sheffield silver platter . . .

Chairs in rows and heaps. Caned bottom, slat bottom, bottomless altogether. Chairs upholstered in plush or horsehair. Chairs with broken rungs and springs protruding. A rosewood Salem rocker. Kitchen tables, scarred by knives and marked by hot dishes. Parlor tables, their veneer warped and peeling. A Chippendale tilt-top table that will send the bids soaring.

Dressers with stubborn drawers and missing handles. Commodes, always pungent. Spool beds, four posters. Braided rugs and musty carpets. Kitchen ranges. Farm tools. Harnesses. Andirons. Lanterns. Hanging lamps with prisms missing, and tangled rusty chains. Mirrors tarnished and mottled. Sea chests with rope beckets, still smelling faintly of tar . . . A hooded cradle . . .

We look them all over, then we set up our camp stools and inspect the crowd. Sharp-eyed dealers, near the front, of course, where they can spot a piece of cranberry glass or Staffordshire. Farm wives, brown-skinned and hearty, thankful to be sitting. Tourists all agog at finding local color. Children everywhere, already demanding root beer or Coca-Cola. Villagers, like ourselves, who leave the halters and the shorts to the tourists and the summer people. Husbands on the outskirts, looking on with careful nonchalance.

Right on schedule the proceedings start. The teller, all business, takes her cashbox to her table. Then the auctioneer appears, ready to make a day of it. He shakes a few select hands, thus conferring status, makes some general remarks, concluding with a joke or two, picks up a jug or a firkin, maybe, and begins.

"Well, folks, what am I offered?"

A good Maine auctioneer is a match for any psychologist living. Each has his own special technique, his own brand of persuasion. Some use the question method. *Five. May I have six? Six. May I have seven?* Some use coaxing. *The dollar and the quarter. Now the dollar and the half.* Some are imperative. *Five make it six. Six. Make it seven.* Some use gestures, snatching out the bids, as it were, turning from one bidder to another with such mounting speed that they are both caught in a rhythm they are reluctant, sometimes unable, to break. Some auctioneers encourage verbal bids, believing that they engender enthusiasm. Some prefer a raised hand or merely a nod in confirmation. (After all, it is easier to nod $15 than to say it.) Dealers are seldom verbal. The auctioneer knows them all, and a raised finger on an unraised hand is enough.

"A quarter I have. Now the thirty-five."

"Thirty-five," someone calls and the thing is his at a bargain. For the first thing up is a gimmick every time.

Then the real bidding begins. There is no telling at the start how it will go. The weather has a lot to do with it. On a hot day the crowd, plagued by heat and sunburn, is often more concerned with cold drinks than with china. On a rainy day people are too busy jostling for a dry place to stand to get worked up over a rabbit-eared chair or an Empire table, though a bottle of furniture polish may be offered as a lure. In wind, behavior is erratic. Likely as not no one will offer a dime for a spool bedstead, but a hatrack started at fifty cents will rise suddenly to $7 or $8. A compote, returned because of a crack before the face and eyes of everyone, will sell a second time for twice as much as before.

The ideal day is cool and dry. The auctioneer shakes more hands than usual. The crowd is good-humored and sociable. Faces seen at other auctions become the faces of friends. Greetings, sometimes confidences, are exchanged. Tips are passed on to known collectors. *Round Pond is the place for ironstone.* Or *Go to Gardiner if you want clocks.* Even the dealers are affable.

"Well, folks, what am I offered?"

Coal scuttles. Picture frames. Boxes of buttons. Beaded lamp shades. Family albums. A coil of rope. A Lazy Susan. A milk stool. A pewter teapot. Old guns . . . .

"Four. Four I have. Do I hear the five?"

The voice rises and falls, tuneless, magnetic. Toes twitch to the rhythm. Knitting needles take it up. Children slow down on their soft drinks to listen. The men move closer.

"Five. Five I have. Do I hear the six?"

Invariably somebody loses his head.

"Two I have from this gentleman in the back. Who'll make it three?"

"Three," the same gentleman will shout, red faced, in answer, determined not to give way to anyone.

I remember one time when two sisters, sitting apart, bid furiously on the same cut glass bowl. "Why did you keep

forcing me up?" one asked hotly, coming over to the other
when the bidding finally stopped.

"I wanted to be sure and get it," the sister said.

And I remember a young couple, homeless, heading across
the country on a motorcycle, who had just stopped for a minute
to look on but couldn't resist bidding, and found themselves
the bewildered possessors of a mammoth golden oak dining
room set piled high by the roadside, awaiting removal.

The crowd relishes it all, peering at every purchase, offering
advice or approval, sometimes doing a little trading on their
own, thus relieving themselves of articles for which their enthusiasm has already cooled. Maybe a paperweight showing
Mount Vernon for two finger bowls. Or a hobnailed pitcher
and three matching glasses for a kerosene camp stove. Or a pair
of bottle-green portieres and a spray of plastic roses for a fold-
ing cot.

Meanwhile the men are carrying things to the cars. Wash
tubs. Dry sinks. Whatnots. Wagon seats. Cobblers' benches.
Cabinets, with doors swinging. A horsehair sofa, hard to grasp.
School room desks. A lawn swing or two. Church pews. Maybe
an organ. And always near the end of the procession some
patient husband tussles resignedly with a spinning wheel.

Oh there's nothing quite so heady on a summer day as a
seat in some farmyard, facing a faded, dusty, odorous helter-
skelter of almost everything in which who knows what may be
hiding, and hearing at the same time the hypnotic, coercing
voice of the auctioneer.

"Four. Four I have. Do I hear the five?"

THE BOAT WAS ABLE

BY J. HARVEY HOWELLS

It was one of those cloudless, wind-free mornings on Casco Bay, rare as a four-pound quahog, when a motionless sea lip-laps the ledges and the tide creeps in as stealthily as a stalking cat. Five miles to the southwest, sparkling in the golden air, Bailey Island looked near enough to pick up. A champagne day.

Framed in the piney arms of Smuggler's Cove, the stripper was a sight to turn a man's heart.

"Built right, ain't she?" said my friend the innkeeper.

"How long?" I asked.

"Long enough. Fella brought a big tuna ashore in one o' them a month back. Alone. Passed a line around head and tail, then stood on the center thwart and rocked it aboard. Nigh as long as the boat was. Five mile out, too."

The vague yearnings of years crystallized into decision. That

day I knew my future summers would be drab indeed without a
strip-built boat of my own.

"Wish you luck," said the innkeeper. "You're a visituh.
You'll tail onto a line o' lobstermen wantin' work boats. A
long line."

"You forget. I'm not a *visitor* any more. I'm a *cottager*."

This was important. What my wife and I think of as "our"
part of Maine is divided into three ethnic groups. There are the
original settlers, who never contradict the inference that they
stem from that tap root sunk in 1607 by old Sir George Pop-
ham and his Colony. There are the resorters who swoop Down
East by Cadillac and Ford for a few lobster-hued days with
their own kind before darting back to Brookline, Westport, or
Chappaqua. We had been of this frenetic persuasion until circumstances — and my wife's determination — had permitted
us to join the third party, those fortunate few who spend all
summer in Maine on their own premises; a *cosa nostra* whose
battle cry, "Cottagers Only!" can be heard rallying the clan to
the tribal rites each 5 p.m. from Independence to Labor Day.

Surely this would give me an edge with the boat builder.
After all, we buy a ton or two of local groceries each year now,
not to mention a poundful of lobster.

"You're still a visituh," said the innkeeper.

Now among the cottagers was a lady of many charms, one of
them newly appealing to me. She was the only non-lobsterman
I knew who possessed a stripper. Of course, Marian was dang
near a native herself, having grown up summers on her late
father's island a scant sea mile from the boatyard. The stripper,
now her grandson's pride, had been their ferry in the old days.

"Maybe I could help," said Marian. "I've known the builder
for — well — quite some time."

Next day we drove to West Point, one unspoiled lobstering
village.

"This is Harvey Howells, Alton," said Marian. "He likes
your boats. Where's Alice?"

With that she vanished into the next room, her part in the transaction accomplished with near-native brevity. In eleven words she had introduced us, flattered the builder, recommended me as a friend with good taste and, by disappearing, made it obvious that business was afoot.

"Lot o' people seem to," said Alton, referring back to Marian's introduction.

"I've admired them for years," I said. "There's nothing like a Maine-built boat. I used to own a Friendship."

"Used to?" Clearly he thought only an oaf would part with a Friendship sloop.

"We were just starting our family," I apologized. "I knew we wouldn't be cruising again for a while. You use the same materials, don't you? Oak frame and cedar planking?"

"Nope."

Stop babbling, Howells. Wait for it.

"Pine planking," said Alton.

I'd been close enough. Emboldened, I tried again.

"They're all the same length over-all, aren't they? Sixteen feet? Do you ever make them longer?"

"Seen where I build m' boats?" He had a gentle voice for his size.

"Just from the water —"

"Gets cold up he-uh in the wintuh."

"So I've heard."

"Use a Franklin for heat."

"Great little stoves. They're all the rage again, down Connecticut way —"

"Shed's nineteen foot long. I got to get between bow and stove when I'm workin'." He stood up, filling the spotless kitchen. "Don't aim to put my arse on a hot Franklin for nobody. Boat's sixteen foot long." He smiled benignly. "If you want it."

It was as easy as that. God bless you, Marian. It's not what you know —

"Can I give you a down payment?" I managed to say.

"Don't need it right now. Later, long 'bout January when I do, you'll get a letter tellin' you your boat's finished. Put down your address" — he handed me an old envelope — " 'n I'll try not to lose it."

My scribbling acted as a signal. Marian and Alice materialized, all shook hands, and we cottagers left.

"I don't have to ask if he quoted a fair price," said Marian. "Alton's a fair man."

"We didn't let sordid commercialism enter into our discussion."

"You mean you don't know?"

"Would you ask Robert Frost what he charged per poem?"

In January I received a post card: *The boat you ordered last summer is now ready at the agreed upon price. Yrs. truly, Alton Wallace.*

"Alton is a State of Mainer," said my wife when she stopped laughing. "He hates to name the figure for fear he shoots low."

"Maybe he didn't want to disclose his business on a post card."

After twenty-four hours of cogitating, I sent off the following:

Delighted to get your card. Can't wait, etc. Proud, etc. Grateful, etc. Stupid, etc. I can't remember the exact price agreed, and I wouldn't want to be off ten dollars one way or t'other. If you'll put the figure in the enclosed air mail envelope, I'll dash off a check by return. Sincerely—

The envelope to keep Alton's finances from friendly eyes at West Point came back promptly. Five hundred dollars. Can you imagine? For a hand-built boat that can go anywhere.

"Kind of hard to be off ten dollars one way or t'other on that," said my wife.

"Exactly the figure I anticipated."

"Don't be smug."

Right here let me say I never ask a price now in my Maine dealings, never dicker, and never feel cheated. Assumption of his honesty disarms the State of Mainer, while bargaining is a call to battle; if you end up with a bloody wallet, it's your own fault for putting up your dooks in the first place.

In early June we returned to our spiritual home. My wife unlocked the cottage door, whereupon my nine-year-old son and I immediately dashed for West Point, leaving his mother to unpack in peace and quiet. Ours was man's work.

"Your boat's down to Marian's brother's garridge," said Alton and grinned, "I borrowed the key from Dana."

Dana's is general store, gas and lobster station for land and sea, post office, Western Union, ship's chandler, town gossip hall, and depository for summer folks' keys.

"That danged Alton," said Dana. "You got free storage, Alton got a free laugh. All I got was my lumps for letting out the key."

She was sixteen feet of grace born of utility. High, round-swelling bow dropped in a sweeping sheer to a square stern; with six-foot-two beam, her deck was wide enough for dancing. The inch strips of pine planking butted one to another with cabinetmaker's skill that gave her a skin smooth as a baby pollock's. All that she needed now was water to float in and a motor to push her.

To fetch the latter down from Bath, next day I borrowed his venerable pick-up from the innkeeper.

My son and I managed to lower the 25 h.p. behemoth over the tailgate to balance precariously on its stand. Between motor and boat, now afloat at an outhaul, lay six parallel knife edges of menacing rock that had to be crossed before outboard and hull could be joined in union. This feat would have to be accomplished before the entire walking population of West Point, strung out just above high water mark. Men, women, children and thirty-seven dogs. Of course, they weren't there to watch me make a fool of myself. Not much.

"How you going to get the motor over the rocks?" asked my son in instant embarrassment. "Djeesh! A hundred and fifty pounds!"

"I'll think of something," I whispered, then raised my voice.
"First we have to fit her out."

Gas tank, anchor, chain, line, horn, bailing scoop, life jackets, oars — I wasn't about to earn a ticket from the Coast Guard.
My audience could see that, even if their collective gaze was
politely fixed on the far horizon.

"Oars ain't wuth much wi'out thole pins," a wrapper-clad
matron whispered into my ear as I passed.

Ouch! I strolled over to Alton's shed.

"Oars ain't wuth much wi'out thole pins," I said.

He cut four and whittled the ends. "You like the paintuh
I throwed in?"

"I was just about to thank you."

"Slapped another coat o' white on her last evenin' after you
left."

"You didn't have to do that —"

"Protectin' my handiwuk."

An only slightly smaller edition of Alton entered the shed
carrying my anchor chain and the twenty fathoms of nylon.
Whistling soundlessly, the newcomer proceeded to rig one
to the other through a thimble, splicing the line professionally
back on itself with banana-thick fingers that moved nimbly as
a maiden's at her petit point.

Alton lit a blow torch.

"You finally goin' to burn the place down like I suggested?"
said the splicer.

"You want that thumb, Dextuh, you better hold stiddy."

"Who you wavin' at, then?"

With the white-hot flame a split inch away from the other
man's fingers, Alton seared the loose ends of the splice. In the
twilight of the shed, with my son watching, the two men intent
on their task, the torch roaring, the act took on a symbolism,
a ritual sealing of the brotherhood of the sea.

"Many thanks, gentlemen," I said. "I always was a lousy
splicer."

"Couldn't be no worse'n Dextuh."

"Alton don't splice. He ties knots — grannies."

Alton gave him a short punch that would have splintered the ribs of an ox, but Dexter only grinned. We walked back out to the sunshine where the outboard stood landlocked to its stand. I heard my son groan.

So, apparently, did Alton. Gently pushing Dexter aside, he wrapped the monstrous machine in a bear hug, straightened up, crossed the jagged rocks in six easy strides, bent over, and lowered the motor into place on the transom.

"The boat builduh" — Dexter spat appreciatively — "a mighty man is he."

I swung gracefully aboard and fixed the gas line with only one fumble.

"How'll you get it going?" whispered my son, red-faced. "Can't we rig the starter? Twenty-five horse! Djeesh!"

Alton beamed down on him. "Easy, sonny." He spoke the next words slowly. For my benefit? "You pull out the choke. You take hold of the cable. You step back a pace — you look up — you pray — and you yank."

With the motor a-roaring, the worst was over. Now all I had to do was negotiate a narrow channel chockful of dories, luggers, and draggers at anchor, with young West Pointers dashing between them in flat-bottomed skiffs, each throwing out a wash to shame a destroyer. But the jam didn't bother me. I've fooled around boats all my life —

"Cast off!"

Standing in the stern, nautical as all get-out I eased my new-won pride away from the rocks. As I did I stole a glance back at the unsmiling launching party. Should I essay a nonchalant farewell wave? As I was pondering this, an invisible force stopped boat and motor dead. I fell forward on the mid-thwart, and my son lay down in the bow to hide his face.

Alton's soft voice boomed across the strait.

"You got yourself hung up on an outhaul."

That nightmare of a daytime stroll down Fifth Avenue in the altogether holds no shame to compare with making a mari-

time idiot of yourself before professionals. Cursing quietly —
I don't approve of swearing before the young — I hauled the
motor up and went to work on the Laocoon coils wrapped
around the propellor. The long reach over the transom didn't
make it any simpler.

"Step in the next boat," called Alton. "Easier to get at it."

The heck I would. I worried at the fankle, growling like a
dog, till the cast cradle was reduced to one last loop. As I rested
a moment, savoring success, a skiff swung in close, the pre-
teenager at the helm leaned over, freed the line with a quick
flip, and sprayed off. The little scene stealer didn't even slow
up.

The going tide drifted us down on a moored dory.

"Grab it!"

My son held fast while I pulled the starter cable. And pulled.
And pulled.

"Push in the choke," called Alton.

"Blankblank it to blank!"

"Dad!"

She started on the next pull. With a wild-horse leap that
nearly tossed me into the drink. I'd forgotten to put her in neu-
tral. The dory squealed in anguish as we scraped a fair amount
of Alton's new paint on her timbers.

Then we were in the clear, headed for the open bay, free
of entangling outhauls, speeding away from too-knowing eyes.
I looked aft to see the West Pointers, the show over, trekking
back uphill to kitchen, Dana's, or the mending of lobster pots.
All except Alton, who straightened to attention and threw us
a perfect USNR salute.

Our jewel has been with us five seasons now, a family re-
tainer that can tote a thousand pounds of humanity without
submerging her water line. She's done a lot for us, not the
least of which is teaching our son the self-assurance that comes
from skippering your own boat no matter how small. In addition, she has brought us acceptance from Alice, Dana, Dexter,

and all. I think they figure any cottager smart enough to acquire an Alton stripper can't be all dope.

Now if I could find a way to put these boats into mass production, we could sell them down to Long Island Sound, delivered, for a thousand dollars easy. We could net a profit of five hundred on each one. Have to put in a steering wheel for the effete New Yorker, though.

But then they wouldn't be the same. Nor would West Point. Nor Alton.

LAKES, STREAMS, AND WOODS

There's still plenty of room left in Maine:
3400 miles of coast,
7600 lakes and streams,
33,000 square miles
of mostly fields and woods
where men and wild creatures
can share the freedom
and solitude of
the out-of-doors.

CROSS ROCK RAPIDS

BY GRACE SHAW TOLMAN

MANY YEARS AGO in late fall a party of young people, including myself, stood on a bank where the St. John and Allagash Rivers meet. We had paddled Moosehead, climbed Mt. Kineo in a rain storm, and got lost on Long Lake in a snow storm. We had portaged all the carries under full pack; had journeyed for many miles, seeing plenty of wild life, but rarely another living soul, and had enjoyed the time of our lives at so little cost, even in 1901, that we had called it a vacation "on the shoe-string trail." We were on the final leg of the famous Allagash trip, and our head guide was giving us instructions about running the last rapid.

"Now, this here last one is called Cross Rock Rapids," he said. "The current runs right down to the rock, and just afore you get there you push off with your settin' pole and slip out on the left side. Follow me, and when you see me pull my hat down, do as I do."

He squinted around, as if to make sure that each one understood, and walked down to the waiting canoes. We had been on the trip since early fall, and had become quite good amateur white water runners.

Mine was the only canoe without an Allagash guide, but my companion, Frank Bailie, was a good white water man, and I was an apt pupil, so I thought.

The river was wide and deep at this point and the pull of the current was strong. Rounding a sharp turn we came in view of the rapid, and it was a beautiful sight in a rugged and awe-inspiring way.

A gaunt black rock in the shape of a rude cross stood in the deep water with swirling waves breaking around its base. "Rock of ages, cleft for me," I quoted softly to myself.

We saw Charlie settle himself and pull down his old felt hat and, like a live thing, his canoe rushed straight for the rock. Within reaching distance the man in the bow set his pole. We heard the familiar ring of steel on stone, and the canoe slid out, and past the rock.

The next two canoes executed the same maneuver and then it was our turn. With pole poised I waited, feeling the thrill that only white water runners can know. Now was the time, and I set my pole hard, as I had seen the others do.

The canoe snubbed, and started to slide off. I lifted my pole — or tried to do so — for another thrust. To my horror, the pole wouldn't move; it was wedged solidly in a cleft of the rock. Frank saw my predicament and yelled, "Let go!" At the same time he backed water furiously.

I did let go, and the pole sprang back, giving me a bat on the head as it came down. There was no time to think or plan and I suppose that I acted on instinct, to keep the canoe from striking the rock and capsizing.

Throwing myself out along the bow, and hooking my toes under the seat, I reached my arms as far out as I could. I was none too soon, for at that moment Cross Rock and I met with an impact that almost tore my arms from their sockets.

A thousand needles stabbed through my hands as they struck the rough and solid rock. Water swirled over my head, nearly smothering me, and the steel plate on the bow of the canoe cut cruelly into my neck and chest.

"Push!" shouted Frank, and I could have cheerfully killed him.

I *was* pushing — with arms that felt shattered, and during suspended seconds of time that seemed unendurably longer than years. Just as I thought I must let go and slide into the water, I felt the canoe slip sidewise, and in a few more measureless moments we were in the quiet water beyond the rock.

A ragged cheer went up from the canoes ahead but, too near gone to care, I lay along the bow like a bedraggled figurehead. I had to get my weight off the bow and back into the canoe, and it was the hardest task of all in my bruised and numb condition. Moving slowly, inch by inch, I slid back until at last I lay face down, with my head in a fish basket and my feet in the cook pail.

Before long we were on shore, and I was being wrapped in blankets and offered everything from Scotch to peppermint tea from a half dozen hastily-proffered thermos bottles.

After I had told my story, and had assured everyone — myself included — that I was not badly damaged, we set out once more. I rode in state in the duffle canoe, with old Charlie fussing over me like an anxious hen with one chick. Just before we rounded the turn that would shut off our view of the rock, I turned for a last look, and a feeling, almost of nostalgia, swept over me.

"I will never forget it," I murmured, half to myself.

"Come putty nigh bein' your tombstone, Miss Shaw," said old Charlie solemnly.

Now, when memory takes me back to that swift and unforgettable episode, or when I tell the story to some interested listener, there are two questions that I always ask and that will never be answered.

First, why didn't the canoe capsize? I have seen them do it with a tenth of the provocation.

Second, is my pole still lodged in the cleft of Cross Rock?

LOONS ARE NOT SO CRAZY

BY GENE LETOURNEAU

MANY PEOPLE CALL HIM "crazy," but the American loon, largest and handsomest of the diving birds of Maine, is far from stupid. My father, who was a lawyer as well as an ardent fisherman, always contended that there was a reasonable doubt as to the loon's alleged lack of intelligence. Events have proved Dad right. Despite its reputation for weird behaviour, the loon has exhibited a remarkable capacity to win friends and to survive. Both federal and state laws guarantee him peace to live out his life unmolested on lakes and coastal waters. Natural predators may overtake him during his first summer or ice imprison him in his old age, but during the years in between he lives a lonesome yet happy existence. So popular has he become in Maine over the years that at least seventeen places in the state bear his name — nine lakes and ponds, six islands and a bay and a stream — not to mention numerous hunting and fishing lodges and summer camps. If Maine hadn't accepted the chickadee as its state bird, it — instead of Minnesota — might have chosen the loon.

My first recollection of seeing a loon dates back to boyhood fishing trips with my father. Invariably, when we went fishing on a lake, Dad looked around for a feeding loon. The bird, he explained, located schools of small fish for him, and he knew that wherever chubs, dace and minnows congregated there were sure to be larger fish around to prey on them. Sometimes, when the fish were biting well, he would call a halt long before we had boated our limit. My brothers and I would wonder why, and Dad would point to the loon and say, "If you take only what you need, like that loon, there'll always be some to enjoy."

Some fifty years have passed since I first saw a pair of loons. During that time I've listened to their lonely, eerie call on quiet wilderness ponds in the night, watched their frivolous courtship in the spring and seen them defiantly raise their young from black powder-puffs to the flying stage in time to migrate in the fall and perpetuate the cycle of the species. Always, I've admired their beauty and grace, whether they were swimming or diving in the water or flying in for a landing. And I've heard old timers say how they tell the weather by loons. When loons are flying, windy conditions may be expected. A long "A-loooo-ey" cry at night means peaceful weather will hold. Continuous calling or "talking" indicates an impending change, perhaps a thunder shower; while unusual quiet among the loons is a sure sign of moderately foul weather — mist, fog or light rain.

The common loon, also known as the great American diver, is found all the way from the northern United States to the Arctic Circle. It's the largest of all diving waterfowl — some 30 inches overall, from the tip of its short, peaked bill to its abrupt tail, and weighing up to 12 pounds. Black and white forms its principal coloration. Both back and wings are black with white spots, while the head and neck are a glossy black and green with white streaks on the neck. Like most waterfowl, it reaches its finest plumage during early spring. Perhaps its most unusual characteristic is the location of its webbed feet. Their position is farther back than on other diving birds — a handicap for walking, perhaps, but a definite asset for diving and swimming under water.

As lakes clear of ice in the spring, loons fly north from their winter habitat along the coast. They time their arrival at nesting areas perfectly and never crowd one another. Often a single pair are the only loons on a wilderness pond of 50 to 100 acres. The courtship soon after their arrival is a spectacular show, with the male bird the star performer. Beating his wings and mixing every call at his command, the courting male dances on the water as long as he can keep his balance. When he isn't dancing he makes short flights around the pond with a series of exciting takeoffs and landings.

Once mated, a pair of loons selects a site for their nest. They prefer a small island or ledge that has some vegetation growing on it. Such a location, surrounded by water and visible from any side, reduces the hazards of predatory attack. No great care is taken with the nest itself; it is simply an area hollowed out in grass or other low growth. Usually, the female lays only two eggs, which are light brown and spotted and slightly larger than those of a hen.

Both the male and female loon take turns setting on the nest. When the young are hatched, they are not long in taking to the water to feed on aquatic life and small fish. They either paddle behind the mother loon or ride on her back. In their first few weeks of life, baby loons require at least three dozen small fish a day for food. Adult loons, on the other hand, consume their own weight daily.

During the period of nesting and until the young loons can fly, adult loons will risk their own lives to defend their progeny. While on the nest the parent birds resort to various tactics to draw attention to themselves and away from the nest. As soon as the young take to the water, the parents continue their deception, one trying to lead an invader away while the other guards the offspring.

Last summer two game wardens in Seboeis saw a loon drive off a moose that had gotten too near its nest. The loon rushed at the moose, beating its wings and screaming. The moose, in turn, laid its ears back and chased the loon out into deeper water. The strange duel went on for some time until the moose moved away from the nest.

Perhaps the most fascinating period for observing loons is when the young are reaching maturity. They begin flight training in August, beating wings and feet on top of the water in their attempt to become airborne. Adult loons often join in the fun.

Loons require longer runways to take off and land than most waterfowl. A lot depends upon wind conditions. On calm days loons are apt to have difficulty becoming airborne and often make landings that would hardly satisfy a flight officer. I have seen loons swimming in a still, small pond become restless and try to take off when they heard other loons crying in the distance. They'd taxi to a point which provided the longest runway and, using both feet and wings, attempt to leave the pond's surface. When they realized they had used up too much runway, they would cut motors in disgust and swim back to try again.

A landing loon is something to watch. Nearly always it heads into the wind with neck outstretched and comes in at speeds of about 45 miles an hour. Even when waves are rolling it touches down gracefully, skimming the surface for some distance before reducing speed by braking with wings and feet.

One day on a quiet wilderness lake I saw a loon blunder. With me was a veteran bush pilot who often remarked that he had stolen flying lessons from geese, ducks and loons. A two-inch ripple on the water indicated a light breeze as we watched the loon come in to land.

"Two to one he makes a turn into the wind," the pilot said.

But, much to his surprise and mine, the loon plummeted down-wind into the water with a resounding splash.

"Now then," the pilot remarked, "he really fouled that one, but, who knows, maybe he was running out of fuel."

Generally, however, a loon seems to know how much run-way it needs to land or take off. Sometimes it requires a half mile. This may explain why loons are seldom seen on small ponds or on beaver flowages fringed by tall timber.

Weather conditions determine the time when loons migrate in the fall. As soon as fresh water starts to freeze they leave for open salt water along the coast. Some remain off the Maine seaboard throughout the winter. Once in a great while, an old or ailing loon will be frozen in a lake or pond. A few are rescued each year by conservation officers and bird lovers. People seem to want to help the loons leave so that they will be sure to come back to Maine's wilderness lakes another spring. Loons seldom resist such assistance. They're not so crazy after all.

THE HOLLERING ON SPENCER

BY SAMUEL CLARK

NORTH OF THE OLD CANADA ROAD on the far side of the Dead
River lie the two Enchanted towns, the Upper and the Lower
Enchanted. How they came to be called that still remains a
mystery. Perhaps some surveyor, or timber cruiser or wanderer
of the woods found a strange enchantment there that inspired
the name. Certainly there was enchantment in the little buck-
skin bag of gold dust and nuggets the size of pea beans a forgotten lumberman picked out of a brook and brought back
with him at the end of a spring drive. Even lumbermen, who
dealt strictly with the facts of life and were not given to fantasy,
sensed the eeriness of the region while working there in the
winter months long ago.

Along the western boundary of the Lower Enchanted ran
the Spencer, a driveable stream with several lumber camps
nearby. On a night in mid January, black and cold, at an
hour when all men slept, there came tumbling out of the dark-

ness a long-drawn call pitched in a strange lilting cadence — "halloo, hal-loo, hal-loo-oo-oo." Before the call was repeated, every man jack was standing on the floor or scrambling over the deacon's seat.

"A lost man! All out to find him . . . "

As the men struggled into their woolens, the call sounded again and awoke strange tremors in the back of the neck. Out the men streamed into the night, following the flickering light of the hostler's lantern.

"Over here," they shouted into the darkness. "The road's over here." But there was no answer. Back they trailed to camp and to fitful sleep, to wait for morning and hope to find the lost man's tracks in the snow.

In the morning they searched again, but found no tracks. They discovered only that men in three other camps near the Lower Enchanted had been called out by the same cry, and they, too, had not found a trace.

Winter passed, and men returned to tell the tale in homes and country stores. Hearers said it must have been an animal. One suggested a wolf, but others answered that a wolf does not howl like that.

"No," said the men who had heard the cry. "It was a man — or else."

The Enchanteds are still up there today. You may go to see them. Perhaps you, too, may pick up a little sackful of gold on the borders of an unnamed stream, and in the hour of deepest darkness listen and hear coming out of the night the same long "halloo, hal-loo, hal-loo-oo-oo."

TIME STANDS STILL

Have you never said, "Oh! That *was* a good day!"?
And when memory is written on the printed page,
time stands still.

A DAY WITH CAP'N JIM

BY EDWIN D. MERRY

MY FIRST MAGNIFICENT DAY with Cap'n Jim, my father's oldest brother, was back in my boyhood before World War I. It was spring, and the wind blew out of a streaked sky all day long and out-talked the ebb and flood of water in our beloved Sheepscot River, some ten miles deep into tidewater Maine.

That was a magic day of boats and adventure which my brother Tom and I shall never forget.

Cap'n Jim, tall and stern, had appeared at our farm at chore time the night before. It was then that we heard the exciting question directed to our father: "Got any use for these fellers tomorrow? Me'n Bill Paterson's goin' over to the island. Got some caulkin' to do on the scow. Maybe we'll float her off on the afternoon tide and fetch her into the Old Log Cove. I thought them fellers might like. . . ."

So it was that we trailed Cap'n Jim and old Bill along through the morning woods while the sun slanted in against the

west wind and toasted warm against our backs. In shaded ra-
vines patches of snow still remained, coarsely granular around
the roots of the trees.

At the Point Shore the Cap'n said to Tom and me, "You
fellers stay here. I'll take over Will and the paint cans first."

When we went over in the tiny green punt, Tom sat in the
bow with his mittened hands about a clam hoe while I squatted
between Cap'n Jim's enormous rubber boots. No one else
rowed like our deep-water uncle. With him cockleshell ferrying
was a religious ritual. His pull had about it all the deliberation
of a fisherman hooked lightly to a great fish. Then on the back-
stroke he would turn his wrists so that the oar blades cut like
a skipping stone over the green, frigid water.

We came in thus sidewise to the sun-warmed east side of Leh-
mans Island. No wind entered here beneath the pines, and the
tide was up so that we could step out onto the fourth plank
step of Cap'n Jim's boat house. The scow, the *Wild Rose*,
flung up her one mast just north of this tar-papered, basking
house of treasures.

Tom and I entered and were never the same thereafter.
Above a bench we found a breechloading horse-pistol and cart-
ridges, green with verdigris. Along the walls there were lobster
traps, eel pots, coils of silvery rope, bottles with false bottoms,
and hand-hewn buoys. Over our heads a minnow trap shared
a wooden peg with a dip net. In a little room of lower roof, we
lay upon our bellies beside a three-legged forge and stared
into the pale water-over-ice that showed plainly through the
cracks in the floor. "Gosh," I exclaimed to Tom, "this is a
heck of a lot better than our room at home. Wouldn't you like
to sleep in a room where you could see water like this — maybe
catch a fish right out of bed?"

It was in this darker room of lower roof that we found a
whole barrel filled with wooden decoy ducks. There was net-
ting enough here to fence in all the alewives that might come
nosing up into the creek at Jinneys Bridge in the month of
May.

Back in the main building we found marine engines with shiny oil cups. There were anchors of various sizes; one hung by a chain from a beam so that I could swing on it when Tom pushed me. One wall was beautifully festooned by a squirrel-chewed sail. The floor space was principally occupied by the mutely potent power boat, the *Halcyon*. Once we heard sounds like organ notes, and we pressed our faces against glass to gape open-mouthed at a flock of geese gliding in against the Point Shore pines.

Up in the shop loft we found even more fabulous wealth: a bicycle, a treadle-operated printing press, a compass in gimbals which could be put in motion like ocean waves. From one box under the pine-swept roof we removed shining minnows, frogs with hooks for tails, four gorgeous jackknives, fishing reels, and other wonders that were entirely beyond our knowing.

While Tom and I explored, Cap'n Jim and his man were busy in their hip rubber boots driving oakum up into the seams of the scow's bottom. From time to time we could hear their voices like bird cheeps cutting in the continuing battle of the wind and the gurgling sound of the Sheepscot water going back to Hendricks Head and the open Atlantic. That was a day of rare quality. Even then I think that Tom and I had some knowledge of its lasting significance. We appreciated our Uncle Jim. I remember Tom's solemn words: "We must leave everything just as we found it. It wouldn't be fair not to."

At noon they called us to partake of enchanted food (ham and eggs and potatoes) in an enchanted little room redolent with the smells of bilge water, three-and-one oil and oakum — to say nothing of the appetizing odors of the food and of driftwood ablaze in the stove. This was the cabin of the *Wild Rose* where the slow ticking of a brass ship's clock wonderfully filled all the silences.

That evening just at sunset the magical ship came afloat and swung away from her wintering timbers. Tom and I were a couple of tired boys upon her vibrant deck. We had explored the dark island, dug a bucket of clams, and finally retreated to the warmth of the ship's cabin where two rifles and a shot-gun rested on slats above our heads. There were two chained-up bunks and a crawl door that opened into the dank and mysterious hold.

In the gathering spring dusk we floated in to the Old Log inlet. Lines were heaved ashore and made fast to hornbeam and oak. Then we trailed Cap'n Jim and old Bill up through the sap-sprung, twilight woods to home — and bed.

ISLESBORO FIREWORKS

BY H. G. BOARDMAN

SAFER AND SANER we may be, but something has gone out of the
local scene with the passing of fireworks in our island village.
For weeks before the Fourth of July, we Islesboro boys used
to save up our scant and precious pennies toward our annual
festival of sound and light. Most of us bought bunches of the
small Chinese crackers whose pungent smell lingered after the
cheerful crackling. Bigger boys, with lucrative employment as
caddies, laid in a good supply of cannon crackers. Even the
small ones had their sparklers. And great was the rivalry as to
which of us could be the first to break the silence of that glorious day. Dawn and the roosters were no earlier, and proud was
that boy who first woke the neighborhood with the biggest
salute in his hoard.

From then on, the day was a bedlam of noise. Old tin cans
or empty barrels were wonderful ways of magnifying the din;
fairly large stones could be lifted in the air by a good sized

cracker; some profligate lad might light a whole bunch of Chinese crackers, and who can forget that gorgeous sustained crackle? Small fry whose stock was low scrambled to garner those stray pieces that blew away from the bunch without exploding. Very few of us were ever "hoist with his own petard." There were, of course, some burns and even a contusion or two; but we managed in our town to reach manhood without any real tragedy — unless you count an occasional runaway horse. I seem to recall that Al Gilkey's old Turk ran from Williams Brothers' store to the Town Hall four miles away without stopping, the time a firecracker went off under his feet.

But while the joy of the island youth was great, there was also a memorable affair among the more sophisticated summer residents. For many years, Mr. and Mrs. John Turner Atterbury and their four lovely daughters were hosts to the summer colony at an annual party and fireworks display at their summer home *Dramora*, whose broad porches and spacious lawns offered an unsurpassed vista of Gilkey Harbor and the Camden Hills. This festive evening was one of the highlights of the season, ranking not far behind the annual arrival of the New York Yacht Club, headed by the J. P. Morgan yacht *Corsair*. Every family of the summer colony was there by invitation, crowding the porches.

But the summer people were not the only spectators. In the shadows of the shrubbery bordering the lawns of the estate, an almost equal number of onlookers had gathered. Island families had an early supper in order to hitch the horse and drive down the island to be within walking distance. We youngsters pedaled our "wheels" down through the dusk to get choice stands among the rhododendrons.

And worth the trip it was! The guests had been served a collation and spirits were high. Out on the front lawn the huge chests of fireworks were ready. Roman candles awaited to shower their variegated balls of fire in clusters that vied with the "Volcanoes" or fountains, and the spinning pinwheels. Stands had been built for set pieces and chutes arranged to guide the rockets. No ten-cent two-inch rockets these; they were big and able to soar high over the grounds to fall at last in the harbor, although it was probably never true that one carried clear across to Charles Dana Gibson's place on Seven-Hundred-Acre Island. When dusk was deep enough, John Field, the Atterbury caretaker, with his sons Edward and Laforest, gathered around the mammoth chest, lighted their punk sticks and proceeded to the display.

But even from the happy memories of long-past youth, one show will ever stand out as the most spectacular I have seen. All was ready; guests had been fed and refreshed; in the shadows the town people held their breath as John and his sons approached the big chest. Then it happened! From the very first piece lighted, a stray spark blew back into that box, and everything in it went off more or less at once. The Roman candles shot in streams in every direction. The pin-wheels whirled inside the box, churning the whole into a Hades-like cauldron. Rockets were taking off to land and sea. Screams from the veranda where the guests were gathered; screams from the bushes where the self-invited watched; cheers of unbridled joy from us urchins to whom destruction was better fun than art. One large rocket went through a plate glass window into the music room, and ignited a divan. It was long to be remembered, this Glorious Fourth!

Nowadays we don't have the fireworks we used to. No longer may small boys on a Maine island save up their pennies for bombs and rockets. At best, we may contribute to a community display, set off sensibly by the local fire chief. But we who are now sober "senior citizens" can still thrill to the memory of "the night the fireworks blew up."

OLD BAR HARBOR DAYS

BY MARIAN L. PEABODY

I FELL IN LOVE with Bar Harbor at first sight. I was ten years old and we had come to visit my uncle, Robert Amory, at the *Eyrie*. How well I remember the thrill of seeing my first mountains as the boat came in sight of Mt. Desert. Then the first glimpse of the rocky, thickly wooded islands in beautiful Frenchman's Bay completely took my breath away.

My father, the Rev. William Lawrence, later Bishop Lawrence, had been coming here since he was a Harvard freshman to visit his friend, George Minot, but my mother, busy with young children, had never come and indeed never *wanted* to, as she had an idea it was a rather "wild place where girls from New York and Philadelphia walked up mountains swinging their arms." In Boston you kept your hands in a muff in winter and in summer clasped over a purse or card case at your waist. So my young father came alone for a short holiday.

After our first visit to Bar Harbor in 1886, however, we continued to come almost every summer for the rest of our parents' lives. We first rented the Shingle Cottage on Mt. Desert Street where we children played croquet on the grass patch in front and watched the three pretty Sturgis girls, beautiful Lulu Morris and fascinating gypsy-like Marie Scott, tripping back and forth between Lynam's Hotel and the Parker Cottage next door to us. We greatly admired these young girls and copied their costumes for our paper dolls.

After a few years my father built a house on Schoolhouse Hill at the head of Mt. Desert Street, just below the summer home of his cousin, Frank Lawrence. The latter's house was struck by lightning in a midnight storm some years later and burned to the ground in a few minutes while the family were on the train on their way to Bar Harbor for the summer.

During the gay 90s I doubt if there was a spot in the world where that decade was pleasanter. A group of interesting people had settled here. Among the early comers was the artist, William Morris Hunt, who built *Mizzentop*, and Captain Mahan, the naval expert and historian, Dr. Weir Mitchell, Mr. George Bowdoin, whose family founded Bowdoin College, Dr. Robert Abbe, Mr. Johnston Livingston and his daughter and son-in-law, Count and Countess de Laugiers-Villars, and Mr. Morris K. Jesup. The latter two were our near neighbors on the hill. Along the shore some larger summer cottages had been built by Dr. Hasket Derby, Mr. and Mrs. John Kane, Mr. Edward Coles and his sister-in-law, Mrs. John Markoe, Mr. Gouverneur Ogden, Mr. Montgomery Sears and Mrs. Cadwalader Jones. A little later *Kenarden Lodge* was built by Mr. John Kennedy, a delightful Scotsman, who gave us our first ride completely around Mt. Desert Island in his small and fast steam yacht. Also at this time the British, Turkish and Austrian embassies had their offices at Bar Harbor to escape the summer heat of Washington, D.C.

The Vanderbilts bought beautiful *Pointe d'Acadie* from Mr. Ogden, and after old Mr. Vanderbilt died, Mr. George Vanderbilt built two houses on his land, one for the William

Jay Schieffelins and the other for Mrs. John Trevor and her family. I am reminded of a ball later on at *Pointe d'Acadie*, with the guests all at supper at little tables, when suddenly all the lights went out. Imagine the confusion in the kitchen and pantries, but the guests, fortunately all seated at the tables, went on talking in total darkness until a small flicker of light appeared at the top of the steps leading from the supper room, and we saw Mrs. Vanderbilt, tall and stately, holding aloft one candle stuck in the neck of a champagne bottle.

The 90s were the days of Flower Parades — of ladies driving their own phaetons completely covered with flowers, from the horses' ears to the groom's seat in the back, including the lady herself, who wore a dress to match or contrast the flowers she had chosen for decoration. There were also canoe parades from the Canoe Club on Bar Island, a couple in each canoe under a canopy of flowers. These parades were held off the attractive Club House situated on the bay side of Bar Island. Some of the summer visitors equalled the Indians in their skill in handling canoes, notably Mr. Llewellyn Barry, who usually came out in the finals of the races against the young son of Big Thunder, who seemed to be the head of the tribe.

The Indian Village was where the baseball field is today. We used to go from tent to tent buying sweet smelling baskets and admiring the cunning children and papooses. Lovely young Alice Shepard (later Mrs. Dave Morris) went every week to give the Indian children a Sunday School lesson.

A popular excursion in early days was to drive to Eagle Lake, take the little steamer which ran back and forth across the lake and then walk through a beautiful hardwood forest to Jordan's Pond. This path through the woods was called "The Carry," because the Indians used to carry their canoes along it on their heads. We would often row across the pond to the Jordan's Pond House, dine and drive home in a buckboard by way of Schooner Head. The first — and only time — my mother tried this with three young children, someone forgot to order the rowboats to come meet us at the end of the Carry. Mother was in great anxiety as it grew dark and after we had hallooed and yodeled in vain for hours. Finally we built a big bonfire, which attracted someone's attention, and we were rescued.

Motoring is the dangerous occupation of the young now-adays but we used to "go canoeing" on any sort of day, our escort often standing to paddle, and I, for one, could not swim a stroke! We also climbed the cliffs at the Ovens and Otter Cliffs, the favorite picnic spots, and we jumped the chasms by moonlight, stumping each other to do more and more dangerous things. How well I remember the little mossy path leading to Otter Cliffs and, as we picked our way through the thick woods, the roar of the sea and the surf and the mournful sound of the bell buoy grew louder and louder until we emerged on the high flat shelf of rock, dotted with blue-bells, where we had our picnic. Afterwards came the ride home through the Gorge on a three- or four-seated buckboard, three on a seat, bouncing along and singing at the top of our lungs — the pair of horses taking the hills at a gallop, which we were told was what they preferred to do.

We early settlers went up Green Mountain (now called Cadillac) in various ways. First by cog-railway to a cupolaed hotel on the summit; then on foot, always the best way to appreciate the scenery; next by the "carriage road," and finally by motorcar. One beautiful full moonlit night early in the century a few of us in a buckboard, chaperoned by young Mr. and Mrs. Dave Morris, drove slowly up the mountain, shivered on the top until the Vanderbilts' butler (also up there with his friends) lent us some wood and matches for a fire, after which we thoroughly enjoyed the moon over Eagle Lake and then the dawn and sunrise over the sea, returning to the Morrises' with a great appetite for a 6:30 breakfast.

Every year the North Atlantic Squadron visited Bar Harbor, at first under Admiral Gherardi, who had two sons the age of my sister and myself. We spent much time, at their invitation, on the ships or on excursions in the ships' barges or launches. The barges were huge, heavy boats rowed by about a dozen sailors, and it was pretty to see the oars all go up in the air at once as we approached the ship or dock. Later on our warships were accompanied by the British Bermuda Squadron, and then there were gay times indeed and beautiful parties in the large galleried ballroom of the Kebo Valley Club. There was much more color in the uniforms in those days. The tall, slim British officers were most beguiling in their tight-fitting Eton jackets and ropes of gold braid. They taught us the Kitchen Lancers, which was a very lively square dance, quite different from the stately lancers we had always danced, and considered much too rowdy by our chaperones.

Once, when the British ships were here, the Montgomery Sears gave a party for the officers, and in return the British Admiral invited all the guests to a picnic lunch aboard his ship and a trip around the Island and up Somes Sound. This was probably the first time a warship had been up the Sound since the battle there in the War of 1812. It was pretty to see the sailors on each side of the deck "throwing the lead" to see if it was deep enough water for the big cruiser.

One day a strange looking vessel came into Bar Harbor. It proved to be the *Roosevelt* on her way to the North Pole. She stopped here so that Admiral Peary might say goodbye to Mr. Jesup, who was largely financing the expedition. Mr. Jesup took my father out to see the ship and meet Peary, a fine, simple appearing man. He told my father he had 160 pounds of candy aboard to treat the crew at Christmas and for bartering with the Eskimos.

Around this time a young musician named Damrosch appeared. He was engaged to one of the Miss Blaines. He gave a series of piano recitals at the Belmont, in which he interpreted the Wagner Operas. My father and I attended these with great enjoyment.

The Kebo Valley Club was the center of all the social life. There we played in tennis tournaments, golf tournaments, rode in gymkhana races, watched baseball games and horse shows, and danced evenings. There were staged elaborate charity entertainments, which consisted of lovely tableaux vivantes and various dances — Spanish and Scottish or elaborate minuets. Old Mr. Peter Marie came from Newport and had miniatures painted of the prettiest girls for his collection.

I remember one domino ball held only a short time before the big clubhouse burned down. Our coachman came running into the house one evening saying, "The Kebo Club has burned down and the fire is coming through the woods as fast as I c'd run." My father told all of us, and the household, to leave the house at once, not waiting to take a thing. My mother put the baby into the clothes basket with anything she could grab and two of us carried him down the hill, the coachman and groom following, each leading two very agitated horses. Coming up the hill to fight the fire were shouting men and a cutunder dragging a firehose; and all over the town, and over us, were sparks and flying embers.

After the Kebo Valley Club burned, the horse shows were held in Robin Hood Park, a most beautiful spot under the shadow of Newport Mountain and on the Gorge Road just before it plunged down to the Tarn between the mountains. Here there was a wide field with a race course around it, a perfect place for a county fair or horse show. We used to ride around this course with the riding teacher to learn how to take jumps. So when the golf links swallowed the racecourse at Kebo, a grandstand was built here, with boxes along the front and the judges' stand opposite, and there never were prettier horse shows anywhere. Col. Edward Morrell of Philadelphia had beautiful horses and a coach and a brake and usually got the prize. He was a most picturesque figure as he drove his handsome four. There were always six or eight coaches, and many smart little turnouts driven by ladies. Mrs. Edgar Scott had a very pretty pair of horses and drove a phaeton or "surrey with a fringe on top," not only in the show but every day over the many beautiful drives. Then there were the children's classes which were delightful to watch. David Rockefeller was very cute on his vivacious pony; and there would also be a prize for the best-looking cutunder and horse.

Croquet must also be mentioned, for that game was once taken very seriously. Many people turned their grass tennis courts into croquet grounds and exciting tournaments were held; so exciting that we did not even stop to eat, our lunch being brought out to us on trays — and sometimes dinner, too — and we ate it hastily between shots. There were umpires, who often had a rather hard time of it, and real silver cups for prizes.

How many remember Colonel Bush and his delightful receptions at the Pot and Kettle Club! He was one of the most genial of Kentucky colonels, and the Pot and Kettle was a perfect spot for his parties — in fact, for all entertaining, as the food was the best on the Island, and many were the big dinners we attended there. Both at the Pot and Kettle and at Jordan's Pond one met interesting people from all over the world. Acquaintances turned up that we might have seen last in England or Italy or the Far East, and the Pot and Kettle for some seasons had a group of musicians of international fame — Paderewski, Kreisler, Bauer and Schelling, as well as our own singers, Myron Whitney and Frank Rogers. Arthur Train, the writer, made an amusing toast-master.

During the 90s the churches were fuller than they are today. Every Sunday the Episcopal Church had campchairs on either side of the aisles to accommodate the crowd. Once, when the great preacher Phillips Brooks was with us, my father would not let any of us children go to church because he wanted our seats filled by people who might never have heard him. At that time old Mr. Leffingwell was rector. He was a saint, and looked it, with his deep-set eyes, erect carriage and long white beard. I always thought the prophets might have looked like him. His was a very humble character, and he shrank from preaching to the big summer congregations. My father knew how he felt and had told him that he would preach for him if he needed him at the last moment. Accordingly Mr. Leffingwell would announce, "Next Sunday the Rev. Mr. Lawrence will preach *unless* I can find someone else in the meantime." On the occasion of the baptism of a baby, Mr. Leffingwell would turn to the congregation before starting the service and say, "*Should* the child cry, let no one be embarrassed." For fifty years our family half filled the west transept of St. Saviour's.

One of the most picturesque sights of each summer was to see the yacht club cruising fleets come in. Both the New York Yacht Club and the Eastern came every year, often together. The New York club sometimes had forty or fifty yachts, which would come around the point, all sails set, like a flock of beautiful, huge, white birds. The great steam yacht *Corsair* always led, as Mr. J. P. Morgan was commodore for many years. Following her might be eight or ten other big steam yachts. Then would come the schooners and the big sloops and then the smaller ones, as they raced in classes up the coast. The *Corsair* would stay in harbor usually for perhaps a month. Every Sunday morning she would take a party over to Northeast Harbor to hear Bishop Doane, who was an old friend of Mr. Morgan. Our family sometimes went on these parties if the weather was fine. We would start about nine o'clock, having had our breakfast, but Mr. Morgan would *not* have had his breakfast and expected everyone to have theirs with him; so all would repair to the dining-saloon, sit around the big table and watch Mr. Morgan eat. His coffee cup held at least a pint. He had it made for him, as his doctor had told him one cup of coffee was all he could have. As we went around Great Head, where there is apt to be quite a heavy ocean swell, the conversation of the ladies would begin to languish. Mr. Morgan's very bright black eyes (with a somewhat mischievous gleam in them as they glanced around the table) would take note of the growing depression and finally he would say, "Don't wait for me if anyone prefers the deck," and there would be an immediate but dignified exit toward the companionway and fresh air.

The Eastern Yacht Club from Massachusetts and our friend

Amory Gardner, on the schooner *Mayflower*, would bring in a number of Boston men. Mr. Gardner liked to join our family "hymn sing" on Sunday evening, when the whole hill would re-echo to familiar, old hymns. One day my father and I went to an interesting sailing party on the *Mayflower*, on which were Sir Randolph Churchill and his wife, parents of Winston Churchill. Lady Randolph was the beautiful Jennie Jerome of New York, still very handsome and attractive, although her husband was a tragic figure. In the midst of a brilliant Parliamentary career, his health had given out and he was over here in a last desperate attempt to retrieve it. Years later I read about this yachting party in Lady Randolph's autobiography.

One morning in the summer of 1914 my husband got up and looked out the window, then called me and said in a tone of utter amazement, "There's an ocean liner in the harbor." Everyone knows the story of the *Kronprinzessin Cecilie*, how the news of the war had overtaken her in mid-ocean with her cargo of $10 million in American gold and a full complement of 1200 passengers. We had all been wondering what she would do, and only the evening before Arden Robbins had been over at our house and said, "I expect by this time that Captain Polack has got that gold to some German port," and now here she was, lying peacefully in the still waters at Bar Harbor and looking so colossal that the town seemed dwarfed. She seemed to reach from one end of the village to the other and her smokestacks topped the church steeples. Our neighbor, Armar Saunderson, took us out on his launch right after breakfast and, as Mrs. Saunderson had made a voyage on the *Kronprinzessin* and knew the captain, we went aboard. I remember how anxiously the stewards asked us, "Has England declared war?" Most of the passengers had gone ashore to catch trains for Boston or New York, but Mrs. Hinkle and her daughter, who had left Bar Harbor less than a week before for a trip to Europe, moved back into their Maine house. No one aboard had known what the captain was going to do, but they knew they were not headed for England or France as they had expected. When the Hinkles waked on this lovely summer morning and saw a chain of mountains, they decided they must be nearing the Azores. As they came nearer and recognized the familiar outline, one can imagine their surprise. Mr. Ledyard Blair was a passenger and had seen something of the captain. The latter, faced with the problem of the best disposal of his passengers and cargo, had decided to race for the nearest neutral port, and so had consulted Mr. Blair. He had suggested Bar Harbor and offered to pilot the ship in, as he was familiar with the coast and harbor, having often steered his own steam yacht over the course. We met Captain Polack, a big, hearty, German sailorman and liked him.

The ship was interned in Bar Harbor for weeks and months, and the Captain and officers became popular with the summer residents. As the war progressed and casualties began, it was suggested that there should be a benefit for the Red Cross, and Armar Saunderson asked my husband and me to join a small committee to plan a benefit. On this committee, besides the Saundersons and ourselves, there were Mr. and Mrs. Edgar Scott and Mr. and Mrs. Ernesto Fabbri and Mr. Alessandro Fabbri. Mrs. Fabbri had been coming to Bar Harbor often since a child with her family, the Elliott F. Shepards. Since her marriage she had run a typical Italian menage, consisting of three generations, in a beautiful, large villa on Frenchman's Bay, the background and view equally reminiscent of the larger villas on the Italian lakes with the same taste and style and family life within. Mr. Alessandro Fabbri called to mind Lorenzo the Magnificent, as he enjoyed life with zest and vim. His every whim was gratified, and his charming personality won people in all walks of life. He it was who had heard on his radio (one of the first there was) that the *Kronprinzessin* was coming to Bar Harbor, and he had taken his moving picture camera (also the latest thing) and gone out in his launch to meet her and take pictures. These pictures were shown in the New York theatres the next day, I believe.

The Fabbris were very kind to the homesick Germans anchored off their place and continued to be all the time they were there. Soon after the arrival of the German ocean liner, Mr. Fabbri gave his powerful radio to the government, and it was installed at Otter Creek and became the one on which the official war news from Europe came in and was published in the papers. A tablet on a boulder at the former radio station tells about it and memorializes Mr. Fabbri (DOWN EAST, November, 1964).

In planning our Red Cross benefit, we decided to have a ball at the Swimming Club, now the center of the social life of the community. It was located on West Street, where there was a large natural pool warmed by the sun and changed by the tide, several fine tennis courts; a clubhouse with a ballroom and stage and wide piazzas where a part of the Boston Symphony Orchestra played every day. We set to work at once to organize a really good party. Captain Polack was anxious to help and lent the ship's band, all the flags for decoration and sailors to help hang them and the lanterns around the grounds. It seems hard to believe now that the terrible World War I could start in such a cooperative and amicable way with the Englishman Saunderson, the Italian Fabbris, the German officers and us Americans all working together for the Red Cross. If only this spirit in Bar Harbor could have been kept, and spread throughout the world!

WHEN ALL WAS NOT HARMONY ON THE HARMONY LINE

BY ALBERT O. PORTER

In 1866, LEADING CITIZENS of Pittsfield, Maine, organized the Sebasticook and Moosehead Railroad with the intention of running track as far as Moosehead Lake, where they hoped to tap the wealth of the great north woods. Construction began in July of that year and by fall the road was opened to Hartland, seven miles away. Hartland remained the end of the line for several years, then the track was pushed farther north along the east side of Great Moose Pond as far as Main Stream. In 1901 it reached Harmony, where it ended. It never got to Moosehead.

Pittsfield was not only the southern terminus of the Harmony branch; it was also the junction point with the main line of the Maine Central Railroad between Waterville and Bangor. Something was happening all the time at the Pittsfield station. Fourteen passenger trains a day went through town and all but two of them stopped. Freight trains were also frequent. During

the summertime the high point of the day came about three
o'clock in the afternoon when the eastbound Bar Harbor Express arrived. It didn't bother to stop; the engineer crashed
through at full speed to get momentum for the upgrade to
Detroit. Compared with the Bar Harbor Express, with its fifteen
to twenty Pullman and parlor cars, often with a private car on
the end, the brass on the observation platform shining, the
other trains were an anticlimax.

My uncle, Dr. Edwin A. Porter, practiced medicine in Pittsfield for many years, and we used to visit him for a part of
every summer when I was a boy. His house on Railroad Avenue, right across from the railroad station, was a wonderful
place for watching trains, a pastime to which I became addicted
at an early age. The present generation has difficulty realizing
the important place a railroad held fifty years ago in the life of
small towns situated along the line. Often it provided the only
outlet to the outside world. If you went anywhere, you went by
train. Freight trains supplied the life blood of the town, from
bales of raw wool for the mills to groceries and buggy whips.
As parcels were not delivered in those days, even small ship-
ments moved by express. Mail deliveries, of course, were gov-
erned by the train schedules, which most people in town knew
by heart. A new engine was a conversation piece, and small boys
accorded the train crews the hero worship now given to air-
plane pilots. The railroad station was the heart of the town,
for that was where the action was. In Pittsfield in those days
there was plenty of it.

I shall never forget one afternoon when I was at the depot to
watch the afternoon train for Portland come through. The
engineer came down the grade from Detroit just a little too
fast and didn't bring the train to a stop until it was four car
lengths farther down the platform than usual. The station
agent had left a hand truck loaded high with express where the
express car usually stopped. Cursing the engineer under his
breath, he started pulling the truck down the rough board
platform. As it bumped over the planks, a large barrel on top

of the load teetered back and forth and fiinally fell off right between two cars. It promptly burst with a wet plop and hundreds of live eels went slithering in all directions. Somebody panicked and yelled, "snakes," and all hell broke loose. Passengers getting off the train turned and tried to get back on. People on the train got scared and tried to get off. Women screamed and men attacked the eels with all available weapons from suitcases to canes and umbrellas. One woman lost her head completely and ran screaming up Main Street and didn't stop until she reached the Universalist Church at the top of the hill. It was a good twenty minutes before calm was restored and the train got under way. I learned later that the station agent was spoken to quite severely.

In spite of all the activity on the Maine Central tracks, I was somehow fascinated more by what went on along the Sebasticook & Moosehead line. At that time, the railroad had a little tin teakettle of an engine, an early American eight-wheeler with a lot of brass on it, which the engineer polished with tender, loving care. The engine also had a cracked bell that rang with a dull clunk — a museum piece even then. In addition to box cars for freight, the train hauled one combination baggage and passenger car, which was in charge of a conductor. He was a large, impressive gentleman named Bert Pettengill. I can still see the afternoon train leaving for Main Stream: the little locomotive up front, a string of four to six box cars, the combination car at the end, and Conductor Pettengill in a freshly pressed uniform with a gold conductor's badge on his cap handing the passengers up the steps of the battered coach with all the dignity and presence of a conductor on the Twentieth Century Limited. Then with a lordly gesture he'd signal the engineer to start, catch the rear platform as it came by and swing up the steps with a practiced grace, giving a condescending wave to the station loafers as the train pulled out of town.

My Uncle Ed was a born story teller and his tales of hunting in the wild woods used to keep me enthralled for hours. One of his best stories, however, had nothing to do with hunting.

It seemed that in the late 1890s he was awakened in the middle of a cold and frosty night by a man pounding on his front door. Uncle Ed stuck his head out the bedroom window to find out what was the matter.

"Doc," the man said, "you gotta get up to Hartland right away and fast. Our doctor went hunting this afernoon and fell in the woods and broke his leg. They just brought him in, and besides there's a woman about to have a baby. You gotta get up there and set the Doc's leg and deliver the baby."

"All right," my uncle replied. "You go over to the Lancey House stable and have them hitch up my horse. You drive it back and I'll be ready when you get here."

"Don't bother about no horse," the man replied. "I'm the engineer on the railroad and I got the engine."

Uncle Ed looked across to the station. Sure enough, there it was. He rushed into his clothes, grabbed his bag and hurried across to the station and climbed aboard the cab. It's seven miles from Pittsfield to Hartland, and Uncle Ed swore they made it in seven minutes flat from a standing start. He said he was never so scared in his life. Doing better than sixty miles an hour on that rough and bumpy track, he was sure they were going in the ditch at every curve. It was a day of miracles, however, and they made it. After Uncle Ed's medical chores were successfully concluded, the woman's husband drove him back to the Hartland station, where the engine was waiting for the return trip. Uncle Ed said he told the engineer if he did more than twenty miles an hour he'd shoot him. The trip home was more sedate, but the engineer was quite grumpy. He wanted to prove to Uncle Ed he could do sixty again.

One summer when we returned to Pittsfield, we found quite a change. Like other short lines, the Sebasticook & Moosehead had been taken over by the Maine Central. The ancient eight-wheeler and the combine were gone. Newer and heavier engines were on the branch run, the cars were somewhat more modern and the worst of the bumps had been taken out of the track. The next few years marked the high point of service on the Hartland branch, or rather the Harmony branch as it was now called. A passenger train ran down from Harmony and back in the morning. There was a mixed passenger and freight train at noon, and the main train ran in the late afternoon. This train usually consisted of an express car, a combination baggage car and smoker and one coach. Sometimes there was business enough for a second coach. Conductor Pettengill was still in charge, his dignity more impressive than ever.

I rode the branch quite often that summer. As a result, I learned first hand about the row Pettengill had with the camp owners along the shore of Moose Pond. When the line was originally extended north from Hartland, it went quite close to the pond. People who owned camps there gave the railroad a right of way across their lots in return for making their camps flag stops forever. Uncle Ed had bought one of these camps and we spent some time there. For him it was ideal. He could catch the morning train in his backyard and get to Pittsfield in time for his office hours. Then at the end of the day he could ride back to camp on the late afternoon train. It was also an ideal arrangement for housewives. They could stop a southbound train, ride to Hartland for a nickel and have forty-five minutes to an hour to do their shopping. Then they took the train back on its return trip.

The situation was far from ideal, however, for the train crew. They had to make six flag stops within a mile, some of them only 100 feet apart. Going southbound was bad enough, but northbound was worse. There was a slight upgrade along the pond which made it difficult to stop and start the train. For Conductor Pettengill it was an unmitigated nuisance. He had to make out a cash fare slip for each nickel collected, and if half a dozen women accompanied by small children got on at the camps, he hardly had time to do his paper work before reaching Hartland. He decided, therefore, to do something about it.

He soon found a way, but it backfired. When the local owners leased the Sebasticook & Moosehead to the Maine Central, they felt that they had an obligation to take care of Pettengill.

Consequently, a clause was inserted in the lease providing that he should continue to be employed until such time as he should quit or retire. This raised something of a problem for the Maine Central, for whom Pettengill had worked earlier in the switching yard at Lisbon Falls. During a strike he stayed on the job when the other men went out, and when the unions won the strike, he was finished as far as they were concerned. As soon as word got around that he was to work again for the Maine Central, this time as a conductor, there was a big to-do and a fine labor battle was in the making. Fortunately, it was settled by a compromise: If Pettengill stayed on the Harmony branch, he could serve out his time; but if he set foot on a main line train, the Maine Central could expect trouble. This arrangement confined Pettengill to the branch, but still left him with a lifetime job.

He should have been satisfied, but, unfortunately, he assumed undelegated authority. He began to issue orders signing himself, "Superintendent, Hartland Division, Maine Central Railroad." Local people were at first amused; they thought he was trying to be funny, and the subjects of his orders were trivial anyway. Then one morning some people at the Moose Pond camps came out to get the morning train, and it went by without stopping. Looking around, they found a "general order" tacked to a tree abolishing all flag stops as of that day. An impromptu indignation meeting convened at once around the tree and broke up with the camp owners in one of the highest dudgeons ever seen in central Maine.

At that time the general superintendent of the Maine Central was a peppery Scotsman named MacDonald. The first he knew that all was not harmony on the Harmony branch was when he received a long, collect telegram sent to him in Portland by one of the camp owners. The gist of the wire was that since the Maine Central had violated its agreement by not observing a flag stop, the right of way across his lot had reverted to him, and from now on Maine Central trains would cease and desist from trespassing on his property. The telegram went on to say that the ban would be enforced by the sheriff, and if that officer failed to do his duty, rifles and shotguns were available. No sooner had Superintendent MacDonald read the telegram, than a message was sent to Pettengill that blistered the wires, and flag stops were restored that afternoon.

Pettengill's next attempt at independent command got him into real trouble. The Maine legislature had just passed one of the state's labor laws, establishing a forty-eight-hour week. The first week after the law went into effect, business was unusually brisk on the Harmony branch with one or two extra freights and a lot of switching. On Saturday morning the train from Harmony failed to arrive and the agent in Pittsfield telegraphed to ask what was the matter, thinking there must have been a wreck of some sort. He got an answer from Pettengill saying that he had kept careful track of the time the crew had put in and that they had finished their forty-eight hours on Friday. The agent sent back a hot wire telling Pettengill to stop fooling around and get going. In return, Pettengill told him he could not violate the law of the state and the crew was through until Monday morning. The mixed train didn't come down at noon and neither did the afternoon passenger train. By that time there was a large group of indignant passengers stranded in Pittsfield station, to say nothing of mail and express and a long string of freight cars in the yard.

In the meantime, all this had been reported to Superintendent MacDonald in Portland. He was too mad to send a wire; the telegraph was too impersonal. This foolishness had to be settled once and for all, face to face. He ordered his private car hitched to the Bar Harbor Express as far as Waterville and then had a light engine ordered out to run as far as Harmony.

According to the story, the meeting with Pettengill was epic. First, Superintendent MacDonald explained that the new forty-eight-hour law specifically did not apply to railroads, trolley lines, steamships or any other form of public transportation; then he went on to give Pettengill a monumental chewing out that left the conductor white and shaking. Next the superintendent ordered Pettengill to round up the crew and get ready to go. They got up steam about 7 o'clock that evening, and MacDonald made them run all three round trips, one after another. He paid the rest of the crew overtime, but Pettengill didn't get a cent, even though it was after three in the morning before he finished. After that nobody heard of any more special orders from the "superintendent of the Hartland division."

When passenger business began to decline, service on the Maine Central was canceled on the branch lines first. One after another, branches to Bucksport, Skowhegan, Hartland and Dover-Foxcroft were designated "freight only." When this happened there was no longer a need for separate train crews; the local main line freight could serve any branch when necessary. The casual life on the Harmony branch ended and with it an era in Maine railroading. Characters like Pettengill don't exist any more. But with their passing much of the fascination and color of railroading has passed as well.

MAINE WINTER

Contrary to popular opinion, Mainers generally do not
hibernate in winter. Some live snugly in their
kitchens, to be sure, but most venture
forth to find zest in outdoor work
and sport, meeting the
snow and cold
head on.

LET WINTER COME

BY MARJORIE SPILLER NEAGLE

THE TAUT DRY DAYS of summer relaxed as fall drew near. The grass lost its brightness and turned to amber brown. The royal purple of milkweed faded, and Bouncing Bet's soft pink blooms grew rusty.

The birds began to gather and hold noisy conclave. For a week the air was filled with the sound of their clamoring as they twittered and scolded and darted from tree top to clothes pole to barn roof, making plans for their flight. We watched them for most of one day. The next morning they were gone, and our small world seemed strangely sad and still.

Midway in September we children tramped to school along the dusty Maine roadside where the goldenrod blossoms had begun to turn into gray ghosts of themselves. We sniffed a change in the air . . . a coolness, a crispness not noticed before. It was the smell of coming frost and it intensified the scent of ripened apples and the wild grapes on Cole's Hill. It arrived late in the month, leaving the merest trace of white, and then was gone.

But with October it returned. As we ran across the lawn and fields we heard the frozen grass crunch under our feet, and saw that the squash and cucumber vines were black. Mother brought in her house plants. Father and the boys gathered the corn, leaving the shucks standing like lonely dried up brown old men. After supper when we raced each other to the edge of the garden where they leaned together we heard their rasping whispers and the rattling of their skeleton bones as the rising wind blew against them. Then we ran pell mell back to the house ahead of the swiftly gathering shadows.

On Saturday we wheeled barrow loads of pumpkins and squash to the barn. We drove Old Dolly to the mile-distant ocean beach and brought back cartsful of pungent seaweed with which Father covered the exhausted ground for its long rest.

Indoors we helped Mother peel and stew the tomatoes, and set jars of their red juicy pulp on cellar shelves. We strung apple slices and hung them in the spare chamber to dry. We "put down" cucumbers in crocks of brine, and made jelly from the grapes that hung in purple clusters from trellises alongside Mother's small vegetable garden. Early and late the tantalizing smell of vinegar spices filled the kitchen.

In October chestnuts burst through their coverings and fell silently to the ground. We filled our pockets with them, as avaricious as the squirrels scampering to their holes in the oak trees, their cheeks bulging with acorns. Chickadees called from the apple tree outside the kitchen window, and a red-headed woodpecker drummed incessantly in the orchard.

October brought days when mighty gusts of wind tore even the most tenacious leaves from the trees, scattering and lifting them to swirl and dance against the landscape, then piled them in drifts along the fences. They scrunched deliciously when we waded through them, knee deep.

A week or two of this with the frosts growing heavier and

the brook in the lower pasture deeply edged with gray lace, and then came the quiet, lazy days of Indian summer, that illusive, shadowy time when everything seemed to stand still . . . waiting. But we could not keep this false summer forever. It went, and the frosts returned, and the pinching morning air.

On clear days we caught glimpses of Mt. Agamenticus brooding behind the thin blue veil of smoke that rose from a hundred pyres of burning leaves. When darkness came we sat at the orchard's edge around our own bonfire of leaves and dead apple branches, and listened to the tales Father told of the Indians who had once roamed these fields and woods. That night we dreamed of naked painted warriors dancing around camp fires, brandishing tomahawks.

In November daylight hours grew shorter, and everything took on a more somber hue. There were days of cold driving rains when we were glad to stay in the barn, playing hide and seek. We hid in the woodshed, the hayloft, the corn bins, and even the empty grain barrels.

Through the spyglass bequeathed to us by some unremembered seafaring ancestor we gazed from the cupola windows at the ocean beyond the trees, not knowing where its grayness began and that of the sky left off. From the opposite window we saw only the slanting rain.

When the storm raged for days on end Mother made her mincemeat and tore strips of wool for rug braiding while we children helped Father husk the corn. The barn was a world in itself, warm and secure with the wind rattling the sturdy doors and the rain beating on the roof. The cattle munched their cuds contentedly, and the horses neighed to each other. The sweetness of clover-scented hay mingled with the acrid smell of harness leather, and the golden ears of corn piled higher as we worked without knowing that it was work.

A night came near the month's end when we heard a turbulent honking. Running to the windows we saw in the clear November light a long gray wedge moving across the face of

the moon. The wild geese were flying south, and winter trailed
in their wake.

With December each dawn came reluctantly. Sky and land
were of the same monotonous pewter gray. Even at noon the
sun was cheerless and seemed glad to escape early behind the
clouds that grew thicker and grayer with each passing hour. A
deep silence pressed upon the land. It was so quiet that the
long-drawn whistle of a train carried to our ears while it was
still far off. We counted the strokes of the clock on the Town
Hall, and they seemed to come from close at hand. The raucous
cry of the blue jay at the farthest end of the orchard was clear
and loud.

In the late afternoon of such a day we were in the barn
with Father. While he did the milking we pitched down hay,
and measured oats, and fed the barn cats the warm milk Father
poured from the pail into their saucers. When he had finished
the chores and assured himself that all was well with the "crit-
ters" he motioned us to go ahead. One of us carried the lantern.
Another opened the door. Outside in the dim rays of the lantern's light we saw the snowflakes, big and swirling, settling
rapidly on the walk and steps and on our coat sleeves. We felt
their wetness on our faces.

We raced ahead of Father and burst into the kitchen.

"It's snowing!" we yelled.

"That'll mean a lot of wet shoes and mittens," was Mother's
only comment.

But when Father came in she said, "The children say it's
snowing. It's a good thing you got their sleds painted in time.
This probably means real winter."

"Well, let it come," answered Father complacently.

The harvest was gathered. The vegetable bins were filled.
Barrels of Northern Spies and Baldwins sat in rows in the
cellar. Shelves were stocked with jars of fruit and berries and
jellies. A butchered hog hung in the barn.

Corncribs overflowed. Tiers of dried stove wood, higher
than Father's head, lined the walls of the woodshed. Every foot

of the house and barn roofs had been inspected for possible leaks. Every clapboard was secure. Weather strips had been nailed along every doorsill. Windows were tight. The house was banked with sawdust topped by branches of fragrant fir and cedar.

"Let winter come," repeated Father, spreading his hands to the warmth of the stove. "Everything is in order, and we are ready for it."

MOUNTAIN LUMBERERS—OLD-SCHOOL

BY CHARLES G. WILSON

THEY WERE A STRANGE BREED, Mister, those familiars of the forest who all winter long felled pine, spruce, birch and maple. They were tough and strong and unbelievably enduring, as well they might be to stand waist deep in snow, buffeted by wind, and topple the big trees with their double-bitted axes and cross-cut saws.

They were set apart from townspeople by an indifference of manner, a conscious pride, even a mite of arrogance, especially among the young river drivers. They walked with the springy step of a buck deer until years of cold wind and cold water stiffened their joints. Teamsters, choppers and rivermen — they were all nimble. They had to be to twitch a big log from a frozen pile with plunging horses; to saw a tree to the exact point where it began to crack and tremble for the fall, giving the men but a second's time to jump aside and dodge a wicked "widowmaker," to ride a log in a roaring spring freshet, to work loose a jam and scramble over the moving logs. All these things combined to give them qualities that set them apart from average men.

But let me tell you, Mister, they were humble, despite their pride — cloaked in humility as the fellow says, for they saw the stark values of life and death in the silent wastes of snow. They had worked so long with danger that it had become as commonplace as the yellow dog that hung around the cook shack.

At dawn's light they would leave the village on the long wagon-sleds, and as they went through the streets we villagers lying abed could tell what the weather was by the sounds of their passing. If the snow squealed protestingly beneath the runners and the pole bells rang loud and clear, then a cold day was beginning. But if the horses plodded by, "shuff, shuff," and the sled runners made a sighing sound, and the bells rang softly, then it was warming up to snow.

The horses were grand! Great Percherons with feathered fetlocks, dyed plumes swinging on either cheek from the bridle stalls — the hames and harnesses bright with brass. When the teams returned in the winter dusk, the tinkle of the pole bells as they breasted the rise of the hill and plodded down to the village with their heavy loads of birch and rock maple brought a homey gladness to the heart.

Believe me, Mister, our mountain lumberers were a daring breed. There was nothing that could stump them, no chance they wouldn't take. They'd survey a fine stand of spruce on a high narrow ledge or a pretty bunch of "punkin" pine which it seemed only winged creatures could reach. They'd look up at the trees calculatingly, take a little tobacco in their pipes, and with their teams and simple tools — don't forget the hooks on their eyebrows — they would start inching up, and soon the axes would ring in triumph.

How do you dare drive a team with a ton and a half of logs down the "ram-downs," the steep places, Mister? Well, you keep the reins pretty tight and drive by the feel in the seat of your pants and faith in your Creator. You'd better have faith, for if the sled sluices and swings off into a jackknife, that load of logs can do a lot of damage to horseflesh, not to mention the teamster.

How do you stand the cold, Mister, knee deep in the snow all day long? I reckon you have to be born to it. Born, huh? I wasn't born; I was just an icicle on the porch eaves. My old man came out of the kitchen one morning and saw me hanging there . "Son," he said, "I calculate you're big enough to earn your keep." And he broke me off, stood me in the snow and put an axe in my hand. I've been cutting wood ever since, except when I was river-driving.

Yessir! They were a tough breed, Mister.

DIARY OF A MAINE TRAPPER

BY ARTHUR W. WALL

Arthur W. Wall, who was born in Rockport in 1899, first adventured at sea, then obeyed what he felt to be a stronger call to the Maine woods. A "loner" by nature, he spent a number of seasons running traplines from an abandoned lumber camp in Township 11, Range 10, which is the four Musquacook Lakes country, northeast of Churchill Lake and midway between Big Machias and Long Lakes. The trapper described the region as "an area of 6x6 miles, where I am the only population, monarch of all I survey."

In the winter of 1948-1949 a bush pilot flew him to Musquacook for the trapping season. He took along provisions for two months and a cat for company, but forgot to bring any reading matter. However, he had a pencil and a notebook in which he kept a day-by-day account of the wilderness life. Although each day's weather and his

*monotonous meals were important events in the stark rec-
ord, observations of wildlife and snatches of personal revelation contribute to its mounting drama. Of necessity,
Mr. Wall's diary has been abridged greatly.*

DECEMBER 27, MONDAY 6:16 p.m. Temperature −4 degrees. Left
Portage at 12 noon in good weather but Musquacook country
lives up to its reputation. We struck snow squalls and a hurricane at 2000 feet. Couldn't see the earth and at 1400 feet could
just make it out. That plane did everything but turn bottom
side up; even scared the cat. The plane had to come in another
trip to bring the rest of my supplies — two trips for $24. The
camp is just starting to warm up. Flapjacks and molasses for
supper. Looked at some traps I left set when I went out two
weeks ago and had one big weasel.

December 28. −4 degrees. I have a sign on my door designat-
ing this as Camp Agony, and I call this place the Never Never
Land, because it never clears off. Heavy westerly snow squalls
all forenoon. Beef stew for dinner; supper ditto. Cut wood most
of the day.

*The trapper kept a tier of half a cord of wood inside the
camp at all times. The camp itself, built in 1930, was the
only one of a lumbering compound left standing. It was a
cabin 20 feet square, built of four logs to a side. The floor
also was of logs, faced up on two sides by a broad ax, laid
snugly together and leveled off with an adze, and was
about a foot thick. It had a double roof of cedar splits
with about 6 inches of dirt between.*

December 29, +34 degrees. Raging northeast blizzard.
Caught a Canadian lynx — about 45 pounds of him. Damnedest
looking thing I ever saw. Legs are as long as my arms, feet
bigger than my fists, a ring of 4-inch hair surrounding his face
like a beard and a tuft of coarse black hair growing from the
tip of each ear straight up . . . Flapjacks and beef stew for dinner and supper. Company tonight at 5 p.m. — two men with
a tractor hauling a sledload of boards in to Musquacook to

build a camp next summer, about seven miles northwest of
here.

December 30, +14 degrees. A ripsnorting northeast blizzard,
almost two feet and still snowing hard. Never left camp all
day. Those two men haven't come back yet; there's a little
camp on Third Lake, and they must be holed up there; don't
believe they had grub or blankets or anything. Also two fellows from Ashland were supposed to come to Fourth Lake by
plane yesterday for beaver trapping, but I never heard any
plane and if they did get in, they must be holed up too. If
they are denned up there tonight, I have neighbors seven
miles northwest and neighbors seven miles southwest; getting
crowded. Nothing moves in these Northern Maine woods'
blizzards — not even the animals.

December 31, +24. Never Never Land still whooping her
up — fifty hours so far without a break. The old year is going
out a-roaring. Those two guys who went in Wednesday back
here at noon, cold, wet and half starved. I filled 'em up on pancakes, beans and coffee. They upset their load and broke the
sled; nothing to eat and that camp was locked; crawled in a
window and cookstove wouldn't work. A plane was supposed
to fly another man and some grub in for them Wednesday afternoon, but this storm started Wednesday noon, so no plane, no
grub. They took off at 2 p.m. for Ashland with their tractor
and set of sleds behind, and without too much gas. They should
have stayed here 'til it cleared when a plane would be on the
hunt for 'em and could fly in some gas. I doubt if they get
out tonight, but tomorrow is open season on beaver, and that
tractor is breaking my road for several miles right by beaver
ponds, so they're saving me a lot of hard snowshoeing.

January 1, 1949, Saturday, +32. Open season started at 12
noon. Nasty going — bushes sheathed in $\frac{1}{4}$-inch ice and wet in
woods. Got one pond set. Hot dog roast in the woods for dinner, beans for supper.

January 3, +20. Haven't seen the sun for six days. Big lynx

within 100 feet of camp last night. Heard my cat howling, I guess. Down to my traps; caught one beaver, an old monster. Cut a mile of trail to another pond. Can't walk through the woods without chopping your way; everything iced up and bent down to the ground. Good snowshoeing though. Another lynx crossed my trail. As soon as they find a few beaver carcasses to eat off, I'm going to have fun catching them — $15 bounty and the skin's worth $5-$6. While I was fixing my traps a big otter came down the brook about 100 feet away. Weenie roast in woods; flapjacks and molasses for supper.

10:37 p.m. same day. I'm listening now to something not one person in a million ever heard on January 3rd in this latitude — a frog croaking. He's been croaking for an hour under the floor, under the stove. I suppose it's warm down there in the dirt and he thinks it's spring.

January 4. No sun, no wind, no nothing, just so great a quiet that it's noisy. It seems as if I hear a dull muffled roar in the air — probably my ears making fun of it. Bread, cold boiled salt pork and tea for a "picnic" dinner on Lost Pond outlet, where I put in two sets for beaver, two traps to a set.

January 5. I'm a wreck tonight; toes sore from snowshoe harness, both legs lame, ribs and shoulders sore from pack straps, dead tired and a bad cold — otherwise I feel fine. Forgot my boiling pail, so no tea, no dinner, but a handful of raisins, five miles from camp. Put in another set, two traps, but no beaver. Staggered my way home. Fresh deer track in my trail; lynx chased him out of the deeryard. The state won't raise the bounty on cats above $15, even if they kill every deer in the country. If they would pay $25, a man could take a hound and shotgun and make a living just on cats, but it's a lot of work for only $15. Never saw so many lynx tracks — at least 5 inches in diameter, where a big bobcat track is never more than 3 inches at most.

The trapper, feeling ill and discouraged, snowshoed ten to twenty miles a day, setting and checking traps, but not catching beaver. So he set traps for lynx, and took a day

"of rest" at Camp Agony to bake beans, replenish his
woodpile and cut cedar splits to make beaver stretchers — a
platform 3½ feet square. It turned cold on January 11th,
but woods travel did not improve.

January 12. 33 below this a.m. at 6:30. All over hell today.
No luck, no dinner, either; too cold for a picnic. Put another
set in over the McNally; took a big drink of water out of the
hole where I'd set my traps, rolled a cigarette, tightened my
belt, yelled "Dirigo" and lit out for camp — five miles. Used
to go through the woods like a moose; still do — a sick moose.
Warden flying over again this p.m. Funny he don't stop at my
camp.

January 14. One more day and one more beaver; guess I'll
make expenses anyway. Saw a couple of deer tracks, but they're
not plentiful in here, although two moose are yarded on the
north side of the ridge.

January 15, 12 below. Went over the ridge to Squirrel Pond
and found one colony of beaver in the outlet, set two traps.
Jumped the two moose and all they did was stand and look
at me; probably they never saw a man before in their lives.
I'd like one of them for meat, but I don't dare hardly look
at them, let alone shoot one. So I settled for three rabbits — so
plentiful in here I can shoot more than I can carry home. Anyone who never was in a place like this, where the silence is as
big as all the world, can't imagine just how small and insigni-
ficant a human being really is. My frog is croaking as usual
tonight.

January 19. +20 and snowing hard. This record is for last
night, because I wasn't here last night. I'm tired, lame and
sore and about $35 richer. Started for McNally yesterday morn-
ing and saw a fresh fisher track heading north. Went back to
camp for more grub — boiled salt pork and pancakes — and
took his track about 8:30 a.m. Last night I was ten miles north
of here, and said fisher was still traveling, so all I could do was
camp out under a tree until daylight. Had to cut wood half
the night to keep from freezing. Took up the track east at day-

light, then back south another mile or so. Found him holed up in a hollow cedar. Dug him out and he was a small female, about ten or twelve pounds. Got here about 4:30 p.m., fell into the bunk and passed out for about three hours. I don't want too many nights like last night.

January 20, −8 degrees. No beaver, but got an otter in a beaver trap. Mind you, these beaver sets are always under ice, where there's 8 inches to 2½ feet of water. Lots of work to it: shovel off the snow with a snowshoe, cut a hole about a foot square and set the traps on the bottom, using poplar, white birch, brown ash or whatever wood the place affords, but they don't like soft woods or alders. They don't eat the wood anyway; just the bark and smaller twigs. Nice dinner in woods today; cold boiled rabbit meat, cold flapjacks and hot tea. Flapjacks and molasses for supper.

January 21. Got myself lost. No sun and thought I was traveling northwest, but after looking at my compass, found I was on a westerly course which would have taken me to Second Musquacook Lake.

January 22. Saw a plane go over flying low, heading east, about noon. Guess he made it; didn't start to snow 'til about 2:30. Been talking to the cat, but it's kind of one-sided conversation. Wish I had something to read. Did you every try reading labels on tin cans? Been reading them backwards for a change.

January 23, Sunday, 10 below. Three beaver today — two blankets and one smaller. These blankets are 64 inches and over — measured by the total of both diameters, so if a skin is stretched out 38 inches and 32 in width, it makes a 70-inch beaver pelt. Guess I'll smooth up some handmade stretchers for otter and lynx.

January 24. Found an old last year's beaver flowage, but no life this winter. I walked over to the house and noticed the top was white with frost where it stuck out of the snow. One side was ripped open about 1½ feet and there was a bear curled up in it asleep. He filled the whole place — about 3'

diameter and 1½′ high. He'll probably snow under completely — good luck to him anyway.

January 25. I'm half scared to go into the woods with the
wind the way it is. Always a mess of junk coming down —
old stubs, dead branches and even live fir tops. Never know
when one is going to clobber you, and probably wouldn't know
it if it did. Game warden flew over this noon. Haven't seen a
soul since December 31, but there's never a dull moment.

January 26. Made fifteen miles or more. Busted a snowshoe
but patched it and got running again. This is one form of
travel that no one has been able to improve since the days of
the Indians, and the more snow the better.

January 26. Took up traps at Lost Pond: one small beaver
and two weasels. Listening to the wind howl and the snow
driving against the window and hissing down the hot stove-
pipe. I wonder what purpose a human being serves on this
earth. Even a tree serves some purpose: helps hold the earth
together, holds the water back and makes shelter and food
for the animals. All a man does is take and take from the earth,
never putting anything back in, just a parasite. In my eyes the
more I see of nature, the smaller I become.

January 28, 31 below. Deathly still all day, a profitable one;
tired tonight though. I build a big fire right where the beaver
are caught and skin them there. No job to it, and saves carrying 50 pounds, soaking wet. It's camp work, where it's nice
and warm, to flesh the skin and nail it on the board. Boy,
it's cold. The stars are snapping and I can hear a tree crack
like a rifle shot once in awhile. These winters make me feel
good all over: no flies, no mud, no sweat, just plain old-fashioned comfort.

*The trapper's supplies were running low, but he had a
20-pound lard can almost full of frozen rabbit meat. His
meals of beans and flapjacks or flapjacks and meat were
cooked on top of a sheet iron heater, with no oven. At
the end of January he baked potatoes under a pan on top*

*of the stove "kind of crusty on one side but edible. I've
still got thirty days to March 1st."*

February 1. Got eight skins to clean — an hour's work to a
skin — a greasy, messy job, but part of this work, so what? Here
goes for the first one; water heating for coffee first.

February 4. A long hard trip over to Little Musquacook
Stream. 7:30 when I got home tonight, about all in, but at
least I have heat, light and food. I remember a few nights in
my life when I *didn't* have them. I wonder what makes a man
grow old; not only that, I wonder how he even lives to grow
old. Picked about a quart of frozen high-bush cranberries over
by the brook today; make good sauce, if you like 'em for a
change.

February 7th. Worst blizzard of the winter. This northeast-
erly blows right in front of camp, which faces south, clearing
the snow almost down to the ground. These nights I think of
when I was working in the Warren woods and wonder what
all my friends down there are doing. I lived in East Warren
from 1914 'til 1926 and I do get homesick, but probably never
will go back there. I can't do this for many more winters as
I feel the years creeping up on me. I never knew the full
meaning of being tired until the last few years.

February 8. Had one beaver and two marten in the weasel
traps. I'm supposed to turn these marten skins over to the game
warden, according to law. But I haven't forgotten what they
did to me once when I turned in three muskrat skins, caught
accidentally. They took me to a kangaroo court on an illegal
possession charge, resulting in a $10 fine for each skin and costs
of $9.95 — a total of $39.95 — and revoked my trapping license
for a year. You can't help catching them if you're using meat
for bait, as they're not scared of a trap. Their natural food is
red squirrels, but any kind of meat will take them, and I'm
using half rabbits for all sets except otter and beaver. Martens
are pretty little animals, not much bigger than a gray squirrel,
brownish red and with a face something like a small fox. The
fisher is about the same, only grizzly gray with a long tail, al-

most black, also larger, up to 10 or 12 pounds. The fisher is also called black cat, pekan, pennants marten. Don't know where they got their name — they don't eat fish and don't look like a black cat.

February 9, 6 below. Made the rounds today, down Squirrel Brook, up thorofare to Third Lake and home by 5:30, about $200 richer. Had six beaver and a big lynx in a trap I had set for a fox. Too tired to eat supper.

February 10. Cleaned beaver skins. Took dry ones off boards and nailed on green ones. I have four boards and put two pelts to a board, one on each side. Take about three days to dry. Fox skins are taken off the stretcher half dry, turned fur side out and hauled back on a stretcher to finish drying; same with marten and fisher. Mink, otter, rats and cats are left pelt side out 'til dry.

February 11. Cleaned up the rest of my hides. Had to nail three on the walls, making beautiful interior decorations. Good old roast beaver for supper — tastes just the way it smells: awful. I would like to have two good apple pies and a dozen doughnuts; maybe a few bananas.

February 19, 9 below. A graveyard all day, no wind and a hollow roaring in the air. I can't explain it: always seems to be in the west, but there's nothing west of here for forty miles, just endless forest, ridge after ridge with cedar swamp between, nothing that possibly could make any sound. That noise seems to start with a low rumble like distant thunder, thin, building volume 'til it fills the whole western sky; it suddenly fades away for a couple minutes, then starts all over again. Kind of creepy, to say the least.

February 20, Sunday. Another day, another dollar, fourteen hours on snowshoes and wish I had pie. Shifted to brown ash on every set. Good old cold roast beaver for dinner; tastes like paint oil; but it's got vitamins the health experts never heard of.

February 22. Everything buried under snow and no sun, no nothing, just me and my cat in a world all our own. This damn roaring through the western sky when I know there's absolutely no noise there is getting on my nerves. Be glad when I get out of here.

February 25. Flapjacks and pork for dinner, but oh boy, supper was something to talk about. I boiled beaver half an hour, then fried it in its own grease, and there's no word to describe the flavor except, maybe, "ugh!"

February 26. Lazy day: cleaned green furs and nailed them on boards; made weasel stretchers; cut a little camp wood; made an ax handle; patched my snowshoes; made rabbit stew for dinner with dumplings. Saw two planes today: I think one was Chapman from Ashland. Wish someone would set down here on the pond.

February 27, Sunday, 4 below. Cleaned up traps and hung 'em in a tree, ready for next winter.

February 28. If I don't get "kilt" getting out of here tomorrow, I'll be in clover. Went by the beaver house, where the bear is snoozing, just a big mound of snow. The first thing I'm doing when I get out is hit a restaurant and order a whole custard pie. All I've got to pack is my frying pan and cat. But I've got to get the skins bagged and down to the pond to put aboard the plane in the morning. I tramped a trail the length of the pond just before dark, and then tramped out the words "No Slush" so Thanny Coffin will know there's a safe landing when he gets here from Portage Lake. It's clear, the stars almost snapping, and the air so cold you can hardly breathe. My frog is croaking; guess he'll quiet down after I leave and the fire burns no more.

I have 55 beaver, 6 foxes, 3 fisher, 28 weasel, 4 lynx, 4 bobcat, 6 otter and 3 mink.